SWASTIKA IN THE GUNSIGHT

MEMOIRS OF A RUSSIAN FIGHTER PILOT
1941–45

IGOR KABEROV

TRANSLATED AND ABRIDGED FROM THE ORIGINAL
RUSSIAN EDITION BY PETER RULE

SUTTON PUBLISHING

First published in 1975 by Lenizdat Publishing House, Leningrad

First published in this abridged and translated edition in 1999 by
Sutton Publishing Limited · Phoenix Mill · Thrupp · Stroud ·
Gloucestershire · GL5 2BU

ISBN 0 7509 2240 0

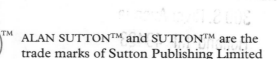 ALAN SUTTON™ and SUTTON™ are the
trade marks of Sutton Publishing Limited

Typeset in 10/12pt Plantin.
Typesetting and origination by
Sutton Publishing Limited, Stroud, Glos.
Printed in Great Britain by
Biddles Limited, Guildford, Surrey.

CONTENTS

Preface

I was a fighter pilot during the terrible years of the war and played a part in the defence of Leningrad, fighting Hitler's air aces in the vast expanses of the Baltic skies.

Turning over in my mind the events of those years, re-reading the yellowing pages of my diary, which I kept every day throughout the war from first to last, I recall my wartime friends, the pilots and technicians, our fearless flight commanders and the heroic people of Leningrad.

The war was cruel, the losses and the suffering of the townspeople, encircled by an enemy blockade, were heavy but they held out, thanks to the bravery and heroism of its defenders.

Literary fame did not attract me when I took up my pen. We have many books written about the war. But nevertheless, I think that the word of a living witness to those distant battles has its value. Leningrad's unparalleled feat must be preserved in the memory of generations to come.

I. KABEROV
Hero of the Soviet Union

Translator's Introduction

Igor Aleksandrovich Kaberov, a much respected veteran of the Second World War, died at the age of seventy-nine on 2 October 1995. In the Novgorod newspaper, *Novgorodskiye Vyedomosti*, of Wednesday 4 October, notices from the town and regional war veterans, the headquarters staff of the Leningrad military district, the military commissariat of the Novgorod region and the town and district committees of the Communist Party of the Russian Federation were printed expressing sincere condolences to his family and friends. His burial took place on 6 October in Novgorod's Western Cemetery.

His obituary, signed by many of the town's dignitaries, appeared in the same edition of the newspaper and bears witness to the respect and affection in which he was held:

> Beloved by his fellow-countrymen, the distinguished military pilot and Hero of the Soviet Union, has passed away. Destined for greatness, he was born in April 1917 and shared with his homeland many of its sorrows and joys. Before the start of the Great Patriotic War 1941–45 he completed his studies at the Eysk Naval Aviation School. From the first days of the war he fearlessly defended the Baltic skies, took part in many operations, including those to liberate Tikhvin and break through Leningrad's blockade.
>
> Bravery, valour and the highest professionalism characterized this fighter pilot who became a wartime legend. His war service ended over the Pacific Ocean. Igor Aleksandrovich Kaberov completed 476 military sorties, took part in 132 aerial battles and shot down 28 enemy aircraft. His country valued highly his military feats and awarded him many orders and medals, honouring him with the title of Hero. He gave the Motherland more than twenty years of faithful service, and when discharged into the reserve worked for yet another thirty years with young people in the flying club, developing their technical skills and training about a thousand qualified parachutists.
>
> Igor Aleksandrovich took part in several Victory Parades on Red Square in Moscow, including the Jubilee Parade. He was at the head of the enterprise which raised funds for the regional celebrations to mark the 50th Anniversary of Victory in Europe and did a great deal to render material and moral support to veterans.
>
> He loved life, loved people, and was devoted to the town of Novgorod and carried the title of Respected Citizen with honour. We grieve the loss of such a man as Igor Aleksandrovich Kaberov, whose blessed memory will always remain in the hearts of the grateful people of Novgorod.

Ronald Clutterbuck (Flt Lt A.R.D'A Clutterbuck, DFC) had corresponded with Igor Kaberov since the inauguration of the twin towns, Novgorod and

Watford, in 1984. In May 1985 Igor Aleksandrovich came to Watford as a member of an official Novgorod delegation to attend the mayor-making ceremony of Councillor Mrs Irene Tunstall-Dunn. During his stay, he visited the RAF Museum in Hendon where Mr Clutterbuck had arranged with the keeper of the museum for Igor to be allowed to sit in the cockpit of a Hawker Hurricane, one of the types of aircraft he had flown in defence of his homeland during its Great Patriotic War. Photographs and souvenirs of his visit have been kept by Joyce Clutterbuck, Ronald's widow. One of these, a copy of Kaberov's memoirs, she showed me in 1987 and, having read the book, I decided to continue the correspondence which her husband had started. An exchange of letters followed and when my offer to translate the book was accepted, Igor sent me a copy in 1992.

The task of publishing this translation has been made possible only through the assistance of kind friends who have loaned me equipment, given me helpful advice with its use, printed the text and read these proofs. I am particularly indebted to Llewellyn Watkins and Mel Carrie for their technical advice and help, and to David Reader, Vic Smeed and Igor Kaberov (grandson and namesake of his famous grandfather) for reading the proofs. Lastly, I must thank my son Edward, and daughter-in-law Anne, whose word processing skills made possible the task of abridging this memoir.

Igor Aleksandrovich Kaberov received the translated text in May 1995, on the Fiftieth Anniversary of Victory in Europe, and, with the help of his English-speaking grandson, read and, after making some corrections, approved and returned the text. He died in Vologda, the town of his birth, during a visit there in October of that year. Now that this translation is published, it is my wish that any royalties should go to the author's family or be paid into a memorial fund for Novgorod's beloved hero and respected citizen.

PETER RULE
Croxley Green
July 1999

Russian Names

Russian names usually consist of a forename, a patronymic and a surname. The patronymic is taken from the forename of the person's father. The full name of the author of this book is Igor Aleksandrovich Kaberov. This tells us that he was the son of Aleksandr Kaberov; the suffix -ovich meaning son of. Female patronymics have the endings -ovna or -yevna. The full name of the author's wife, whom we meet in the first chapter of his memoirs and several times later, is Valentina Ivanovna Kaberova. This tells us that she was Ivan's daughter. Female surnames, of which the masculine form ends in -ov, usually take the ending -ova.

When politely addressing or referring to anyone, the forename and patronymic is used. Thus when the Brigade Commissar, S.S. Bessonov, arrives from Kronstadt to conduct an investigation, he is referred to as Semyon Semyonovich. And when Igor Kaberov is injured making a forced landing, he expresses his gratitude to Zinaida Mikhailovna, a village housewife, whose surname is Petrova, for rendering first aid.

Most people are referred to by their forename or its diminutive. Thus Mikhail Fyodorov is called Misha or Mishka by his fellow officers, Boris Godunov – Borka, Sergey Sukhov – Seryozha and the author's wife – Valya or Valyusha.

The title 'commander' or 'comrade commander', several times used by ground staff when addressing officer pilots, seems strange to English readers, but it was a term used after the creation of the Red Army to replace the title 'officer'. Ranks, shoulder boards and the title 'officer' replaced that of 'commander' only in July 1943.

CHAPTER ONE

The Young Flight

Midnight Siren

On a June day, evening was near and a marching song could be heard coming from the street:

> We don't want an inch of foreign soil,
> But neither shall we surrender ours.

Approaching the open window, I involuntarily became lost in admiration for a column of sunburnt sailors as they kept step in perfect formation. Their song echoed above the garrison.

Six months earlier I had been a cadet at the Eysk aviation school, wore the very same uniform as these young naval cadets and sang the very same song while marching in the ranks. But now we were lieutenants. Like fledglings from a nest, my flying-school friends had flown to different fleets: some to the Barents Sea, some to the Black Sea, some to the Pacific. For my part, I dropped anchor in the Baltic at this small garrison which was only a stone's throw from Kronstadt.

It was Saturday; work had finished and preparations were going on to give us a pass into town. Suddenly the door burst open and the Orderly Officer came into the room.

'Lt Kaberov wanted in the corridor!' he announced. And quietly to me, 'Your wife has come to see you.'

I was in the corridor in a flash. Two months had passed since Valya and I had seen one another, but to me it seemed an eternity. I couldn't take my eyes off her. A smart summer dress, an unruly lock of hair over her forehead and such joy in her eyes.

'This time I have come for a whole week,' she said happily. 'Everything is fine at home. Ninochka is well; she's started to walk and is so amusing. She can already say "Papa" and "Mama".'

I took my wife's case and we made our way to Volodya's place. A mechanic in my flight, his real name was Vladislav Dikov. But at first acquaintance he said, 'Call me Volodya,[1] it's simpler.'

He was held in great respect in the garrison. Even as a young man he had taken part in the battles on the Karelian Isthmus. Volodya and his wife Vera lived in a small room in one of the houses built for headquarters staff. They were cheerful and kind people and we spent the evening with them at the club, returning home at midnight. Over supper we discussed how we would spend the next day. It was agreed that we would go to Leningrad in the morning: my wife and I had long intended to visit St Isaac's cathedral to look at the town from the observation platform. We also wanted to go to the zoo and walk along Nevsky Prospect. All this was soon forgotten: the silence of the night was broken by the wailing of a siren.

'The alarm!' shrieked Vera.

'Why don't they let people sleep?' grumbled Dikov, dressing hurriedly. 'How many nights in a row . . .?'

Alarmed by the sound of the siren, Volodya and I ran on to the street and plunged into the cool of the night. The loudspeaker roared: 'Red alert in the garrison! Fleet, prepare for immediate action!'

'Lieutenant,' said Dikov as he made his way, 'I remember when the fighting started on the Soviet–Finnish frontier, we were given exactly the same commands.'

'We'll find out presently. Things will be clearer when we're at our posts.'

We mingled with other pilots and ground staff who were running to the hangars. The doors were wide open and those who had arrived first had already wheeled out the aircraft. Someone started up an engine. You might have thought he was in the aircraft when the alarm went. Tireless people these mechanics!

'Who's here? Well, give a hand!' The familiar voice of the Flight Commander, Bagryantsev, reached us.

Dikov and I began pushing an aircraft, helping to roll it out of the hangar. I turned to Bagryantsev.

'Red alert and prepare for immediate action. What does it mean?'

'Generally speaking, it means prepare to do battle.' He stopped. 'Get ready for immediate take-off. Tell everyone. Test the aircraft and taxi them over to the river. They must be camouflaged. Do your stuff here and I'll be back in a moment,' he said, walking away to the headquarters dug-out.

Aliyev and Khripunov, pilots from my flight, taxied over to the river. I had warmed up the engine of my plane when Bagryantsev returned. He drummed impatiently with his fist on the side of the cockpit. I reduced the engine speed.

'Where's Fyodorov?' shouted Bagryantsev.

'There, to the right. Also warming up.'

'Listen carefully. Presently we are going on reconnaissance. Don't switch on your navigation lights. We are flying independently. You take off last and keep to the left. Understood?' He ran up to Fyodorov's aircraft. In a couple of minutes our fighters took to the air, cleaving the twilight.

At altitude it is considerably less dark than at ground level. I kept an eye on the skies. Beneath us was the Finnish Gulf. Visible to the right and just behind us was the island of Kotlin, on the eastern side of which is the naval base of Kronstadt. Ahead, the shore of Vyborg Gulf grew dark. Beyond was Finland. Could our neighbours really be picking a quarrel with us again? I remembered my younger brother, killed during the military conflict unleashed by Finnish reactionaries, and involuntarily looked towards Vyborg. Somewhere there, on Kyamyarya station, Yura lies in a common grave. A nineteen-year-old lieutenant, a company commander! If only he could have lived!

Bagryantsev turned to the right towards Vyborg. For a time we followed this course, then turned to the left and the enormous Vyborg Gulf was behind us. Somewhere was the state frontier with Finland. Its dark shore, indented with silver fjords, stretched far to the west. Not a light anywhere. We made for home. In the area where we were based, we descended to 200 metres. At this low altitude, we flew towards the airfield itself and surveyed the land. Two bonfires were burning to mark our landing place.

Climbing out of the cockpit, Bagryantsev smiled. 'Well, nightfighters, how are you? Did you see anything?'

'Of course we did,' answered Fyodorov.

'But what, precisely?'

'Islands, the Finnish coast,' said Mikhail. 'But nothing else. Not even lights.'

'Quite so, not one light,' said Bagryantsev, lost in thought. 'Perhaps this bodes ill. All right, that's what we'll report.'

Meanwhile, the pilots and technicians gathered round and asked one and the same question: 'Well, how was it?' The question was about the newly supplied aircraft in which we had flown and, of course, what we had managed to see. But then a green flare shot into the air and an announcement was broadcast: 'Bagryantsev, Fyodorov, Kaberov – take off!'

'Carefully reconnoitre the vicinity of the Kronstadt base, and go again where we were before!' Bagryantsev shouted as he ran towards us. Our engines roared and we took off straight from where we had parked. In a few minutes, Kronstadt was beneath us. The famous forts lay like a horseshoe on the gulf. Further to the right, quite close, we could see Leningrad silhouetted in the morning mist. In the outer roads of Kronstadt, a launch was visible. We circled the base twice and flew once again towards Vyborg. Nowhere were there signs of trouble. When we landed, it was already light. The Squadron Commander, Maj Novikov, and the senior political officer, Isakovich, came towards us. Pilots, technicians and engine fitters gathered round them. Everyone wanted to know why the red alert had been given. Absurd rumours had reached some about a mysterious mine, supposedly dropped on Kronstadt.

The thought that something serious had happened was with us all. Someone phoned the operations room but got no definite reply to his question. Someone else was convinced that in five or ten minutes there would be an all-clear. This he knew since he heard it came from a source close to the group commander. But above the parked aircraft yet another flare went up – a signal that our flight was next to take off. We circled for almost an hour above Kronstadt but discovered neither foreign aircraft in our air space nor ships in the gulf. At dispersal, hardly anyone was to be seen.

'Evidently the all-clear's gone,' I thought. 'Now I can see Valya and go into town!' I was overjoyed.

We taxied and switched off our engines. Bagryantsev was a little ahead, but Fyodorov's plane was next to mine.

'Well, how are you, Misha?' I shouted at him.

'Excellent!' he said, climbing from his cockpit. 'Yes, today we worked well. Not long ago, we could only dream of such flights.'

I embraced Dikov, the technician, who had run up to the aircraft. 'Thanks for the aircraft, Volodya.'

'Comrade Commander!' Dikov interrupted me. 'It's war!'

'How can there be war?' I was taken aback. 'But we've only just. . . .'

'War with Germany! Go there quickly.' He pointed at the people surrounding a loudspeaker, which had been placed beside the dug-out. 'They're broadcasting from Moscow.'

Taking off our flying helmets, we walked towards the dug-out.

This Ancient Word 'War'

They were transmitting the Soviet government's announcement about the invasion of our country by German forces. It expressed the unshakeable confidence that our valiant army, the fleet and the brave 'hawks' of Soviet aviation would do their duty for their homeland and the Soviet people, and would deliver a crushing blow to the aggressor.

'The government urges you, citizens of the Soviet Union, men and women, to defend our glorious Bolshevik party and close ranks around the Soviet government. . . . Our cause is just. The enemy will be crushed. Victory will be ours.'

The voice which came from the loudspeaker stopped and for some time we stood in silence as if rooted to the spot. Then everyone moved towards the Squadron Commander and Isakovich who was standing with him. A confused conversation began about the situation which had arisen. We young pilots also exchanged opinions. The usually calm and leisurely young lieutenant Pyotr Khripunov unexpectedly and fervently shouted:

'Lads, frankly speaking, I've been itching to get my hands on these dirty swine for a long time. It will be fine to have a real fight with the Fascists rather than practise.'

'Of course, splendid!' agreed the Squadron Adjutant, Lt Anikanov, who had joined us. 'But now my friends,' he pointed at a tent which had just been erected, 'the barber awaits you. If you need a trim, please step this way.'

We crowded into the tent. In wartime, a head of hair is a hindrance. 'Let's cut our hair like Kotovsky!'[2]

At two o'clock I met my wife. We walked in silence some distance from the Dikovs. Beside the clubhouse, in the dense shade of the acacia bushes we stopped.

'Well, what can I say, Valyusha my dear?' I began, somewhat constrained. 'Things haven't turned out so well. . . .'

We couldn't believe that peaceful times were over, that the word 'war', for every one of us, had become a reality. Fighter aircraft, taking off from the airfield, roared over the clubhouse. Valya looked up and, shading her eyes from the sun, watched as they passed.

'They are going to war,' Valya said quietly, not taking her eyes off the planes.

The fighters flew higher and higher and, when they dissolved into the blue sky, my wife turned to me. 'My soldier boy!' she said, affectionately running her hand over my prickly scalp. 'Presently, you too will fly away.' Her lips trembled, her eyes were moist and tears fell from her eyelashes.

'Look, there's no need for that.' I embraced my wife. 'Calm yourself, Valusha dear. Everything will be alright.'

'I won't cry any more,' she said quietly, putting her handkerchief to her eyes. A bell rang in the clubhouse. At any minute, a meeting of servicemen's families was about to begin there. The Duty Officer asked those who had gathered to go into the hall.

'Well, I must go, Igor dear,' said my wife, hurriedly preparing to leave. For a moment she pressed close to me. 'You look so funny without your hair. When it grows, don't cut it again. Agreed?'

'Aye-aye, Commander!' I laughed, laying my hand on my bare head.

'Go on with you. What else will you say? Commander indeed!' she gently reproached. 'Well, I must go. One thing I beg of you, Igor dear. Don't worry about us, and write.'

The sun was baking hot on the street. I walked slowly towards the airfield and came up to the dispersal area. It was like a disturbed ant hill. They were repairing the old shelters. Here and there they were digging new ones. They assigned the headquarters dug-out for the use of staff. Fyodorov and Godunov decided to adapt an enormous plywood container in which, at one time, an aircraft had arrived from the factory in parts.

'Not a house – a dream!' said Godunov, fastening a door hinge.

We had supper – field rations, as if we were at the front – and spent the night in the dug-out. Tired after the day's work and even more so after the previous sleepless night, everyone soon dropped off. Of course, after comfortable quarters, snow-white sheets and a soft bed, it is not cosy to sleep on a plank bed; but aircrew get used to anything. I would have liked my raglan coat; it's what a greatcoat is to a soldier. He can lie on it, cover himself with it and use it as a pillow.

In the morning, they roused us at first light. The squadron was set a military exercise: to defend the naval base of Kronstadt from the air. Lt Kostilyev's flight was to fly first. Waiting for take-off, some lay resting on their plank beds; others wrote a 'summary to the homeland' as we jokingly called our letters. Matvey Yefimov found a chess set and, setting out the pieces on the board, relished the prospect of presently beating Sergey Sukhov.

I worked on my field news-sheet. The day before, on the first day of the war, two leaflets had been published; a third was being prepared today. I had found a place at the adjutant's table and, paying no attention to his grumbling, I went through the notes I had received the previous day and buried myself in my editorial work. Meanwhile, Maj Novikov, the Squadron Commander, came up to me. Of average height, unhurried, with a good-natured open face, wearing as always his flying helmet with the ear flaps tucked under the elastic of his goggles, unhurriedly he quietly tapped me on the shoulder. 'Get ready for a flight to the naval base.'

I jumped up from my chair. 'Aye-aye, to the base!'

Novikov frowned. He didn't like bombastic phrases; didn't like anything ostentatious; and even this service expression did not seem necessary. Giving me time to control my excitement, the Squadron Commander quietly defined more exactly what I had to do.

'Don't go far from Kronstadt. In particular, keep an eye on the skies. Take off in ten minutes.'

'I understand, Major,' I answered as calmly as possible, feeling my face redden.

Putting on their flying helmets, Aliyev and Khripunov followed me out of the dug-out. On the way, I gave out the necessary instructions. Dikov, who was beside the plane, helped me into my parachute harness.

'So it's off to war, Lieutenant, is it?'

'Yes, Volodya, to the war.'

'And when shall we climb St Isaac's?'

'Probably that'll have to be after the war.'

'Aye-aye, after the war.' Dikov saluted, laughed and helped me into the cockpit.

I had already revved up to taxi for take-off when Dikov jumped on to the edge of the wing and shouted right in my ear. 'Come back in one piece! Good hunting!'

I smiled in reply and nodded to him. Dikov jumped from the wing. Running aside, he waved to me as we taxied out.

'The young flight', as the Commander once called us, was given the task of carrying out a military patrol on its own. To my right was Khripunov, to my left Hussein Aliyev. We flew, gaining height along the western shore of the Karelian Isthmus, towards Vyborg. Visibility was good. Across the gulf, Finland was clearly visible with its forests, lakes and coastline cut with fjords. It seemed as though not a soul was there. I turned and led the flight, first towards Krasnaya Gorka, then towards Kronstadt. We didn't come across a single aircraft. Having made a final circle above the naval base, we turned for home.

Then I remembered that we had not trained in formation flying for some time. This was a suitable moment. In the present conflict it would be much needed. Quickly banking and aligning the flight between Kronstadt and the sun, I gave the signal to fly in open formation. Having made sure that both pilots had obeyed the command, I performed a barrel roll. The I 16, at first somewhat unwillingly, and then with unexpected ease, completed the manoeuvre. I looked at my friends: they followed suit. I performed a loop and for a moment found myself upside down. Aliyev and Khripunov joined me. Then all three of us dived towards the sea. Pulling the aircraft out of the dive, I glanced at my friends. Fine pilots, they kept close, as if fastened to me by invisible threads. At full speed and losing altitude, I led the flight back to the airfield. We flew low over Peterhoff Park directly above the Great Cascade and came out at the landing strip where we made our landing.

'Well, "Eagles", congratulations on your first wartime patrol! What did you see?' I asked the pilots.

'Just now it's quiet,' said Aliyev. 'What it will be like is difficult to say.' I reported to the Squadron Commander that everywhere was quiet.

'That's bad,' said the Major. 'When it's quiet, then it's not quite clear what's happening.'

'Is there really information about our neighbour's restless behaviour?' I asked.

'Nothing special, but. . . .' The Major took a pencil and went up to the chart. 'Yesterday morning, right here, some kind of vessel was blown up by a mine.' With the point of his pencil, he circled the place where the ship had gone down. 'Somewhere here in the shipping lane.'

So that's what it was: the mysterious mine they had spoken about the day before. It wasn't simply rumour. It turned out that Finland was helping Hitler's Germany, cooperating with her. The bombardment of Sevastopol, Kiev, Murmansk and the mining of the waters around Kronstadt were carried out at the same time. I sat down on my plank bed, pulled a map from my map case and, where the shipping lane was marked, drew a sinking ship and next to it on the blue of the Finnish Gulf wrote: 'First casualty of the war. a.m. 22nd June 1941.'

Only many years later, long after the war, reading an article by Victor Konyetsky, 'In the Sea Channel' (in *Leningrad's Feat*), did I find out the details of the 'First casualty of the war'. As it left its moorings in the port of Leningrad on the first morning of the war, the steamship *Rukhna* was blown up by a mine dropped by an enemy aircraft. Trofimov, the badly wounded pilot, found the strength to reach the wheelhouse of the sinking ship as it lifted its prow and, at the last moment, turned the ship to one side. The *Rukhna* moved from the middle of the channel on to its side and when it sank left the fairway free for the passage of ships. Chance willed that Trofimov should stay alive. He was lifted out of the water on to a lifeboat. On the next flight covering the naval base, we looked for the place where the ship went down and flew over the masts sticking above the water. The whole flight made a steep climb and saluted with a burst of machine-gun fire.

Only a few days had passed since the beginning of the war but how everything had changed on our airfield. The aircraft stood beneath camouflage nets and now they were difficult to spot among the overgrown bushes. Everything superfluous had been removed from the dispersal area and fir trees grew on the roof of the dug-out. The armourers concealed their tent in a thicket on the river bank. At long last, the word 'camouflage' carried weight with us. There was one occasion, returning from patrol, when I didn't recognize the airfield. My flight had found it necessary to circle over it twice before it became clear that we were nowhere else but home. Both of the hangars and the large storehouses as well as the water tower were painted with grey, brown, and even crimson stripes and spots. Maj Kutsov, the Chief of Staff of the regiment, had conceived the idea of concealing even the airfield itself from the enemy's eyes. It was proposed to lay sand-strewn paths haphazardly across it. They managed to lay one such path and even this transformed the appearance of the airfield.

Barrage balloons appeared above Leningrad and Kronstadt. Their gigantic bodies swayed rhythmically on fine wire cables. Fighter escorts began to fly no lower than 3,000 metres. On one of the patrols, we noticed a reconnaissance aircraft over the Karelian Isthmus. Cutting across the Finnish Gulf, we followed a course from north to south straight for Kronstadt. Leaving my comrades to cover the naval base, I started to gain height in the hope of intercepting the plane. At about 6,000 metres, it became difficult to breathe. Meanwhile it turned out that there was no oxygen mask in the side pocket. On these flights none of us had flown at a great altitude and the technician had removed the mask because it wasn't needed. The reconnaissance aircraft passed above me at a height of about 8,000 metres. It was moving fast and I knew that I would never catch it even with an oxygen mask on.

I carefully examined the enemy aircraft; there was no mistaking the long nacelles which supported the engines. It was a Ju 88. I was breathing like a fish cast on the shore. Green, red and yellow circles flashed before my eyes. Recognizing this as a symptom of oxygen deficiency, I winged over with a last effort before losing consciousness. My aircraft plunged earthwards but I no longer saw or heard anything. I came to at a height of about 2,000 metres. The machine was in a vertical dive and there was whistling in my ears. I pulled the aircraft out of its dive; my hands and feet trembled. The vapour trail from the Ju 88 spread far away to the west. I cannot express the annoyance I felt within me. Beneath was Volosovo and the railway line to Narva. How could I have given up the chase for the reconnaissance aircraft? I imagined to myself how people on the ground following my flight would shake their heads reproachfully. 'Oh, laddie!'

To the east of our airfield – I saw this from afar – something was burning. Bad news awaited me on the ground: comrade-in-arms Pyotr Khripunov was dead. Returning from the naval base, Aliyev and he were coming in to land. At the same time, a pilot from a neighbouring squadron, Okopny, reacted late to the warning rocket as he made his approach in his MiG 3 and there was no wireless communication. As he turned, he struck Khripunov's aircraft as it touched down. Helplessly, we watched from a distance as the remains of the two machines burned. It was impossible to approach too close; ammunition was exploding.

'So our Pyotr Falaleyevich is no more,' said one of the pilots. 'Oh, how he longed to fight; how he wanted to do battle with the enemy.'

We dined in silence. Then Maj Novikov reminded us once more to be vigilant in the air, and about the fact that, since Finland had entered the war on the side of Fascist Germany, the situation had become much more complicated.

After dinner, the Squadron Adjutant, Lt Anikanov, a really smart staff officer, who was always busy looking after our welfare, arrived. 'Comrades, pilots, I have pleasant news!'

Everyone fell silent. To be sure, each one of us wanted to hear news, especially good news.

'From today,' Anikanov began slowly, 'aircrews will take a rest in the village of Nizino.' The last word he pronounced with particular exultation as if he were expecting an ovation.

Sergey Sukhov spoke: 'Is that all the news?'

'What?' Anikanov was confused as he gazed at our faces which expressed no delight.

'I don't understand,' Sergey continued. 'All of us here are for waging war, but you talk to us of some kind of rest.'

'If you, Anikanich,[3] were to send us to the front where it would be possible to fight the Fascists,' said Fyodorov, 'that would be pleasant news.'

Seizing the opportunity, we gathered round the Adjutant, trying to find out if there were plans to transfer us closer to the front. Would it not be possible to move to a unit conducting military operations? Anikanov withstood all the attacks in silence, uttering finally:

'The transport has been ordered. I beg you to be seated.'

It was a pity to leave the homely dug-out, but orders are orders. Our vehicle stopped at the very end of the village of Nizino. We entered a house, beside which stood a guard. The quartermaster was taking good care of us; on the beds shone snow-white pillows and peeping from under the blankets were sheets. That night we took a glorious rest.

In the morning, Novikov and Isakovich informed all their personal staff that our forces to the west of Vyborg had joined battle with the enemy. Now it became clear to everyone that soon we would be faced with a struggle with the Fascists. Leningrad prepared to fight on two fronts. As a result of the general regrouping of forces, some kind of changes took place in our regiment; only three squadrons remained out of the five. The rest were transferred to other units and flew off to western airfields.

Our flight was rather lucky. Several days running we were instructed to take off first; so it was on this occasion. All of us (2/Lt Godunov, a pilot from Kostilyev's flight was sent to make our third) had already taken our places in the aircraft awaiting take-off to cover the naval base, but take-off was cancelled. An order came through to fit auxiliary fuel tanks and report to the Commanding Officer. The task we were set was unusual. We were ordered to determine the position of the front line and how far the enemy were from Leningrad. Having listened to Maj Novikov, we looked at one another in astonishment.

'Don't you see? The situation at the front is so complicated, and reports about it are so contradictory,' he said, 'that staff at the command headquarters of the naval air force must order us to reconnoitre.'

Looking at his watch, Novikov warned us that headquarters had given us until six o'clock in the morning and that our orders left us only minutes to take off. Then the CO took my map case and, having pointed out exactly the route on the map, explained once more: 'Go to Pskov and, if necessary, further. Go until you encounter flak. You must fly at altitude. Keep between 1,500 and 2,000 metres and you'll be all right. Apart from that, act according to the situation.'

'Until you encounter flak.' I remembered the CO's words as I turned to set course for Pskov. A strange mission! Aliyev's and Godunov's aircraft flew as if attached to mine. But we were making our way towards the front line and close battle order does not guarantee the repulsion of a sudden attack by enemy fighters. We had to open out.

We passed Volosovo; Lake Samro, large and round, like a five-kopek piece, appeared to the right. For the time being, with a long way to go, we stayed at an altitude of 3,000 metres: at this height, less fuel is used. Below the wing, villages, fields, woods and swamps floated past. To the right, the shore of Lake Chud and the town of Gdov were already visible. In the area of Pskov, our flight was hindered by cloud. Where would they open fire on us? I confess I was disturbed. I carefully searched the skies. Our height was now 800 metres. We were flying beneath the clouds. The town of Ostrov appeared on the horizon. To the right, something was burning. Clouds of black smoke covered the town. To the left, a little farther away but just visible, were the centres of two fires. Tanks were moving along the road to Pskov, raising a cloud of dust. No doubt enemy armour, but nobody opened fire on us.

When we were already at the outskirts of Ostrov, two aircraft came from the left on course to meet us under the very edge of the cloud. Possibly they were enemy fighters; I turned back. I felt my heart beating violently and tried to control my nerves, but by now the aircraft had disappeared. The black puffs of shell-bursts unexpectedly blocked our way, one of them causing my aircraft to rock perceptibly. We gained height but shell after shell persistently burst close to us. A tongue of flame flashed and I was immediately enveloped in dark smoke. Of course it wasn't very pleasant when they shot at you, but we soon got used to it. It was nothing to fear. Diving steeply, we pulled out low and discarded our empty fuel tanks (in the event of combat they would only have been a hindrance). I saw how Aliyev's auxiliary tanks turned somersaults oddly as they fell. The enemy artillery evidently decided they were bombs. The intensity of gunfire immediately diminished.

We headed for Pskov. More and more tanks were moving along the road; and what large numbers there were! How I wanted to discharge some part of my ammunition at them! But what was the point of such a strike? Just the same, I could not restrain myself. I turned the flight towards the column and dived. Despite the dense cloud of dust, the black crosses on the tanks were easily distinguished. Like reptiles they were creeping towards Leningrad. In a rage, I pressed the trigger and, having strafed the column, moved away from the road. My comrades followed my example before joining me in formation. The enemy's fire was confused and we treated it calmly. The situation was perfectly clear: we set course for home.

After landing, I jumped out of the cockpit with particular ease. Novikov, Isakovich and some officer unknown to us, but evidently a representative from command headquarters, met us. I made a report of everything as it had happened and pointed out on the map where they opened fire on us, where and in which direction the enemy tank column was moving and which point it had reached. The headquarters representative thanked us and, walking away, he glanced under the fighter in which Aliyev had been flying to examine the bomb racks.

'What's this, did you take bombs with you?'

'No, we had auxiliary fuel tanks,' said Hussein, 'but Kaberov and I released them when we strafed.'

'And where did you release yours?' I asked Godunov.

'I thought they were of use to us and wanted to bring them home,' answered Boris, 'but then I became angry and dropped them on the enemy column. I thought: "Let the fascists take them for bombs. Let's see them dash for the ditch in fear."' Godunov's mischievous answer caused us to smile. Ivan Romanovich Novikov praised his wit.

'Now what, Comrade Commander?' said Isakovich. 'Now they have been strafed and it can be said that they have seen enemy forces.'

Novikov smiled warmly and urged us to go to lunch. 'Go on, or it will be cold.'

However, we didn't manage to eat in peace. The lads swooped down on us with questions: 'Where have you been? What did you see?' The information that the Germans were already near Pskov disturbed everyone. I moved the uneaten plate of goulash aside. I could not get the enemy tanks out of my mind. I could still see those steel monsters moving along the road and raising a dust. Couldn't our forces stop them there?

Yet another mission followed. So, once again, we were in the air; only this time there were five of us. Yegor Kostilyev led the group; Boris Godunov was second-in-command; then the whole of our flight, Hussein Aliyev, Nikolay Sosyedin and me. Our orders were to give cover to the bombers in their flight to and from the target, the target being the column of tanks near Pskov. We met ten SBs over an appointed place near Gatchina. We knew nothing about the pilots in this group, nor their Commander. We knew neither the nature of the bombing, nor the altitude set, nor basic instructions about cooperation. Our aircraft were not in radio contact. But in flying school they taught us. . . . Yes, but that was school, this was war!

Kostilyev and Godunov flew to the left and just behind the bombers at the same altitude. Sosyedin, Aliyev and I kept a position a little higher and to the right. For the first time I was close to the bombers in flight and became lost in admiration for them. Ten SB aircraft were flying in a wedge formation, as we call it. They rocked majestically on their resilient wings. Fine machines! But I had heard they had suffered losses from enemy fighter attacks. Broken clouds began to appear and soon the bombers moved into them as a group. At first, the ground was visible through the cloud but then our vision was obscured and the bombers could no longer be seen. Kostilyev feared a collision and led us below the clouds. We looked around but could not find Sosyedin's aircraft. Where was he? What was he doing? Never mind, he'd catch up. But five minutes passed and Sosyedin did not appear; and the bombers had vanished.

There was the railway from Pskov to Dno. To the left was the large station at Karamishevo. I had noticed it before on the reconnaissance flight. We flew round Pskov from the eastern side. Everybody looked about them but neither the bombers nor Sosyedin's aircraft were to be seen. Our altitude was 600 metres. Kostilyev led us to the road running from Ostrov to Pskov; here the flak was heavy. To the right a burning SB aircraft fell out of the clouds. The uncontrolled machine dropped, leaving a curling smoke trail in the sky. It was impossible to help the crew. The remaining SBs bombed the enemy from the clouds and perhaps were repulsing enemy fighters. We were stooging about beneath the clouds.

Kostilyev led the group towards Pskov. The town was almost completely enveloped in smoke. On the southern edge, fires were raging as if they had just bombed it. There were no tanks on the road. Possibly, there in Pskov, a battle was going on. But where were the bombers? I understood now how difficult it was for our leader Kostilyev; but it was no less disturbing for us and our feelings of helplessness grew to despair. The fuel was running out but we still circled near Pskov, vainly trying to find our comrades. We could not think of flying out through the clouds. We did not know their thickness; we might crash with the returning bombers. Only radio communication could have saved the situation. I looked at the small wireless receiver mounted on the instrument panel and indignation overwhelmed me. It worked, but there was such a lot of interference.

A few days before, the wireless operators fitted it into my machine and said they would test the reception between ground and aircraft. Crowds of interested people gathered. The experts dragged a radio transmitter into the open. I was ordered to climb to a height of 2,000 metres above the airfield and carry out instructions from the ground. I wore a flying helmet with built-in earphones. The wireless operators tested everything once more and

I took off. I reached the prearranged height and through the crackle in the earphones a distant voice broke through: 'Aircraft, aircraft, ground here. If you can hear me, rock the plane from wing to wing.' I did so. 'Excellent! Turn to the left. . . . And now to the right. . . . And now aerobatics!' I carried out all the commands and finally heard: 'And now Kaberov – spin!' I switched off the gas and lifted the nose of the plane; then dropped into a spin. One turn, a second, a third, a fourth . . . but the command to pull out did not arrive. Order or no, I had to pull out. It turned out that the radio receiver had packed up. From then on all was silent.

I looked at Kostilyev's aircraft. He was leading us away from Pskov but at the same time changing course. Evidently he was trying to find the bombers and Sosyedin, who had lost us. What would I have not given for a radio! It was difficult to return without first completing our mission. Yes, but was there enough fuel? Near Luga the needle on the petrol gauge was perilously near empty. I started to look round. Where could we land? And how about the others? I had only started to think about this when the engine snorted and fell silent, then revived and finally stopped. For the first time in flight I looked helplessly at a motionless propeller.

'Keep calm, keep calm,' I said to myself. My eyes feverishly scoured the earth, seeking out a strip on which it would be possible to land. Ahead, just to the right, a lake could be seen; next to it – a large field, but in the field – horses. As I came in to land, I saw another aircraft behind me come gliding in, propeller motionless. According to instructions, when landing outside the airfield you were not supposed to lower the undercarriage; but it was a pity to damage the aircraft. Besides, in front of me was a level field. Without changing my mind, I lowered the undercarriage and quickly lost height. Manoeuvring between the grazing horses, I landed safely. But it wasn't a field; it was a real airfield! It was as if someone had tidied it up for our forced landing. I jumped out of my plane and watched my friends make their approach.

Aliyev made a good landing. After him, Godunov came gliding in. He went a little to the right. A horse stood in front of him, so I tried to point it out but a collision seemed unavoidable. However, something strange occurred. Somehow, the horse incomprehensibly flew lightly across the pilot's cockpit and, without denting the tail fin, fell to earth. When his plane stopped, Godunov jumped out and ran frantically round the machine. He touched the propeller and felt something on the cowling. When Kostilyev landed, Aliyev and I ran up to the spot where all this had taken place. Godunov was collecting pieces of plywood in the grass. These, it now became clear, were pieces of the horse. Several other plywood horses were grazing here and there in the field.

It turned out that we were on a real airfield which had been camouflaged in this way. Several days before, one of the aviation units had flown from there to the front. In the meantime, the Commandant of the garrison had decided to disguise the airfield as pasture. Soon we got to know this young man who held the rank of captain. He told us that he was left in the Cheremenyets garrison on his own.

We quickly refuelled but could not manage to start the engines straight away. It turned out that the batteries were flat. But the enterprising Commandant obtained a piece of an old shock absorber, and a device for swinging the propeller was soon ready. We only succeeded in starting Kostilyev's aircraft. I was entrusted with the task of flying to my unit for a technician and an accumulator. I was home in half an hour.

'What's happened? Where are the others? Why aren't you in your own plane?' My service comrades poured questions at me. Having found out what happened, they sighed with relief and informed me that Sosyedin lost us and made a landing at Kotly. I hurried to the CO with a report, but Snigiryev stopped me.

'Something has happened here . . . Matvey Yefimov hasn't returned from patrol.'

'Yefimov! From which patrol?'

'After you, approximately an hour later, another group of fighters took off to accompany the bombers. Yefimov led them to their target in the region of Pskov. Not long ago, before your arrival, they returned. What happened to Yefimov we don't know, but 1/Lt Kirov said that they simply lost sight of him.'

'If their CO has gone missing, whom do they look to now?'

Gripped by bitter feelings, I ran to make my report. Novikov met me in silence. He made no comment while I told him about our flight. Then, marking the landing place on a map with a circle, he stood up, gave orders for the preparation of a UT 14 aircraft by morning and said: 'Take Dikov and take off for Cheremenyets at dawn.'

In the morning, when Dikov and I were already airborne in the twin-engined fighter-trainer UT 14, which had neither armour nor armaments, I decided to fly the 170 kilometres to Cheremenyets at low altitude. Along our flight path, telephone poles, trees and bushes swiftly rushed to meet us and disappeared under our wings. Beyond Luga, we saw a column of troops marching along the highway. They were moving towards the front and I thought I would encourage them by waving my wings. But as soon as I turned the plane to one side of the column, the soldiers dived into the ditches as if blown there by the wind. They dispersed and lay down on both sides of the road. Sensing danger, I pulled the stick towards me. The UT 14 roared into the sky. Only then did I glance at Dikov. He sat as if nothing had happened and even laughed. 'What a cheerful chap you are, Volodka!' I thought at that moment. 'They shoot at you and you laugh. . . .' The airfield was nearby. We landed safely. I taxied over to the other aircraft and switched off the engines, then jumped from the cockpit and dived under the plane. Of course I didn't have to search for long. There they were – bullet holes. One of them had pierced the engine cowling; another had penetrated the fuselage just beneath the technician's cockpit. While I looked for holes, Dikov talked cheerfully to his comrades, who had come over to us, and told them how we had thoroughly scared the infantry and then climbed steeply above them. When I invited my technician to look at the aeroplane and pointed out the bullet holes, he looked at me wide-eyed.

'Where did these come from?'

'What do you mean? You serviced the aircraft for this flight, yet still you ask!'

Then he understood. We examined the engine. It was clear that a bullet had hit a strut of the frame beneath the engine casing, ricocheted off it, made a small mark on the engine casing and, evidently losing speed, fell out of the cowling. The leader of our group, Lt Kostilyev, came up to the aircraft with the Commandant. Reporting the completion of the operation, I did not hide what had happened and, of course, in justification, tried to explain my motives for my flight over the column of infantrymen. Having examined the bullet holes, Kostilyev crawled out from under the plane.

'It seems you aroused their fighting spirit; and they nearly gave vent to it on you. Well then, next time cut it out! If you take liberties when flying, things can end lamentably.' Kostilyev looked at me sternly as if he wanted to be sure that I understood my mistake, then asked: 'What news from the base? Any news about Sosyedin?'

I told him about Sosyedin and of course about Yefimov. Kostilyev thought for a moment. 'Yes, we must hope that he has made a forced landing somewhere.'

The engines started easily and we were soon in the air. I looked at the wooden horses that were left in the Cheremenyets field and at the Commandant's service cap which he waved at us. 'Goodbye, Captain! Shall we meet you again sometime during the war?'

'Now You'll Have To Press The Trigger'

The situation in Leningrad was becoming more and more tense, as the town conducted a desperate war on two fronts. The Finnish forces were breaking through on the Karelian Isthmus. Hitler's hordes had entered the outer limits of the Leningrad region. Mortal danger hung over Tallinn, the Baltic fleet's main base.

On the morning of 13 July 1941, three of our comrades, Vladimir Khaldeyev, Mikhail Bagryantsev and Mikhail Fyodorov flew to Staraya Russa, and Yegor Kostilyev's flight flew to Kuplya. They had been posted to these other airfields. Having summoned the remaining pilots, the CO said that apparently, one of these days, someone would have to fly to Estonia. With this he looked in my direction and I thought that they would probably give the responsibility for that task to our flight. The CO continued to speak but I was already imagining to myself the narrow, ravine-like, medieval side-streets of Tallinn and its broad naval harbour full of ships.

The Major's voice rose: 'Do you understand, Lt Kaberov?'

I was so lost in thought that I hadn't heard his last words and looked at him half awake.

'Do you understand, Lt Kaberov?' the Major asked again. 'You and your comrades have become the base's main pilots. Your flight will remain here in any circumstances. Covering Kronstadt is your chief task.'

The CO looked at his watch and reminded us that only eight minutes remained before the next take-off. We stopped beside Aliyev's aircraft. 'So they've posted you to Tallinn!'

'Never mind, Tallinn is not in the main line of advance,' said Hussein as if consoling someone. 'The main battles, evidently, will be here.' He wanted to say something else but a green flare soared into the air and we took our places in our cockpits. I started the engine and thought: 'You know, Hussein was right for sure. We face arduous battles here; but they are still in the future, and in Tallinn now there is much for our brother to do.' But how boring was this 'blessed patrol' over the naval base and the Marzikovaya Luzha.[4] Not for nothing had Novikov long called us naval-base pilots.

We were already moving when a technician ran out to intercept us, making a cross with his arms. The figure of Anikanov popped up beside the cockpit. The slipstream from the propeller blew the adjutant's cap off. He ran after it, returned and hurriedly informed us that, during the night, the Fascists had bombed Klopitsy, and that now, apparently, an order had come to close this airfield.

'And what now? Do you expect a second raid?' Anikanov smiled and shrugged his shoulders vaguely.

But the very next minute a command was heard: 'To Klopitsy!'

We took off straight from dispersal. I experienced a joyful feeling. 'Fine, for once it's not to the naval base.'

The village of Klopitsy, with a white church in its centre, was next to the airfield. There were no aeroplanes on the ground. It was interesting that the Germans should have dropped bombs here during the attack. What did they see at altitude from the night sky in this empty field and in this thicket, which made a green wall along the northern perimeter of the airfield? Small bomb craters made dark circles as if coins had been rolled there. Aliyev and Sosyedin were near me. Again I examined the bomb craters. I tried to imagine how here, above this field and woodland, the enemy aircraft had circled at night. 'In daylight, we could see them and settle the score,' I thought. 'At some time, we must destroy at least one Fascist. Are we so young that it is impossible to believe this?' Time was running out. We made a last circuit over Klopitsy. I looked at the airfield as it floated past under my wing. How could I know that soon our tent would stand next to it in the dense woodland and that right there in Klopitsy events would unfold which would remain in my memory all my life?

After landing, I reported to the Adjutant about the flight. It was quiet in the dug-out. Isakovich was writing something as he leaned over the table.

'You've heard nothing about Yefimov, Comrade Commissar?'

'No, nothing. It's already three days without news. And where have you flown from? The base?'

'No, we've been covering Klopitsy. It makes a change, but it's annoying just the same. When the Germans bomb, we aren't there and when they leave, we arrive. And there's nothing to guard there. It's an empty airfield.'

'How do you mean, empty?' the Commissar broke off from his work. 'Recently I was in Klopitsy and I know very well that you patrol there.'

'We protect the forest. Apart from that, there's nothing there.'

'And in the forest, have you noticed nothing?' he asked. 'Well, if you've noticed nothing, that's fine. That is very important information and we'll convey it to the head of intelligence at the Klopitsy garrison.'

Isakovich told me that long-distance bombers were on the airfield, concealed by trees and that, as far as possible, we must keep them concealed and guard Klopitsy. There was a post there ARIS (aerial reconnaissance, information and signals), located there to prevent the Fascists bombing the airfield with impunity. I could hardly wait to find out who would fly to Klopitsy and I wanted to ask Mikhail Zakharovich about this but the CO came into the dug-out. 'Haven't you calmed down yet?' he said to me. 'Are you still putting out feelers?'

I was silent. The Major, with a gesture, invited me to sit down and sat himself on a plank bed. 'Listen, Kaberov,' he said. 'This is my third war, and I know very well what things are like. Carry out the orders they give you to the letter and everything will be fine. A great turmoil faces us. You have never felt that your number was up. Try to get as much as possible out of each flight. Prepare yourself. Understood?'

'Yes, Comrade Major.'

'Well then, go and prepare your machine. Take-off is in fifteen minutes. I will accompany you as we escort the bombers. Aliyev and Sosyedin will go alone to the naval base.'

Our SBs had to bomb the enemy at the Strugy Krasniye railway station (south-west of Luga on the way to Pskov). Two I 16s from the army joined us to give cover to the seven bombers. The weather kept fine. There were no enemy fighters over the target and the SBs released their bombs without incident. We accompanied them to Siverskaya and returned to our airfield.

'Did you see?' Novikov asked me when I went up to report to him on the completion of the exercise.

'Yes, Comrade Major, I saw how the SBs dropped their bombs, how they burst and caused a fire. I saw everything.'

'I'm not talking about that. Did you see what kind of strength they had? Two I 16s to seven SBs! It means it's difficult for the army pilots unless some days they ask us for help.'

That day we made three more sweeps covering the base. In the morning, an order came to send a flight of fighters to Klopitsy. Announcing it, the Major summoned Kirov, Godunov and Tenyugin. He briefed these pilots and ordered them not to delay their departure. Ageyev had to transport the ground crew to Klopitsy in a U 2 aircraft. Orders were given to dispatch equipment there for the starter – a special machine for starting an aero-engine.

After Kirov, Godunov and Tenyugin had taken off for Klopitsy, I began to think that they didn't trust us. Another day passed and the routine flight to cover the base seemed quite unbearable to me. In order to maintain the fighting spirit of the pilots, I calmly explained to them the instructions for the flight over the base, which they already knew, and added that, having carried out the patrol, we would conduct a mock battle over Kronstadt as a training exercise.

So, with Kronstadt beneath us, when the time for patrolling was at an end I gave a prearranged signal and battle commenced. It was a dizzy display of aerobatics. At brigade headquarters, however, it was no joke; they were alarmed. Somebody thought that a dogfight with enemy aircraft was going on and soon a flight of I 16 fighters came to help us. Seeing no enemy aircraft, anti-aircraft gunners nevertheless fired a dozen rounds as a warning. Thinking the flak meant the appearance of enemy aircraft, we took the I 16s for enemy fighters and were about to attack them. Fortunately, in the nick of time, it became clear that they were our own. It only remained for us to take our leave and set off to our landing strip.

My friends were waiting for me at dispersal. They had glum faces. I turned to Aliyev. 'What's the matter, Hussein? What's happened?'

'Oh, nothing,' he answered evasively. 'Somehow, things aren't good.' He removed his flying helmet and turned it over in his hands. 'When will there be an end to this routine?'

'I don't understand you,' I replied in astonishment.

'What don't you understand?' His eyes flashed with rage. 'People are dying out there and here we swan around! Why do they feed us?'

Usually reticent, even-tempered and not without a sense of humour, Hussein, at this moment, was not himself. He looked at me as if it were my fault that until now we hadn't had a real fight. Of course, to explain anything to him now was useless. Moreover, what could I explain if I myself was inwardly disturbed by the absence of any real military action?

The whole squadron was up. Khaldeyev, Bagryantsev and Fyodorov were in action somewhere near Staraya Russa. The Commissar was saying that Bagryantsev had shot down two Junkers there and a third enemy aircraft had been rammed. Fyodorov and Khaldeyev added a Messerschmitt each to the score. Kirov, Godunov and Tenyugin had flown off to Klopitsy only the day before. That day they had fought a tough battle with bombers attacking the aerodrome and Kirov had brought down a Junkers. Somewhere over Narva, Kostilyev and Sukhov were in action. In one of the engagements, the tail unit of Kostilyev's aircraft was damaged and he limped back to the airfield with difficulty. Sukhov covered Kostilyev's departure and single-handed fought a battle with four Messerschmitts. Yes, that really was aerial combat! What luck the lads were having! And day after day, we patrolled the main base. It was as if we were chained to it.

'Do you know what, Hussein,' I said to Aliyev after a short pause. 'Let's go and discuss this once more with the CO.'

Maj Dushin, the Regimental Commander, met us affably. 'Well, you pilots on base patrol must be tired, for sure.'

'Not at all,' we replied. 'We are bored stiff flying over Kronstadt, Comrade Major.

'Presently, Maj Novikov will brief you on a new mission.'

We glanced at one another. Novikov unfolded a map on the table, looked at me and, with a hardly perceptible smile, said, 'Well, this will put an end to your suffering. Now, at last, you will have to press your trigger.'

He Landed His Fighter

'The target is an important enemy, mechanized column on the road between Sabsk and the settlement of Osmino,' said the CO. He indicated these populated areas on the map with the point of his pencil. 'Your mission is to attack the enemy column. There are six rocket missiles on each aircraft as well as machine-guns; so you have got something to hit them with.' The Major grinned to himself when he saw our smiling faces. 'No questions? Take off in ten minutes.'

Once in our aircraft, we started the engines and took off. Volosovo village passed beneath us. To the right, a huge fire was blazing: the village of Ivanovsk was burning. Ahead, like a blue ribbon, lay the Luga river. The village of Sabsk could be seen; somewhere beyond it we expected to find the enemy. A few moments more and I could see the enemy column distinctly. I reformed the flight in an echelon to starboard and dived. Spotting us, the Fascists sent up a hurricane of flak; but it was already too late. The deadly missiles tore themselves from their mountings and, tracing a fiery trail, struck the enemy column end to end. Explosions followed, one after another, throwing clouds of earth and pieces of enemy vehicles into the air. At about this moment, we saw a sheet of flame and dense black smoke spread across the forest. Passing low over the enemy column, almost touching it, we strafed with machine-gun fire.

Our first real operational flight, our first strike at the enemy! I regrouped the flight for a second attack. We dived again, firing our rockets, destroying more of the enemy's transport. Bursts of machine-gun fire raked the Fascists. They replied with light flak. In several places on both sides of the road, the forest was on fire. Vehicles, set on fire by us, blazed on the road. In places, smoke covered the column, forming a curtain through which we flew.

Unexpectedly, Sosyedin broke away and climbed. Rocking the plane from wing to wing, he dived with Aliyev following him. What had they discovered there? Ah, that was it: some men were bathing in the River Saba. 'But are they ours?' I wondered. Bursts of flak dispelled my doubts. Shells exploded in front of Sosyedin's aircraft. I turned to attack the gun emplacement but Aliyev forestalled me. He banked and like a stone plunged towards the gun, almost colliding with my plane. Not wishing to impede Aliyev, I followed Sosyedin who was already strafing the bathers. They leaped from the water and ran along the river bank into a willow thicket – a group of men dashed into a field. I turned and gave this group a few bursts. There wasn't a living soul left in the river. Finally, Sosyedin and I flew over the 'beach'. Discarded clothing could be seen on the bank – clearly, no one had dressed. Beside a silent anti-aircraft gun, the motionless bodies of four enemy gunners could be seen. We climbed; but where was Hussein? Not having a radio, I could not know where he had gone.

The wind was blowing smoke away from the road. Again the enemy's transport column could be seen. Sosyedin and I delivered one more attack on it. Before us tracer bullets rose like fireworks. Still Aliyev was nowhere to be seen. Maybe he had had to return to base; but no, we didn't find him at the airfield. We reported the result of our mission, including the successful attack by Aliyev on the anti-aircraft battery; but where was he?

Only by evening did it become clear that an aircraft had landed 18 kilometres from our airfield, close to the village of Gostilitsy. People were saying that this aircraft had waged a fierce aerial battle with enemy aircraft and had been shot down. Our men quickly drove out to the place where it had come down. This is what they heard from witnesses: three Me 110 two-seater fighters were flying towards Leningrad at a fairly low altitude. At the same time, our 'hawk', with its engine smoking, passed over the forest. Unexpectedly, he gained height and intercepted the Fascist aircraft. In the very first moments, the leading Messerschmitt burst into flames and began to lose height. The crew abandoned the aircraft and baled out. The other two Me 110s returned our 'hawk's' fire as he attacked them. Soon, one of them started to smoke and plunged steeply to earth. It fell beyond the village in the forest tract. The third turned back, with our fighter in pursuit. He didn't open fire but was obviously preparing to attack the enemy aircraft from the rear. At this moment, the Fascist opened fire and our 'hawk' started to fall. Then he levelled out, reduced height, flew in the direction of the village and disappeared beyond the forest. The collective farmers who ran towards the tiny woodland clearing saw that the aircraft had landed without putting its wheels down. The pilot was dead. They immediately informed Leningrad what had happened. Soon it became clear that the name of the dead pilot was Aliyev.

In the evening, they brought Hussein and his aircraft back to the airfield. It was still light and everyone immediately examined the twisted engine cowling and the damaged engine cylinders. Friends carefully took Hussein from the plane and laid him on a stretcher. In the cockpit, we saw the smashed instrument panel, and on the floor, fragments of glass and spilled blood. Later the doctor told us that Hussein's body had been struck by thirty shell splinters.

When our comrades arrived at the place where he landed, Hussein was sitting in the cockpit of his fighter. He looked as though, had they called to him, he would have turned immediately and a friendly smile would have flashed across his handsome face. In his left hand, he held the throttle lever, which had been broken by shrapnel; in his right, the control column and, as usual, his feet were on the pedals. Hussein gave the impression that he was aiming at an invisible enemy. He had landed but was still flying his fighter; but now he had already flown to immortality.

'. . . As a mountain takes pride in the flight of a falcon, So the Motherland is proud of its fearless son!' These are the last lines of the remarkable poem about Hussein Aliyev, written by the Azerbaijan poet, Mamed Ragim. His motherland valued Hussein's feat highly and posthumously awarded him a government decoration – the Order of Lenin.

The whole garrison was present at Aliyev's funeral. When a salute was fired, pilots, technicians and Hussein's closest friends stood in mournful silence. Soon a burial mound rose between two sad birch trees, covered with wreaths of wild flowers. In the dim light, we looked once more at the photograph of Hussein on the pyramid of earth, at his features, so dear to our hearts. Quietly we dispersed.

Despite the fierce opposition by our forces, the Fascist army moved inexorably towards Leningrad. Our pilots were returning from western airfields. Kirov, Godunov and Tenyugin returned from Klopitsy; Sukhov and Kostilyev from Kuplya. Soon after, Khaldeyev and Bagryantsev arrived. They brought sad news: in a fierce aerial battle brave Misha Fyodorov had been killed. Aliyev and Fyodorov – it was difficult to believe that these ardent young men, who were so in love with life, were no longer among us. We took revenge on the Fascists for their death. 'For Hussein!', 'For Misha!' we repeated to ourselves as we swept down on an enemy column with a tornado of fire. Again fragments of enemy tanks flew into the air, and again we raked them pitilessly with our machine-gun fire. Sometimes, the nerves of Hitler's fighting cocks would break. Seven soldiers led by their officer, from those forces surrounded in the region of Lake Samro, explained their decision to surrender as they were captured by our infantry.

'Better to surrender than to be driven mad by those hellish machines.'

They had in mind Soviet aircraft and our missiles. That wasn't a bad measure of our first military operation. But at that time only a few of the German soldiers tried to think soberly about their position at the front. Thousands and thousands of others were drunk with Nazi propaganda, and, urged forward by the possessed ravings of their Führer, obstinately burst through towards Moscow and Leningrad.

That's What Friends Are For

It was already light when, above the airfield, our twin-engined transport plane, Li 2, appeared. By that time, the pilots' fighting day had already come to an end. We decided to go for a swim and made our way down to the river. But hardly had I entered the water when I heard a shout.

'Lt Kaberov to the CO!'

Putting on my flying suit as I went, I ran to the squadron dug-out. Two fighters were revving up and, having covered me in dust, took off straight from dispersal. Maj Novikov awaited my arrival with evident impatience. 'Did you see the Li 2 over the airfield?'

'Yes, Major.'

'That's the General's aeroplane. We have been ordered to accompany him to Tallinn. Khaldeyev and Sukhov have already taken off. Refuel at Kotly. Arm your aircraft and fly there.'

'Aye-aye, Major!' I rushed to my machine. My new mechanic, Gritsayenko (Volodya Dikov had been transferred to another unit), had already started the engine. Alferov, the fitter, threw a parachute on me as I ran and helped to fasten the lower straps. In a second, I was in the cockpit, another and, raising a cloud of dust, the plane moved forward. At that moment, I heard someone knocking on the wing and stopped. It was Alferov. The CO was running towards the plane.

'Fuel tanks. Where are your fuel tanks?' I could hear.

'We have rocket racks on,' the mechanic started to explain.

'Quickly, to my machine,' said the Major.

Kirill Yevseyev, the CO's mechanic, soon started the engine. Straight away I took my place in the cockpit on the parachute which lay on the seat and, without fastening the straps, accelerated and took off. As I taxied, the cold motor coughed and died but immediately fired again and revved fully. The aircraft tore itself from the ground at the very end of the airfield, almost touching the tall bushes with its wheels. Beads of perspiration stood out on my forehead. However, all went well. I gained height, turned over the forest and took course for Kotly.

The Li 2 aircraft and our fighters were not to be seen. Probably Gen Samokhin, Officer Commanding the Baltic Fleet, was in a hurry and valued every minute. At Kotly I landed, jumped from the cockpit and straight away ran to Khaldeyev's plane. Both he and Sukhov had already refuelled their machines, as had the Li 2. Taxiing for take-off, Khaldeyev saw me and stopped. He shouted to me above the roar of the engines the route they were taking and what altitude to maintain.

I caught up with the group over Ust-Narva. The General's aircraft was flying low over the water, right along the shore; the fighters just behind at a height of 400 metres. I joined the formation on the starboard side, signalled to Lt Khaldeyev (he was the senior pilot) that everything was under control and started to keep a good look out.

From the direction of Finland, two almost imperceptible dots appeared in the sea. At first I took them for our launches guarding the approaches to the islands. But seconds passed and the dots grew larger and obviously came nearer. 'Aren't they aircraft?' I thought. I couldn't understand why they were moving as if in water, but left no wakes. I moved slightly ahead and, with a movement of my aircraft, indicated to Khaldeyev the suspicious spots. He also began to look at the sea anxiously but evidently could make out nothing.

The setting sun hindered observation, but I had already spotted and clearly recognized that aircraft were coming from the direction of the gulf, and of course they were enemy planes. It was no time to hang about, even for a second. They would see the General's aircraft and then . . . . With a sharp half turn, I dived down and gave a burst of machine-gun fire. The enemy fighters climbed at great speed and my bullets missed them. My failure rather discouraged me. Meanwhile, the Messerschmitt 109s (for the first time I could now recognize them) cut across the outline of the shore and vanished into the clouds.

My friends dropped their auxiliary fuel tanks, quickly gained height and took cover in the spreading evening clouds. I hurried after them. But what's this? Where's the lever to release my fuel tanks? My hand felt only the bracket and spindle with the nut at the end, but no lever. It had been removed. I wanted to shout with indignation. How was I to release the fuel tanks? Why hadn't the mechanic, Yevseyev, told me about this before take-off? I was gripped with alarm. My friends were fighting: I should be there with them. And the General – what if the Fascists noticed him? Time and again I checked the levers and buttons. Each had its particular purpose but was not meant to release the fuel tanks.

I accelerated and the aircraft gained height with difficulty. Not for a moment did my hope of releasing the tanks leave me. Feverishly I looked round the cockpit. At a height of 1,000 metres, an enemy fighter tumbled out of the clouds. I banked and tried to get him in my sights but he climbed above me, turned over like a kite and swooped down. I succeeded in putting my aircraft into a sideslip. Tracer bullets passed me by. My mind worked quickly. Understanding that I was not in a very happy situation, I cautiously followed the Messerschmitt.

Coming out of the attack, the pilot repeated his manoeuvre and again flew at me, fired and missed. Evidently, the two unsuccessful attacks angered my opponent. He didn't climb this time but banked the plane into a tight turn. This was something of an advantage to me. The radius of the turn for my aircraft was less than that of the Messerschmitt. It would be fine to get on his tail and give him a burst. But the fuel tanks, the cursed fuel tanks! Because of them, I couldn't bank steeply enough.

Unexpectedly, a sharp blow shook my aircraft as if the fuselage had been lashed by a whip. The plane was thrown to one side. Recovering my position, I saw there was a gaping hole in my starboard wing. The enemy fighter passed over me like a meteor and in a few seconds struck again. My aircraft turned over and went into a spin. With great difficulty, and not before I was close to the ground, was I able to stop the rotation and steer into horizontal flight. My hands were shaking from nervous strain. I looked round. Nobody was behind me; and nobody was attacking me. Strange, where had the German gone? I accelerated and gained height again. Only now did I discover that the port wing was damaged. However, the machine was flying and responding to the controls. I banked round easily to see if the enemy was playing some dirty trick, but he had actually flown away.

This, however, did not altogether bring joy. My thoughts were not carefree. There could be no question of reaching Tallinn. Would the General get there? And what about Khaldeyev and Sukhov? What was the result of their fight? What would they think of me? How would they judge the fact that I had not stayed with them? Never mind, I would explain back at base; they would understand. . . . But they didn't understand everything. Khaldeyev's and Sukhov's faithful report, which they delivered to the brigade headquarters after they had landed at the airfield a few minutes before me, was construed with unexpected severity. After landing, hardly had I taxied to dispersal than I was ordered to disarm and in half an hour the head of the political department, the Brigade Commissar, S.S. Bessonov, arrived from Kronstadt to conduct an investigation for the party.

Such a turn of events had a depressing effect on both me and Maj Novikov. He immediately explained to everyone that at his orders Yevseyev, the mechanic, had made changes to the system for releasing the auxiliary fuel tanks, strengthening the cable and adding a knob on a specially made bracket under the gunsight.

'It's very useful. You should have pulled the knob, Lieutenant. It's here, nearby,' explained Yevseyev to me, recognizing the reason for my unsuccessful flight. In his hurry, he had forgotten to forewarn me about it and now cursed himself for his negligence.

The voice of Bessonov was roaring in the dug-out. 'You are shielding cowards!'

'He's a candidate member of the Communist Party, Comrade Regimental Commissar,' Isakovich calmly reminded him.

'Expel him. Call a meeting and expel him tomorrow.' I saw and heard him no more. In the darkness, I wandered over to a motor vehicle parked not far from the dug-out, climbed into the cabin and lay down on the seat, ashamed of my own tears. 'For what?' I asked myself. 'What crime have I committed?' Only towards morning did I manage to drop off. I don't know whether I slept for long. Volodya Khaldeyev's voice woke me.

'Look where he's settled himself. And we've been searching for you everywhere. Get up. Go to breakfast.'

'I'm going nowhere.'

'Don't be a fool, nothing will happen to you.'

Everything will be OK. Well, they'll criticize you about the fuel tanks, that's for sure. Of course, Yevseyev let you down there. He's also not himself.'

'I fear Bessonov, Volodya. He's frightful!'

'That's not true. Semyon Semyonovich is a fine man. I have known him for a long time. Now and again he kicks up a fuss. He carries a heavy responsibility for everything, brother. But this is how it was: we were giving cover to the General and suddenly we were left on our own. When Semyon Semyonovich heard, the sparks flew. Isakovich has been talking to us about this. There will probably be a party meeting this evening. Have no fear. Tell them everything just as it was. Party members stand up for themselves.'

And that evening there actually was a party meeting. Those who took part sat on the grass beside the aircraft in which I had flown on my mission. The plane had already been repaired. The technicians had patched up fourteen bullet holes. As they told me later, people from all the dispersal points had come to look at the damaged aircraft.

Snigiryev, a senior technician who was party organizer, opened the meeting. Having informed everyone briefly the gist of the matter, he said: 'I think that first of all we should hear what Communist Kaberov has to say.'

'But why should we do that?' said Bessonov. 'Everything, in my opinion, is quite clear. He's a coward. Cowards have no place in the party. I propose we take a vote on it.'

Those present at the meeting started to make dissatisfied noises. Snigiryev raised his hand. He turned to Bessonov. 'Nobody asked you to speak. Here you are, just a communist like everybody else. So please observe party discipline.'

The chairman's fortitude was rewarded with quickly ensuing silence. Bessonov was cut short. 'I beg your pardon. I was expressing the opinion, of the Brigade Commander.'

I was allowed to speak. Once again I related everything as it happened and quietly waited for questions.

'Who then, after all, is at fault for what happened?' Sergey Sukhov unexpectedly asked me. 'Who is to blame for the fact that you broke away from us and took on the enemy fighter after the first attack?'

It was a searching question. And who posed it? Seryozha Sukhov, my friend who finished flying school with me. He looked at me reproachfully, his severe look demanding a reply. The meeting was silent. I had not expected things to take such a turn and felt ill at ease. My calculations that they would take pity on me as a victim of circumstances were destroyed. I looked at Yevseyev, the technician, at the CO, ran my eyes over all the communists and said nothing.

Then Snigiryev asked to speak. 'To accuse a man of cowardice,' he began, 'you must have sufficient grounds. I am shocked by the way this question has been put. I reject this version of events. It wasn't like that. Here was haste, courage and negligence. And by the way, it's not the first time with Kaberov. There was one occasion when he took off without his flying goggles.'

'They know everything,' I thought. Meanwhile, Snigiryev continued. 'Yes, that did happen, but we didn't hold him responsible. But to no purpose!' Snigiryev's voice sounded angry. He said that Novikov and Yevseyev were also at fault in what had happened, but the pilot was most to blame.

'Kaberov did not reply to Sukhov's question. Even now, apparently, he has not understood his most serious blunder,' said Snigiryev, 'but in accordance with instructions, when taking over an aircraft before take-off, the plane must be checked and the technician's receipt signed. Of course, speed in operations is necessary, but simply to jump into the cockpit and set off is not allowed. An aircraft is not a cart, comrades!'

Commissar Isakovich, the squadron's Senior Political Officer, spoke. He explained the situation which had developed near Leningrad and in Estonia and informed us that Gen Samokhin had arrived safely in Tallinn and had sent a telegram in which he thanked the fighter pilots who had accompanied him.

'Maybe Khaldeyev, Sukhov and Kaberov did not act in the very best way but, nevertheless, as we admitted, they engaged the enemy aircraft in battle,' said Isakovich. 'As far as Communist Kaberov is concerned, we know with what energy he has worked during the war. He is, without doubt, a brave pilot. We must not fail to take into account the fact that in this operation Kaberov spotted the enemy aircraft; he warned the Flight Commander of the danger and he was the first to attack the Messerschmitts. True, because of neglectful inspection of his machine before take-off, he found himself in a difficult position. Moreover, despite the fact that he could not release his fuel tanks, he gained height in order to help his comrades in aerial battle. A Messerschmitt intercepted and opened fire on him; even then Kaberov did not give up. He accepted the unequal contest. And that is character, comrades, the character of a real warrior. But I would also say, to take off as he did yesterday on that mission was inexcusable.'

The Commissar cast his eyes over the aircraft, beneath the wing of which the meeting was being conducted and passed his hand along the fuselage.

'To prepare for take-off and not put on your parachute is a serious blunder! To sit in the cockpit and not check that everything is in order is a second. Just think what might happen if others made the same mistakes. I don't even know how to describe it. I'm not talking about the fact that the pilot didn't strap himself in, but that he didn't warm up the engine. Remember that the engine cut out several times on take-off. By doing this you are only one step from catastrophe.'

'What a real blockhead I am,' I thought. 'How could I have made so many mistakes at one stroke?' Before my comrades, I felt such shame. I looked round the meeting. Everyone had serious, strict faces, especially Isakovich.

'I propose,' he said in conclusion, 'that for infringement of instructions governing the operation of an I 16 aircraft, for neglecting to fasten his parachute, and for quite unnecessary bravado, to admonish Communist Kaberov. And furthermore, to ask the Regimental Commander to post him to a forward airfield with Bagryantsev's flight. There let him prove by his conduct that he does not betray the trust we put in him.'

'Yes, that's right!' voices echoed. A lump rose in my throat. The communists now unanimously voted for Isakovich's proposal. It meant that they had confirmed his admonishment.

Major Novikov glanced at me with an embarrassed smile. 'Well, how are you? Was the dressing-down so bad? No Messerschmitt is likely to thrash you like your friends. And that's right. That's what friends are for. I remember, my father would always say, "If I didn't love you, I wouldn't beat you!"'

Kirill Yevseyev, Volodya Khaldeyev, Aleksey Snigiryev and other comrades gathered round.

The head of the political department left the meeting without saying a word. Later, after I had scored my first victory in battle, he sought me out to congratulate me. This time he said much in praise of our squadron collective and Commissar Isakovich.

'But I also want to admit to you,' Bessonov suddenly became serious, 'that immediately after the meeting, I wanted to apologize to you, brother. Pride, you see, didn't let me. So forgive me, an old man, forgive me for two reasons: for being abrupt and for not confessing my fault immediately.'

I said that I also had to confess that the communists had been right to criticize me. Bessonov shook my hand again.

'Well, fight on!'

CHAPTER TWO

Defending Klopitsy Airfield

Another Second And It Will Be Too Late

On 3 August Bagryantsev's flight, in which I was included as a wing man, left to defend Klopitsy airfield. Our young flight had been disbanded; Aliyev was dead and Sosyedin was flying with Kostilyev. Before we based ourselves at Klopitsy, we had to escort the Commander in Chief to Tallinn once again. It seemed that Gen Samokhin had managed to return from Estonia and was flying there again. Inwardly, I cringed when Novikov pronounced the words 'Escort the General'. But the Major didn't even mention my unfortunate flight. He merely explained briefly to Bagryantsev the operation which faced the flight and turning to all of us said:

'Don't delay in Tallinn; little daylight will be left. Set off and go straight for Klopitsy. You must report for duty at first light.'

As it did the first time, the Li 2 aircraft circled over Nizino. This time we took off without hurrying, got into position and flew away. The General's aircraft kept close to the ground. With its green camouflage, it was hardly noticeable against the forest background. We flew just behind and above the Li 2.

Every second I expected to meet an enemy fighter. I thought out, to the last detail, different tactics for a possible fight. But we didn't meet the enemy. We circled over Tallinn's steep roofs, and landed while the General's aircraft set course for Ezel Island. We were refuelling our planes when a man in naval uniform came up to us. It was the aerodrome Commandant.

'Everything here has been mined,' he said to Bagryantsev. 'Touch nothing. Move only along the paths marked by flags. Hurry to take off.' The Commandant left us as quickly as he had appeared. We glanced at one another. It wasn't difficult to guess that the position in Tallinn was serious; that preparations were being made to evacuate our military forces.

After a quick bite in the mess, we again hurried to our aircraft and soon left the airfield. As we circled over the town, I looked for the spire of the Tallinn town hall with its old weather vane representing an ancient warrior. Farewell Tallinn! Farewell Old Thomas! It'll be some time now before we see one another again.

An hour of steady flight and we were in Klopitsy. Kostilyev's flight, which we were ordered to replace, was preparing to return to its own airfield. Kostilyev, Sukhov and Sosyedin had 'bagged' several Junkers and

Messerschmitts. They could have told us much more about this, but the sun was already on the horizon and they had to fly home in daylight. They asked us for news from Nizino. We told them the latest: Yefimov had been found. It turned out that he had been carrying out a manoeuvre to avoid anti-aircraft fire, broke away from his group, took an imprecise course and lost his bearings. Trying to re-establish them, he ran out of fuel and, as his engine had cut out, made a belly landing close to Yefimov station to the east of Tikhvin on the road to Vologda. The technicians there fitted a new airscrew and Yefimov returned home. Now he had flown off to Ezel together with Alexeyev. Kostilyev unfolded a map and, tracing Yefimov's route, shook his head.

'Look where Andreyich has got to!'

The chaps laughed, 'Yefimov has even landed himself near the village of Yefimov. Could it be he has relatives there?'

Kostilyev and Sukhov started their engines but for some reason Sosyedin hurried to his tent. When he returned, he shoved a piece of paper into my hands. 'It's the German timetable for bombing Klopitsy. I advise you to study it.'

My friends flew away. Soon the airfield was plunged into evening twilight. The technicians continued to work beside the machines, preparing them for morning take-off. Squadron engineer Sergeyev decided to help us settle in. Soon we saw the tents for ground staff, which had been erected in the forest between the golden trunks of tall pine trees. On the very edge of the forest, closer to the dispersal area, stood our white tent, our canvas home. 'What awaits us here?' I thought that evening as I went to bed. Sleep did not come quickly and listening to the even breathing of my comrades, I ran through in my mind the events of the last few days.

At 7 o'clock precisely, as forecast on the timetable drawn up by Sosyedin, enemy aircraft appeared over Klopitsy. A couple of fighters swept insolently over dispersal and started to circle the airfield. Bagryantsev gave orders to start the engines. We took off. The Messerschmitts gained height. Then, slackening speed, they made a sharp turn, bringing them close to us. Bagryantsev immediately turned and made for them. The temptation to attack an enemy aircraft which appears in front of your nose is great. Not waiting for Bagryantsev and Tenyugin, I accelerated, but fortunately looked round: behind were two other enemy fighters diving on Bagryantsev's aircraft. Another second and it would have been impossible to help him. I made a hurried turn and gave a defensive burst of fire. So, without even succeeding to open fire on Bagryantsev, the Messerschmitt lifted its nose, turned on its back, began to spin slowly and suddenly plunged vertically to earth.

'Got him, I've got him!' I shouted. My voice sounded strange in the cockpit where no one could hear me. The enemy aircraft kept falling and falling and I didn't take my eyes off him. A few more seconds and the end came. A cloud of dust flew into the air and, blown by the wind, soon dispersed. The plane fell by the church in the village of Klopitsy, half a kilometre from our dispersal.

The aerial battle came to an end. The enemy did not dare to repeat their attack and left for home. I accelerated, overtook Bagryantsev and indicated to him with gestures the place where the Messerschmitt had fallen. The Flight Commander smiled, nodded to me for a moment, took his hands off the controls and, clasping them above his head, congratulated me. After we landed, all three of us drove to the place where the enemy aircraft had crashed. Farm workers, who had gathered round the plane, moved aside when they saw us.

Here he was, the fallen foe. Only a few minutes before, he was still soaring in the sky, but now . . . . The engine and the cockpit, with the pilot still in it, had dug deep into the earth; the fuselage and tail unit with its spiderlike swastika stuck in the air; and the wings had fallen to the side.

Young and old alike ran towards the edge of the village of Klopitsy. Everyone was talking about the aerial battle which had just finished. An old man was noisily sharing his impressions with others.

'I was standing by the church and looking into the sky,' he was saying excitedly, 'and the Fascist plane flew straight at me. "My God, my God," I said. "You mustn't drop your bomb now." And of course, I ran behind the church. I crossed myself, pressed myself against the wall, screwed up my eyes and waited. I heard a whistle. Something's sure to go off now! It dropped but there was no explosion. I opened my eyes and, Holy Mother of God! I was amazed. It turned out it wasn't a bomb at all. Satan himself had come here in person. I'd have taken my spade to him, but my spade was no use; or else I'd have finished him off!'

'Yes, you did a good job,' said Bagryantsev to me. 'Without a doubt, Bessonov should have been here, Igor. He should have seen. Well, thank you, my friend.' He embraced me. 'Thank you for your help. Had you paused for a second, my children would have been orphans.'

'Now look, comrades,' Bagryantsev said, addressing the people standing round us and pointing at the enemy aircraft. 'This will fly no more, and hopefully neither will the rest.'

We asked the farmers to touch nothing on the plane until our technicians arrived. Bidding farewell to the villagers, we climbed into the car. For the last time, I looked back at the remains of the Messerschmitt. After all, it was my prize, not anybody else's.

In the Forest And Above It

I woke before daybreak, and without getting up, I lifted the edge of the soaking wet tent. Damp, cold air breathed on my face. It had been raining for three days and we had not flown during that time; nor had the Germans. We had flown into Klopitsy the week before and the lads were saying that they were tired of inactivity. True, even in inclement weather, the mechanics had enough work: they made a thorough inspection of aircraft during those days. It turned out that the guns on my aircraft needed adjustment. The armourer had promised to work on it as soon as the rain stopped. I listened for the sound of raindrops on the tent tarpaulin: no sound. That meant that at dawn they would start on the gunsight. For the moment, I could lie in. The day before, our bedsheets had been changed, and it was pleasant to loll on clean bedding. It was not the first time that we had rested more than usual. For two days we had slept on as long as we liked, and it turned out that, during that time, Bagryantsev found plenty to talk about, including much that was interesting about himself.

In childhood things had not been easy for him. He was not even six when his father was killed in the war. His large family went without food. Nine-year-old Misha had to work as an apprentice to a tinsmith. Then a dispute arose with his stepfather and he became homeless. Misha wandered about the country for four years until he settled down working in a factory. In the army, his long held dream came true – he learnt to fly. Then, came military conflict between Finland and the Soviet Union, and with them his first battles and victories, his first decoration for bravery.

Tenyugin was asleep in one of the bunks; the other was neatly made up – since Bagryantsev had flown to Nizino. It was raining but he had still taken off. No doubt, if they had summoned him in such weather, something serious was expected.

Bagryantsev was a restless person. When he, Khaldeyev and Fyodorov were at Shimsk, a Ju 88 reconnaissance aircraft appeared above Utorgosh station. It was clearly visible from the aerodrome. Bagryantsev couldn't take off because his flight had only just returned from patrol and the aircraft were being refuelled. But even if it had been possible to catch up with the reconnaissance aircraft, it would not have changed anything. The pilot could summon his bombers by radio.

Remembering that troop trains were standing on the railway tracks, Bagryantsev climbed into a car and ordered the driver to go to the station immediately. The stationmaster wasn't there, but Mikhail Ivanovich found an engine driver.

'Disperse the rolling stock immediately,' he ordered. 'A raid by enemy bombers is expected.'

'I'll do that when the authorities give me orders,' replied the driver obstinately.

'I'm giving you the order!' insisted Bagryantsev.

The driver still refused. Bagryantsev drew his pistol from its holster and did not leave the shunting engine until all the carriages had been moved.

The ensuing strike by the bombers on the dispersed troop trains caused little damage. Meanwhile, our fighters shot down four enemy aircraft. Two of these were counted as Bagryantsev's: one was shot down, the other rammed.

'And did you bale out?' I asked Bagryantsev when I first heard about it.

'No, I had just reached home,' he said. 'Everything happened, do you see, unexpectedly. The last pair of Junkers dived on the station. Well, I caught them up and got them in my sights. I pressed the button, but nothing happened. Evidently, the ammunition had run out. One of the Junkers dropped its bombs and pulled out of its dive sharply. I also pulled out, but my plane was lower and a little ahead of the enemy. Without thinking twice, I pulled on the stick. My machine shot up and a second later struck the Junkers on the tail unit. There was a crash and my plane shuddered and was thrown to one side. It trembled, as if in a fever, but to my astonishment still flew. However, I felt I would not get far so I turned towards the airfield and looked for a place to land.'

According to Bagryantsev, everything happened simply as if by itself. But I know that it wasn't so. He consciously took a mortal risk. He hated the enemy and all his strength, at that decisive moment, was directed to one purpose: to strike and bring down the aircraft, whatever happened. I tried to imagine how it had been in all its detail. I thought about it as I lay on my camp bed in the rain-soaked tent. Somewhere close by a branch snapped. I rose and walked out.

'Who is here?'

'It is I, Gomonov. I'm on night watch. But why aren't you sleeping, Comrade Lieutenant?'

'Somehow, I can't sleep.'

'It's still early. Get some rest.'

I lay down and again began to think about this ram attack. Actually, how unusual everything is in war. The most desperate decisions are sometimes taken in a fraction of a second. It was quiet in the forest; quite unbelievable that we were at the front. It was as if we were in a pioneer camp and about to set off to collect mushrooms and berries. But this was no time for collecting mushrooms and berries. In our hearts we were disturbed and anxious. The Fascist armies were moving towards Leningrad, coming closer day by day. Where were they now? How far from us? Nobody knew. I got up, dressed and went out of the tent. No gunfire could be heard. Only various birdsongs flooded the woods, as if to wish us 'Good morning'. Only, would it be a good morning?

At this early hour the technicians could now be seen near the aircraft at dispersal. What restless people. Whenever did they sleep! I washed and did something like morning exercises, then called in to our canvas abode. I was able to rest only for ten or fifteen minutes. I lay on the blankets and looked at the roof of the tent as it became brighter and thought constantly about the forthcoming operational flights, the enemy aircraft and the aerial tactics adopted by the enemy. Three days before, the Fascists had made an attack on our aerodrome. Judging from where they had dropped their bombs, they could hardly have known the disposition of our long-range bombers. They were so skilfully hidden in the forest that even we ourselves could not make them out from the air. But just the same, how did it happen that in broad daylight six Me 110s could leap out of the forest on a low-level attack? We didn't even have time to take off. And for some reason, they did not ring us from the observation post. Evidently, we still had many faults in our observation and warning system.

. . . And then there were our bombers. Good show! Where did they go? Do you believe – Berlin! When was that? 8 August and today was the tenth. Just two days ago. Well, our neighbours knew all about it. It was a group from their division. They flew, they said, from somewhere in Estonia; maybe from Ezel where Yefimov and Alekseyev went not long ago. Imagine how the Fascists ran when we dropped bombs on their lair. They were saying that in Berlin there wasn't even a blackout. Never mind, a few more raids and they'd understand what it was all about.

Remembering the details of this raid, I observed how the tent canvas was flooded with light, then suddenly heard carefully placed footsteps. The guard keeping watch on dispersal, seaman Vanya Gomonov, came into the tent. Not tall, he was an unusually lively and energetic lad.

'Comrade Lieutenant,' he said in a forced whisper. 'I can hear a noise somewhere.'

I hurriedly threw back the tent and listened. There was no doubt that somewhere, not far off, German aircraft were approaching.

'Raise the alarm, Vanya!' I shouted, made for my aeroplane, and was in the air.

I had hardly reached 200 metres when, to one side, I could see the dark silhouettes of Fascist bombers. Five Me 110s dived on the airfield. I made a sharp turn and aimed for the leader. The enemy gunner in the next plane gave me a burst of machine-gun fire, which beat a tattoo along the wooden fuselage of my I 16. However, the machine kept a normal course so I attacked again, but the Me 110 had already dropped its bombs and a bluish cloud of smoke spread over the dispersal area and the edge of the wood. Any hope that Tenyugin would come to help me was abandoned. I attacked first one, then another Fascist. In defence, the Messerschmitts formed a circle above the airfield. Then they stretched into a chain and flew away. I attacked the last machine and gave it a burst. The tracer bullets went to the left. I corrected the error on the gunsight and struck the Messerschmitt's port engine. Smoke appeared but the aircraft continued to fly away at the same speed. The enemy gunner continued to fire in desperation. There were already holes in my starboard wing. I carried on firing but without success. The Messerschmitts went down to ground level and flew away at great speed. For some time, I pursued them and then returned. Perhaps another group of enemy aircraft might come.

At last, Tenyugin took off, caught up with me and got into position. Well, I felt happier now there were two of us. After twenty minutes, we landed, but it was with a heavy heart that I climbed out of my cockpit. Not one! Not a single aircraft had I destroyed. It was like gunnery school.

I undid the straps of my parachute. Alferov, our fitter, helped me remove it.

'You did well, Comrade Lieutenant!' he said, clearly trying to console me. 'Only, no doubt they're armoured and you can't penetrate it.'

'It's not a question of armour, Boris; it's something else. Remember how Hussein Aliyev fought. In a matter of minutes, two aircraft were destroyed. Then his ammunition ran out or another Messerschmitt would have crashed to earth. That means it's possible to hit them. But we have, as you know, a gunsight which is awry. I have been thinking: in the morning, we'll repair it.'

Alferov's face became worried: 'I understand, Comrade Lieutenant.'

'Well then, tell the engineer and let the armourers repair the gunsight.'

'Aye-aye,' he rapped out. Placing the parachute on the tailplane, Alferov ran to the armourer's tent.

Tenyugin carefully examined my aeroplane. 'You are lucky. There are so many holes but not one bullet hit the cockpit.' He was silent for a moment, turning his flying helmet over in his hands. 'But just the same, you flew to no purpose; you should have woken me. We should have gone together.'

'Every second was valuable, Volodya.'

'Generally speaking, that's so,' said Tenyugin. 'I hardly had time to run to the aeroplane when they started to dive. And they dropped their bombs again in just the same corner that they did last time. And again they hit nobody, only damaged the forest. Three bombs were real; the rest, as before, pieces of tin! They only made a lot of smoke.'

Yes, the Germans didn't know where our bombers were hidden and this pleased us. But what would happen next? There were only two of us. And what if the Fascists came when our aircraft were being refuelled? Moreover, a large group with fighter escort could fly in. What then? Tenyugin wiped his sunglasses with a cloth and looked at me. 'Well, this is what: in fact we'll go to the mess.'

Tenyugin had lived all his life in Ostashkov. Since childhood, Volodya had loved the picturesque countryside of the Upper Volga and the unique beauty of Lake Seliger. He had the calm, even-tempered character of a native of the Volga region. He was straightforward in his judgement, fearless and a man of few words. Looking at him, I thought to myself: 'How good to work with such a type!'

Breakfast over, we went to our tent at the edge of the wood.

'Look.' Tenyugin stopped me, threw back his head and shaded his eyes from the sun. 'Look, what a sky today! It's like the sky over Lake Seliger! Tell me, have you ever been on Seliger, eh?'

I didn't succeed in answering Tenyugin. Vanya Gomonov was running towards us. What was the matter? It turned out that I was called to the phone urgently. Quick, to the tent! I lifted the receiver.

'Lt Kaberov here.'

'Bombers are heading for us.'

'Who's speaking?' Imagining that this call was from the headquarters of a neighbouring unit, I tried to get more information.

'The observer at the observer post.'

'Where are the bombers coming from? Where are they going? From which direction?'

'They're still not visible.'

'But how can that be?' I hung up in a fit of temper.

'Where is it, this observer post?' Volodya and I ran out of the tent. He pointed out to me an extremely tall pine tree. The observer was sitting in it like a cuckoo; sitting at the very top.

'Hey, guard!' I shouted at him. 'Where are the bombers then?'

He raised his field-glasses to his eyes. 'There they are!'

'Very far?'

'No, near!'

We rushed to our aircraft. Tenyugin took his place in his cockpit and started the engine. I couldn't do the same. My fighter, with its tail propped up, was aimed at a tree on which a white sheet of paper was hanging.

'Gritsayenko!' I shouted at the technician. 'What's the matter?'

'We've been testing the gunsight, Lieutenant. It's in working order now.'

I ordered him to take the trestle away, took the plane into the air and chased after Tenyugin. Meanwhile my leader had already signalled to me and turned about. I followed him. And the observer was right. In fact, to the west of the airfield, aircraft were approaching at low level. I looked at my gunsight. 'Don't let me down, my friend!'

The aircraft were already quite close. Tenyugin turned to attack. I also dived at the aircraft nearest to me. There it was, in the centre of the gunsight and my finger on the trigger, when suddenly . . . . It was as if an electric current passed through me from head to toe. I saw stars on the wings of the aircraft. Ours! We were attacking ours! I banked away; Tenyugin also. He rocked his plane from wing to wing, giving me the signal to follow. We gained height and looked about. Well, of course, they were our Pe 2s, evidently returning from a mission. First three, then two aircraft and, following them a long way behind, another one. It was obvious that they'd had a hard battle since they were separated, each at his own pace.

I remembered our observer. Whoever thought of such a post? Well, from the top of the tree, it was only possible to see enemy aircraft approaching the airfield 8 or 10 kilometres away. And what was the sense in that? They would cover such a distance in a minute and a half. While the observer was ringing us, while we were running to our machines, climbing into the cockpit, starting the engine, warming it up and then taxiing, those one and a half minutes would be up. When would we have time to take off? Although formally everything was in order: there was an AOIC post for aerial observation, information and communication – but would we ever finish fighting with such observation and information? The sailor, of course, was doing his best, and he had to be a brave man to carry out his duties in that crow's nest.

When we landed, there was excitement at dispersal. Bagryantsev had flown in. It was cause for celebration for all personnel. People read newspapers and the letters he had brought, and shared their news. Mikhail Ivanovich went off to the headquarters of a neighbouring unit. We waited for him to return soon.

A particularly large group of people had gathered near our tent. Someone unrolled a colourful poster devoted to the feats of the army's fighter pilots, Zhukov, Zdorovtsev and Kharitonov. Each one of them had been awarded the title of Hero of the Soviet Union at the start of the war. An I 16 fighter was drawn on the poster. It was ramming a Fascist bomber. Pieces of the tail unit were flying in all directions. The engines of the Junkers were on fire. Nose down, it was making its last dive. Of course, the burning engines were an artist's fantasy. It's not necessary to ram a burning aircraft: it would crash anyway. As for the ramming itself, that was fine, it must be said.

Someone mentioned the name of the gallant Russian staff captain Pyotr Nikolayevich Nesterov. It was he who, on 8 September 1914, overtook an enemy aircraft above the headquarters positions of the Third Army on the south-west front and struck it from above with the wheels of his plane. It was the first ram attack in the history of aviation. But now such attacks are no longer a rarity. Just the same, a ram attack is a last extreme measure.

Yegor Kostilyev told me how once at Narva, when his cartridges ran out, he tried to ram a Junkers. 'I accelerated to full speed and went after him. Well, the enemy pilot saw, of course, that the distance between us was shortening and that I was not firing. He turned his machine away sharply. No fool, he understood what this meant. His gunner fired at point-blank range. A cone of bright red tracer bullets flashed before my eyes. The fighter's fuselage creaked, but there was no hit. I chased him again until, once more, I was level with the Junkers. I wanted to strike him with my propeller so that my plane remained in one piece. Unexpectedly, a powerful slipstream from the bomber rocked the fighter. The next moment, the enemy gunner opened fire. At any minute, it seemed to me, my propeller would bite through the tail of the Junkers and he would fall out of control. But my joyful excitement abated there and then. It became clear that the ram attack had not worked. My bullet-riddled plane, with an engine losing power, lost height despite all my efforts. Only with difficulty did I reach the airfield.'

Calling to mind this story of Kostilyev's, I cannot help thinking of the man himself. Yegor, an excellent pilot who flew his fighter with perfect mastery, was recklessly brave. Pupil of the Chkalov Central Aeroclub of the USSR, he frequently astonished Muscovites with his masterly aerobatic performances at air displays. Just the same, Yegor never performed a ram attack. And yet these three and Bagryantsev had done so. What sort of qualities must a person possess in order to carry out such a feat . . .?

A Ram Attack That Failed

A shout was heard from the armourers' tent.

'Scramble, fighters, scramble!'

The technicians rushed to the aircraft, but we were delayed for a moment by Bagryantsev, who had arrived breathless from the headquarters of the next unit.

'There's a group of Junkers to the west of us. They are making course for Leningrad above the clouds. To your aircraft!'

We were soon above the aerodrome and gaining height, but I was uneasy. Above us was unbroken cloud. Until then, I hadn't flown in such conditions. True, I had carried out exercises in a covered cockpit. I looked at the small bearing and the needle which indicated the degree of turn; an instrument with the proud name of 'Pioneer' (a device which, no doubt, had been used in aircraft since the birth of aviation). I tried the rudder. The bearing and the needle in the device began to swing. We reached the edge of the clouds. Bagryantsev flew on and we followed. Altitude – 1,000, 2,000 metres. It was damp and uncomfortable in the clouds. I could no longer see Tenyugin. It was impossible to take your eyes off the leader. That was how you should go on and on, maintaining visual contact. But no. . . . On that day, I don't understand why, for some reason, I had to look at the cockpit. When, therefore, I transferred my glance to the leader, he was no longer beside me. I felt he was near, but I couldn't see him. Fearing a collision, I turned away to one side. Now it was necessary to establish a normal flying position. I glanced feverishly at the instruments, the bearing, the needle, the variometer, the air speed indicator and the altimeter. My nerves were tense. The altimeter showed 3,000 metres and I was still flying in the clouds. How slowly the I 16 gained height! I was only thinking this when the sunlight struck me. A milky foam seemed to have settled on the upper surface of the clouds, and above me was blue sky. It was as if my fingers had become part of the control column. 'You have a weak grasp, Comrade Kaberov,' the surgeon remarked at the last fitness test. It would have been interesting to see how much I would have scored if they had given me the dynamometer test at that moment.

I turned and made for the place where Bagryantsev might have been expected to emerge from the clouds, but neither he nor Tenyugin did I discover. Where were they? I roamed about the gigantic mountainous clouds. I flew to the west, as Bagryantsev had ordered, but followed a course slightly to the north so as to forestall the bombers' emergence in that area; but I didn't lose hope of meeting the others in my flight. Where had they vanished? Further to the west, the cloud thinned out. It became easier to find one's bearings. On the way, a separate cloud appeared. I decided to fly into it and get a little practice at flying on my instruments, but the cloud wasn't big and, just beyond it and in front of me at the same altitude, I saw two Ju 88s with crosses as black as coal. In surprise, I banked sharply away and immediately went into the attack. What an unexpected meeting! The Fascists weren't going towards Leningrad but in the opposite direction. Evidently, they had dropped their deadly load somewhere. If only Bagryantsev and Tenyugin could have joined in.

The enemy spotted me and began to manoeuvre. I fired at one of them – black smoke streaked across the sky. Not losing a second, I made another attack – the enemy gunner answered with a snarl. Several bullets rattled along my machine, but I continued my dive without opening fire so that from close quarters I could be certain of hitting him. The first burst was aimed at the gunner, the second, point blank at the engine. Smoke poured from this motor. The Junkers swayed and vanished under my wing. I wanted to see if it had gone down and banked my plane. At that moment, three tears appeared in my left wing. The aileron was hit but, fortunately, its control was not impaired. The gunner in the leading Junkers had scored the hit. Gripped by anger and wishing to give as good as I got, I launched a third attack. The bomber which I had damaged fell back from the one in front. Ah, once more and he will sing his last! I chose the right moment and pressed the button. 'What's happened?' The guns, after several shots, fell silent. In annoyance, I almost struck the Junkers with my wing as I passed close by him.

To reload the upper machine-guns was comparatively easy, but the lower heavy-calibre ones could not be reloaded quite so easily. I flew away from the Junkers and attempted to reload. Difficult, oh so difficult! I lowered the seat, stretched under the instrument panel, grasped the lever and pulled it back. Then I lifted the seat, looked around, brought the aircraft into level flight and started to repeat the process. My strength was flagging and there was no way I could reload the lower machine-gun. Had I been taller, had my fingers been longer, I could have managed easily. But as it was: impossible. I tugged and tugged at the handle, but what was the point? I raised the seat and looked around. Right under me, the railway stretched from Leningrad to Tallinn; on the left, Volosovo station. Kingisepp appeared to float beneath the wing to the right. And the Junkers – there they were! I tested the reloaded guns. I was able to fire only a short burst. They fell silent. 'Can all the cartridges really be spent?' I thought, horrified. 'What should I do?' Meanwhile the bombers had moved nearer to one another. They were flying, as we say, in close formation. 'Ram attack! Ram both at once!' The idea crossed my mind. 'Attack from below; that would take them by surprise.'

I unfastened the harness straps and tested the parachute rip-cord; then descended about 300 metres as if abandoning the fight. Next, I made course to follow the Junkers, gradually overtaking them. Now the enemy aircraft were flying above and just behind me. Lifting my head, I observed them carefully, judging the moment to strike.

Well, this is it! Stick back, full speed! Obedient and responsive, the fighter rose like a rocket into the sky in the direction in which it was aimed. Soon it would be in pieces, breaking its wings and its enemy's. I made a precise calculation, aiming between the bombers. The bodies of the enemy machines momentarily filled the whole sky. They were very close. A fraction of a second more and a shattering blow would end our meeting. My muscles were strained to their limit. I squeezed myself into a ball, expecting the crash. Obviously, I would be thrown from the cockpit. Never mind, my parachute would save me. Now then, what was this? Why no crash? At the very last moment, the Fascist aircraft parted. Immediately, machine-guns opened fire from both of them simultaneously. Tracer bullets flashed like lightning and met on the engine of my plane, shaking it heavily. Pieces of cowling broke away and the cockpit was filled with smoke. Without striking either of the Junkers, my plane climbed higher then, losing speed and as if plunging into an abyss, it turned over and went into a steep, fast spin. I felt as if my head would be torn off at any moment. I moved the stick sharply to guide the plane out of its spin but it didn't stop turning. Something was fouling the stick. It was a dangerous situation so with an effort I pushed the stick forward. At last, thank goodness, the fighter resumed level flight. My hands and feet were really numb from the incredible strain. No, it must be said, a pilot needs physical strength and a lot of it too.

I opened the throttle and, only then, realized that the aircraft's engine had stopped. There was less smoke, but my eyes were streaming, as if I'd been peeling onions. Before making my last attack, I had lifted my goggles so that I wouldn't damage my eyes in the crash. Now they were dangling behind me on a strap fastened to the helmet. I took hold of them with difficulty and covered my eyes. I tried to judge soberly what was going on. Where the bombers were and what had happened to them, I did not know. Clearly, the ram attack hadn't worked. My altitude was 600 metres. I had to choose a place to land.

Beneath me was an enormous swamp. I took my bearings and turned the plane towards Leningrad. To my left was a village and next to it a level field. 'Shall I land here? No, better to land at the next village,' I thought. The fighter was descending quickly and somehow I couldn't see another suitable landing place. There was another village; beyond it a yellowing field of rye. The railway station was visible. The countryside was indented with gullies and uneven with hillocks. I would have to make a belly landing.

Every second was valuable. Nevertheless, scenes from the film *Stories about the Heroes of Aviation* flashed across my mind. I happened to see this film in the spring of 1938 when I was still working in a factory. In one story about the bravery of aviators, the undercarriage of an I 16 failed to lower and the pilot managed to land this high-speed plane successfully on its belly. A cloud of airfield dust, carried by the wind, covered the screen but the smiling pilot climbed out of the cockpit of his aircraft. 'Everything's fine!' he exclaimed. To me it seemed a miracle. Three times in succession I went to see the film and did not cease to be filled with admiration. 'What fearless people these pilots are! How truly romantic was this dangerous work!'

And now I myself had to do the same thing. It would have been fine on an aerodrome, but God knows where else. For some reason, I didn't trust this rye field. 'Have I done everything in order to land? Oh yes, I'm not strapped in!' The alarming thought struck me. I caught hold of the harness, which had fallen behind the seat, but I couldn't fasten it with my free hand. My altitude was only 60 metres. Ahead were the houses of a village. I flung away the harness and, with difficulty, pulled the plane over the roofs of the houses and steered the aircraft away from a haystack which stood in my path. The wings of the fighter cut the ears of the ripe rye, then flattened it. The aircraft made a belly landing. It slid 10 metres and struck an invisible obstacle. I had the impression that a stone wall had blocked the plane's path. It stood on its nose, slewed round, dropped on one wing and then crashed with all its weight into the rye. Lumps of earth, mixed with ears of rye, flew into the cockpit. My flying goggles struck the gunsight and fragments of glass cut my right temple and cheek.

However, I felt no pain. I jumped out of the cockpit and tried to determine my location. On my right lay the village: to my left, the station. Suddenly I was met by the deafening sound of gunfire. Three Fascist bombers were dropping their bombs on the railway station. One of them hit the signal-box and blew it to pieces. I drew my pistol and crawled away into the rye as far as possible from the aircraft. I began to put my thoughts in order. It turned out that I was not in the front line, but, evidently, the station was ours.

Unexpectedly, the gunfire ceased. I got to my feet and looked about. People were running from the village towards me. In the lead were children. One of them, a bright lad, ran up to the plane, climbed on, and examined it.

'Here it is chaps, follow me!'

Three fair-haired little boys ran up to me. 'Put your pistol away, uncle,' said the first lad. 'Don't be afraid, our soldiers are here. The Germans' – he waved his arm – 'they're in that village. It's called Moloskovitsy.'

The boy said something else, but I listened absentmindedly, my attention concentrated on Moloskovitsy. Yes, that was the field where I wanted to make a landing. Meanwhile, aware that I wasn't listening, he grabbed hold of my tunic.

'Uncle, uncle, my name's Zhenya Petrov and he's Volodya. He's our neighbour's son. There was a battle going on here. Look how many tanks and guns are in the village.'

'And we saw how you fought,' said Volodya perkily. 'That Junkers came down in the swamp. There it is behind the village. Only it didn't burst into flames. It flew on and on with smoke coming out and landed in the swamp. But the one that wasn't smoking flew away. Aren't you hurt? There's blood on your cheek.'

Having replaced my pistol in its holster, I walked towards my aircraft with the boys. It turned out that it had struck an enormous stone boulder. The engine was displaced to the side; the barrel of the heavy calibre machine-gun was bent. The fighter lay on the earth like a wounded bird, helplessly spreading its strong wings. It was full of bullet holes. I took the map case from the cockpit and removed the map. Spreading it on the tailplane, I weighed up the situation. Yes, there could be no doubt, the Germans had actually taken Kingisepp and were making for Volosovo.

Workers from the collective farm gathered round. They examined the fighter with interest. The children knowingly explained where the nose and tail were. From my conversation with the grown-ups, I gathered that the Fascists had taken Moloskovitsy early that morning and had moved towards Vruda, but our forces had made a counter attack and stopped the enemy. They also told me that the chairman of the collective farm, Illarion Pavlovich Andreyev, had ordered all the villagers to bury their valuables in the earth and join the partisans in the forest. Then one of the women made herself busy looking after my cut forehead and the bleeding wound on my cheek.

'A car. A car's coming,' suddenly shouted the children.

In fact a car did come from the direction of the station. It stopped outside the rye field. Two soldiers ran towards us. They were both aircrew, a captain and a first lieutenant. They were looking for their comrade who had not returned from his patrol. Both of them confirmed that the damaged Junkers had come down behind the village. The Captain noted down the telephone number of my regiment's field signals unit in order to inform the authorities about the bomber I had shot down.

'You wanted to ram the other Junkers, that's so, isn't it?' he said.

I was somewhat embarrassed. 'I wanted to, but didn't succeed.'

'You didn't succeed because the Fascists guessed your intention from your manoeuvre and moved apart. We'll discuss this interesting event in our unit and without fail will write about it to your CO.' They were prepared to give me a lift, at least as far as the main road, but I thanked them and declined their offer. The man whom they were looking for had a greater need than I. They waved goodbye to us all and ran to their car.

Surrounded by collective farm workers, I walked to the village with my parachute over my shoulder. Bolshaya Vruda is a large village. It is located a kilometre from the railway station of the same name, and 12 kilometres to the west of Volosovo. The woman who had just bandaged my wounds invited me into her home. I already knew her name. It was Zinaida Mikhailovna Petrova. She told me about her two sons and her work in the collective farm as we sat at her hospitably laid table. She appeared to be no more than forty, but her hair was quite grey. Evidently, life had not been easy for Zinaida Mikhailovna. Powerful explosions interrupted our conversation. The whole house shook, and the glass in the window frames rattled.

'It's the shelling, don't take any notice. Help yourself. Eat up,' said this hospitable housewife quietly. 'They've been shelling now for three days, the tyrants. We've got used to it.'

'No, this is no time to be eating,' I thought as I listened to the familiar and increasing din. 'Zinaida Mikhailovna, it's bombing!'

I had just managed to leap out into the hall and take hold of the handle of the door leading on to the porch, when a tremendous explosion deafened me. Crawling out from under the debris, I hurried to find Zinaida Mikhailovna. Meanwhile, the engines of the Junkers roared shrilly overhead. Eighteen twin-engined bombers were dropping their bombs from a height of 500 or 600 metres on the village of Bolshaya Vruda. Houses were burning, smoke stung the eyes, heartrending cries could be heard, and one after another explosions thundered. Piglets, running in all directions through the village from their bomb-damaged pigsty, screeched piercingly.

I didn't immediately discover that there was neither ceiling nor roof above my head. An elderly woman was calling to the housewife; moans were heard in reply. We searched for Zinaida Mikhailovna among the ruins. Soldiers helped us. With their aid it was finally possible to lift the heavy beams aside. She was only just alive. We carried her to a trench.

With difficulty, I retrieved my parachute. It was time to leave, but a frantic shout stopped me.

'Mummy, Volodya's dead!' It was Zhenya, Zinaida Mikhailovna's son, who had found me in the rye. He stood in front of us, his head bleeding, and trembling as if from cold, while repeating the same phrase over and over again: 'Mummy, Volodya's dead.' We carried the body of Volodya, the sixteen-year-old lad, who lived next door, out of the ruins and buried him there beside the ruined house.

And so I walked towards Volosovo, from time to time transferring my parachute from one shoulder to the other. I walked for a couple of hours. Now and again, lorries full of wounded soldiers overtook me, raising clouds of dust. I walked slowly, for my journey was not a short one. Behind me lay 8 kilometres and ahead to Klopitsy another 18. In my mind's eye, I could see Bolshaya Vruda. There near the village in the field lay my fighter. What was I without it? And for that matter, what did I look like in my burnt clothing, smelling of smoke? How stupid of me to have lost my aircraft! Somewhere, at a turn in the road, a vehicle overtook me and stopped.

'Take a seat, soldier-boy, we'll give you a lift,' the driver cheerfully suggested, jumping down from his cabin. 'You won't shoot down much if you have to carry your parachute. I've often given your mates a lift.'

It turned out that my fellow travellers were seriously wounded soldiers. Exhausted by the bumpy ride, bleeding, many not even bandaged, they lay in the bottom of the van. Some were silent, their eyes closed and almost lifeless. Others cried in pain, uttering the name of Hitler with the choicest of phrases. Three seriously wounded men died on the way.

Taking the opportunity when the vehicle stopped, I jumped down and continued on foot. I must confess that I had become frightened by what I had seen. This was where the real war was going on! For some reason, I felt guilty at the sight of these young men who were dying, at the death of the boy, Volodya, and all the people who had died and suffered in the burning of Bolshaya Vruda.

Outside Volosovo, a motor cycle coming from the opposite direction drew level with me and, raising a cloud of dust, unexpectedly stopped.

'Comrade Commander!' Gritsayenko ran towards me. 'Can this be you? Where have you been? I've driven all over the district. I thought you'd disappeared without trace.'

He hugged me in an embrace which made my bones start to creak.

'Thank God you're alive. And we'll collect the plane; just tell me where it is. Oh yes, and to reassure a worried technician, tell me the reason for your forced landing.'

'Sasha, the aircraft worked perfectly. The rest I'll tell you back at base. Let's go!'

When we were back at the aerodrome, it was difficult to express in words my joy at meeting my wartime friends again. They felt sure I would return and now heartily congratulated me. There wasn't much room in the tent and many of them stood outside the entrance while I described what had happened to me, the tragic events at Bolshaya Vruda and the dead soldiers in the vehicle. When I said that Moloskovitsy had been occupied by the Fascists and that my aircraft was lying in a field close to the front line, there was a rumble of astonished voices.

'The Fascists have occupied Moloskovitsy?' repeated Bagryantsev. 'What are you saying?'

He took from my hands the map case and map, and stood up.

'Please give me your attention. As you can see, the situation has become complicated. But between us and the front line there're still almost 30 kilometres by road. So there's no need to be alarmed. Of course, having taken Kingisepp, the enemy will certainly strive to break through, not only to Volosovo, but also to Kotly and Begunitsy. There is a danger of being encircled, but our troops are evidently holding their position strongly, so there is no cause for panic. There will be an appropriate order for everything.'

He straight away lifted the phone, reported the changes in the situation to garrison headquarters and made arrangements to retrieve my fighter. 'Take Gritsayenko, Alferov and go!' Bagryantsev said to me. 'Be careful.'

The CO gave several instructions to the engineer, ordered two men to be detached to reconnoitre the road leading to Begunitsy and strengthened the guard.

The vehicle stopped by the ruins of Zinaida Mikhailovna's house. Bolshaya Vruda and the neighbouring village of Yamki no longer existed; only the charred remains. A soldier came over to us. In reply to a question about the position in the forward area, he shrugged his shoulders.

'Don't think of going near the plane in daylight. The Fascists could open fire.'

In the gardens and allotments, behind the ruins of the bombed buildings, stood guns and tanks covered in branches. Beside them, almost invisible in their camouflaged clothing, army personnel busied themselves.

As twilight fell, we were already by the plane. A little later, Fascist aircraft began to bomb the railway station. It became dangerous to stay in the open, so I suggested to the technician that he stop work for a while and take cover under the vehicle.

'I recently had my overalls washed, Comrade Commander,' said Gritsayenko offhandedly. 'It's dirty, very dirty under that lorry. Somehow we'll carry on.'

'Neither will I crawl under it,' Alferov repeated. 'Our warrant officer is very strict. He doesn't like dirty seamen. "Are you a sailor or what?" he'll say.'

A half moon appeared for a short time in a clear space between the clouds. In its weak light, the dark silhouettes of enemy bombers could be seen. Somewhere nearby, an anti-aircraft gun opened up, then a second and a third. Unexpectedly, bombs whistled, it seemed right above our heads.

'Get down!' I managed to shout, and everyone dropped to the ground. One of the bombs fell so close that lumps of earth, thrown up by the explosion, clattered on to the fabric covering of the wings. We stood up and shook ourselves. The sound of bombing gradually grew quieter.

After a little while, Fascist aircraft again attacked Bolshaya Vruda, but no longer could anything interrupt our work. The fighter was taken apart and loaded on to the vehicle.

The August nights are short, but by first light everything was ready for our departure. Rolling heavily, the vehicle set off across the field, flattening the ears of ripe rye. Hardly had we passed through the village when the enemy began an artillery bombardment. But the shells exploded behind us and we were already out of danger.

In the morning, having achieved superiority on this section of the front, Hitler's forces, at the cost of great losses to themselves, took the village of Bolshaya Vruda, or rather what was left of it.

CHAPTER THREE

Retreat To Nizino

'Girls, Look Who's Arrived!'

Danger hung over the Klopitsy aerodrome. Fascist forces threatened to take it from two sides. It was decided to evacuate the garrison. When they brought my fighter to Klopitsy, everything there was, as we say, ready for the 'off'. All that remained to do was to grab our things and follow the shortest route to Nizino. Bagryantsev and Tenyugin remained behind for a while in order to protect the aerodrome and also the bombers (they were to return to their permanent base near Leningrad).

The vehicle moved steadily along the smooth road and I closed my eyes in a blissful doze. After a sleepless night, I wanted to rest. In my thoughts, I recalled my wife, my little daughter and my parents. Since the start of the war, I had received only two letters from them. 'Everything's fine with us; don't worry. We're all alive and well. Already, Ninochka can run about and speaks a lot,' wrote my wife in the last letter.

I had it with me, so I took it out for the umpteenth time and re-read the familiar lines. 'Everything's fine with us. . . .' The Fascists were in Staraya Russa and were already approaching Shimsk. And in Novgorod 'everything was fine'. Fine, nothing of the sort. And I must try not to worry!

The driver reduced speed. In our path was a large group of refugees. Women, children and old people were driving cattle and carrying bundles, knapsacks and cases on their shoulders. It was painful to look at them; people who had been driven from the places they had lived all their lives and going they knew not where. . . .

Many waved and begged a lift, but we had nowhere to put them, and we drove on without stopping. Suddenly, an old man appeared in front of the lorry. He was lifting up a little girl with a bandaged head. The driver braked sharply so as not to hit them.

'Where do you think you're going, dad? Under my wheels and with a child as well?' he shouted, opening the door.

I climbed out of the car.

'Give us a lift, my son – I'm an old man. . . . We would have made our way to Leningrad only. . . . A Fascist bomb killed her mother, do you hear. And here's my granddaughter.' He straightened the bloodstained bandage on the girl's head and wiped her tears with a trembling hand.

'And the tyrants burnt our log home. We'd like to get to Leningrad, my son.' When he understood that we weren't going to Leningrad, but to the nearest airfield, to repair an aircraft that we needed to strike the Fascists, the old man pressed his granddaughter to his chest and moved aside.

'God help you conquer the foe, Hitler. God help you, my son!'

Beyond Ropsha, the road worsened: the lorry rocked from side to side. The driver had to slow down. Gritsayenko leaned over from the back of the lorry and shouted through the door: 'Comrade Commander, we are approaching the base. Nizino is visible already.'

Home! At war, but home just the same! At dispersal, aircrew and technicians gathered round the aircraft on all sides.

'Hi, everybody!'

'How was it in Klopitsy?'

Gritsayenko's friends embraced him as he jumped down from the lorry and looked over the aircraft we had brought with us.

'No problem, we'll soon repair that. It'll be like new again!'

Uncle Volodya (as we called Linnik, the Senior Flight Engineer), ambled towards us, wiping his hands with a rag. Vladimir Trofimovich warmly greeted us, asked how I felt and immediately transferred his attention to the aircraft.

'Is it seriously damaged?' He stood on the wheel of the lorry and looked at the bodywork.

'Yes, they did hit me a bit.'

'And did you give as good as you got?' Linnik asked, examining the aeroplane.

I didn't answer immediately. I didn't want to tell anyone about the Junkers I had shot down because I didn't witness the crash. But Linnik was waiting for an answer, and I didn't want to disappoint the good man. Knowing that the Junkers, which had come down in a marsh, was lost to the Fascists, I said: 'In exchange, I got a big one.'

'Yes? That means you've now got two.' He shook my hand firmly and immediately began to tell everyone around how proud he was that I had scored a second victory.

'And we'll repair your aircraft, Comrade Commander. You'll fly again,' Vladimir Trofimovich consoled me.

I found out that aircraft from neighbouring squadrons were flying from eastern airfields into Nizino. Gradually, my friends gathered there. The situation remained complex. Fighters landed, refuelled and flew off on their military exercises. Maj Novikov and Commissar Isakovich greeted me warmly, examined the aircraft we had brought back and shook their heads.

'And how are you?' the CO asked.

'Fine, Major!'

'And how about that?' he added, pointing at the right side of my forehead.

'Oh, that's nothing. A scratch from glass. I forgot to remove my goggles before I landed.'

'There, Mikhail Zakharovich,' Novikov looked at the Commissar. 'They always say everything's "fine". They always say "it was nothing". Go and get a meal and take a rest,' he said to me. 'While they're repairing your fighter, fly in mine. I'll find myself another.' Overjoyed at the thought that I would be able to fly the next day, I hurried to join my friends, but the Major stopped me.

'Today. . . .' he began, but hesitated.

'You wanted to say something, Major?'

'Yes, yesterday, Godunov was killed.' He pronounced these words with difficulty and, after falling silent, added: 'Four of them took on sixteen. . . .'

Making no further enquiries, I asked permission to go. Borka, Borka! Such a live wire, so full of fun, a young communist leader, the life and soul of the squadron.

How I would have liked to hear Borya Godunov's voice! It was impossible to believe that he was no longer with us. Nothing was left of the man except our pleasant memories of him. Not even a grave. Nowhere to place flowers. I thought of this and our Finn, Borka, appeared before my eyes. It was he who had called himself thus. 'I have, as they say, the blood of a Finn and I know the Finnish language, but I have a Russian surname.' He was born and grew up not far from Byeloostrov. . . .

I went into the mess – silence – not a soul in the hall. Yet everything was as it had been before the war. The tables were arranged as they used to be. Over there sat our flight, and there Bagryantsev's. Godunov's place was by the wall. I sat down in Boris's chair and, as he used to do, drummed with my fingers on the table. It only remained for me to shout fervently: 'Shurochka, direct your eyes at us, the peasants have come from work!'[5]

It was getting stuffy. I undid my naval jacket and heard unexpectedly:

'Girls, look who's arrived!'

I recognized Shura Verina from her voice. 'Comrade Lieutenant, but they told us that you hadn't returned from patrol.'

I tried to behave cheerfully: 'That was someone having a joke, Shura. How could I not return to such lovely girls?'

Shura ran to the kitchen; the other girls gathered round the table. 'What's going to happen, Comrade Lieutenant?'

'The Germans are still moving towards Leningrad. But let's assume we don't let them get that far. If so, I think that things won't be that terrible. Just remember: don't panic! Chin up and keep smiling.'

'You are making light of things,' said bright, fair-haired Anya, anxiously knitting her brows. 'But if things go badly for us, what then?' No matter what we said, however we tried to steer the conversation, it always returned to one and the same thing.

'Ah, here's Shura, and here's lunch. How appetizing it smells!' I tried to distract the girls from troublesome thoughts. 'Thank you, Shurochka, may you find a fine husband!'

'You're always joking,' Shura looked first at me, then at the girls. 'But just the same, I'm heartbroken. I can't forget for a minute that Boris Godunov is dead. Perhaps it's not true. Perhaps he's still alive. Such as he can't be dead.

What a man he was! Tell us that, perhaps, he's not lost to us. Perhaps he's seriously wounded. Now there are so many stories that you don't know what to believe. They spoke about you and said that you too had been killed.'

Suspended From Flying Duties

In the morning, I took off in the CO's aircraft. The noise of planes on the airfield did not cease. First we went to reconnoitre the enemy's lines of communication, then to give cover to our troops, and finally to escort the bombers and assault aircraft.

Everything possible and impossible was done to help the infantry hold the brutal Fascist hordes from breaking through to Lenin's city. As far as the position of our forces was concerned, severe complications had set in. Despite enormous loss of life, German units did not succeed in overcoming the defences in the Luga line and moved out to the region of Kingisepp–Veymarn, broke through our defences there and sped towards Leningrad. Having broken our army's resistance in the region of Volosovo, the enemy moved towards Gatchina. At the same time, the Fascist tanks moved closer to Ropsha.

Aerial combat went on overhead without a break. Five or seven flights a day had already become normal for us. Enemy numerical superiority of three or four to one became usual. And we were so exhausted that by evening we could hardly remain standing. We should have taken a good rest but nerves were stretched and sleep did not come.

I had almost no sleep on the third night. When I closed my eyes, I was fighting again, firing again, evading the fire of still more Fascist fighters. By two in the morning, I was walking about the room, listening to the uneven breathing of my friends. They were lucky; they were sleeping.

Something like an hour and a half remained until reveille. But I still couldn't sleep. I tried to banish thought, but it didn't work. The lads would say: 'Count to a hundred and you're sure to drop off.' I lay with closed eyes and counted in a whisper. I reached sixty and suddenly before me were the burnt remains of Bolshaya Vruda with the mounds of fresh graves. Then the little girl with the bandaged head appeared and the old man, lifting his granddaughter above his head. 'We'd like to get to Leningrad, my son!' Where had he come from along the dusty front line road? Maybe also from Bolshaya Vruda or perhaps from Begunitsy. 'The tyrants burnt my wooden home! . . .'

Once more, I tried to count. No, I still couldn't sleep. And yet Sukhov counted to eighty-six and fell asleep. How do we know whether Sukhov was telling the truth? He was a great joker, but as far as taking a rest goes, he could always manage it. He had only to jump out of his cockpit and he was already snoring under the wing in the grass. If only I could have done that. Oh, how important it was for a pilot to have a really sound sleep!

'Who were you talking to?' asked the CO, sleepily getting up from his bed.

'I was counting, trying to sleep, Major.'

'And how did it go?'

'I couldn't.'

'Why not?'

'I don't know.'

That morning I was suspended from flying duties. 'First learn to sleep,' said the CO angrily. 'Then you'll be flying.'

For a long time I wandered about dispersal, looking for a place to take a nap but couldn't find one. I came back to the dug-out and lay on my bunk. But there I couldn't sleep for the incessant noise of the gramophone playing 'Rio Rita'.

I was about to stop the record when Sosyedin came into the dug-out. He took off his flying helmet, ran his fingers through his hair and then did something quite unexpected – he broke into a dance. And what's more with an exclamation:

'God rest his soul! God rest his soul!'

The floorboards shook in the dug-out. 'Has the chap gone off his rocker?' I thought. 'He's dancing to "Rio Rita".'

'Listen, Kolya, what's the matter? Whose soul is resting?'

'The pilot of an Me 110. That's who!'

I had never had the chance to see Sosyedin dance. As I watched him he continued to prance, clap his hands to his chest, to the soles of his feet, and finally to the floorboards. Eventually he must have tired. He flopped on his bunk and fixed me with a strange stare.

'Cranks! They say armour doesn't burn . . . but how it blazed!'

'Tell me more but at least make sense.'

'Can you imagine?' He could hardly recover his breath. 'We were flying with the assault planes. Well, they had finished their operation and were making for home. We had only just left the target when I saw that just behind me two Me 110s were following. I let Sergey Sukhov know and he turned aside and he made for them. How speedily he split them. Then I joined him, and that was that! One burst into flames. . . . It's the first time I've seen one burn. . . . The second flew away. Then we hurried back to the assault aircraft.'

'Are you dancing already, you rogue?' Sukhov said, coming into the dug-out. 'Carry on. Today you may, for sure.'

He slapped Sosyedin on the shoulder, took off his flying helmet, hung up his map case, smoothed his sweaty hair and sat down next to me on the bunk. 'What a pity you weren't there. Brother, it all happened! Thousands of aircraft in the sky. But we were lucky; managed to return without loss. What's more, we brought down an Me 110.'

'You did, but I—'

'What are you saying?'

'Well, I'm sitting here. I slept badly, as you can see. But I feel fine.'

'Listen!' Nikolay interrupted the conversation. 'Didn't the Commander of the air force, Gen Yermachenkov, give you a dressing down before the war?

You remember – he came to verify how the pilots were resting before flying. You, after that I think, put together some kind of operational plan. You did. Yes, you did.'

Sukhov became interested. 'Well, what happened then?'

'What then? Then the General went to the Regimental Commander, Dushin. "How can this be, Comrade Major? You informed me that all the pilots slept, but you have a Flight Commander who infringes the regulations by not sleeping before flying." Dushin didn't know how to reply. Then the General said to Kaberov in an imperative tone: "Go to sleep at once!" I remember how Igor flew into his quarters, from fear forgot to undress and climbed under the blanket in boots and trousers.'

'Now you're exaggerating,' I said.

'I don't exaggerate at all.' Sosyedin was carried away by his recollections. 'At the time, the radio was playing in the club; they'd forgotten to switch it off. The club manager almost lost his job for this and the Orderly was sent to the guard-room. The Regimental Commissar was reprimanded; so was the CO. Flights were suspended; and quite right too. A rest for our brother is a necessity now. Now we are at war, the weak and dreamy are soon knocked out.'

The rest of our pilots had returned to their own airfield. The Squadron Adjutant, Anikanov, was again rushing about in the dug-out, hardly able to issue instructions and record the results of flights in the operations log-book. The naval clerk Yevgeny Duk helped him to do this. A calligrapher and artist, he kept the documents in such good order they were a joy to behold.

'They are for posterity,' he would say. 'After the war, our descendants will pick up these archives and find everything accurately and clearly written: where and how each person fought for Leningrad.'

Yevgeny Duk came from a family of Petersburg workers. But since childhood, he had loved aviation and dreamed of flying. He and I were friends and I promised that at the first opportunity I would help him to realize his dream. For the time being, together we published the camp news-sheet. It had come out every day since the beginning of the war. So now, when once again everyone had gone off to carry out their duties, Duk and I set about preparing the next edition. We were so absorbed in our work that we didn't hear the door open. On the threshold a man appeared.

'Anyone here?'

'Matvey!' I tore myself from my place. 'You've just flown in? But where's Alexeyev?'

'He'll be here presently.'

Yefimov, a big strong man in a flying helmet pushed to the back of his head, strode into the dug-out. We embraced. Matvey warmly greeted Duk and Anikanov. 'Well, that's it, we're home!' he said, looking round and taking a seat on the plank bed.

'But where's the CO?'

'He's gone away on patrol.'

'Tell me, how are you, what's new?'

For more than a month, Yefimov, our squadron party organizer, had been away. We talked and grieved for the loss of our fallen comrades. I told him about the successes of our friends.

'And how are things with you?'

'Well, it's like this; I'm suspended from flying duties. I haven't been able to sleep.'

'And what's the cause of your insomnia? Maybe this has something to do with it.' Matvey pointed at the news-sheet.

'Stop, stop.' The Adjutant rose from behind the table. 'I'm pleased you've reminded me or I might have forgotten.' He took from his pocket a small packet and handed it to me. 'The doctor gave it to me. He asks you to take these before you go to bed.'

Matvey wanted to say something else but the door swung open with a crash and pilots burst into the dug-out, causing uproar. They almost smothered Yefimov and Alekseyev, who came later, with their Herculean embraces. Matvey wanted to report his arrival to the CO in the correct way, but how could he do so at that moment?

'I'm pleased, very pleased.' Novikov glanced round at everyone. 'Now the whole squadron is here. . . . Only Khripunov, Aliyev, Fyodorov and Godunov are no longer with us.' Saddened, he removed the flying helmet which had seen so much.

That evening, we made merry. We danced, laughed, sang. The reason for our merriment – a decree by the Presidium of the Supreme Soviet of the USSR about the award of the Order of Lenin to Bagryantsev. The paper with the news of the decree was passed from hand to hand. Just the same, I tried to go to sleep a little earlier than usual.

I woke when it was quite light. I glanced at my watch and was horrified: eleven o'clock in the morning. That's what a sleeping draught does! Everyone was doing his duty, and I . . . . How could this be? Why hadn't they woken me? I dressed, buckling on my equipment as I dashed into the street like a madman.

'Where are you going, Lieutenant?'

I looked round. A driver was standing behind me.

'And why are you here?'

'I was ordered, Comrade Lieutenant, to wait until you woke up and then to drive you to the airfield.' I sat in the car, still not understanding what was happening. At the airfield, I hurried to report my arrival to Maj Novikov. He laughed: 'Well, did you have a good sleep?'

'Just so! Today I slept extremely well.'

'How do you feel?'

'Excellent.'

'Quite so, don't neglect sleep. Otherwise . . .' he paused, thought about something and looked at his watch. 'In half an hour, you will fly on reconnaissance. Have a little rest.'

'Aye-aye, Major!'

Things Remembered

I calculated that I could bathe for half an hour. What an idea! I ran towards the river. It was a little wider than the other stream. It babbled, conversing with the pebbles. There was nowhere to dive in. I undressed, walked into the water and plunged towards the far shore. I lay down on the grass. That day there was a deep blue sky and the clouds were whiter than white. That was how it used to be in Vologda after fishing. I lay on the shore and gazed at the clouds, and what dreams I dreamed!

Now it seemed to me that I really was at home. How fine it would have been to leap and run along the shore of our Vologda river; to see the house of old Edel and his fishing tackle on the shore; to see the house of my friend Foka and, of course, our own home. It stands on a high bank, beside an enormous lime tree. On the way to it is Voskresensky Hill and the church with its peals of bells. Many times have I scrambled into the bell tower and, standing next to the bell-ringer, marvelled at how skilfully he pulled on the ropes, producing the astonishing, inimitable sounds.

Vologda! How many memories were associated with its name. Vologda backwoods: region where the birds are tame. That's how they once spoke of our part of the countryside. But I was born and grew up there. This severe northern region and this ancient town were dear to me. I loved its tiny wooden houses, standing in the shade of leafy silver birches and its wooden pavements. I loved the white nights and the northern lights.

At first, our family lived in the countryside. In 1911, father was called up for active military service. Three years later, he was marching to the First World War. A brave soldier, father was made a warrant officer. After the October revolution he returned to the countryside and, looking for a happier life, moved his family to Vologda and started work in the factory there. After that – the Red Guard, the Southern Front. Father was wounded in the battle with the Whites, and concussion led to blindness. Only many years later did the skilful hands of a surgeon partly restore his sight.

There were six of us children in the family. One of my four brothers, skating on the ice, was drowned in the river. In those times it was not easy for my mother; we were constantly in need. Mother, mother, how I grieved you when I told you that I wanted to fly! You even wept at that moment. You were fearful for my life.

Long ago when I was in the second class at school, I remember how a plane came down near us, just beyond the town. It burst into flames and fell out of the sky. I ran with the lads to take a look. The crew had been killed. In the place where the aircraft had fallen, lay lumps of churned up earth and a pile of the misshapen and burnt remains of wood and metal. My heart was wrung. At home I told them what I had seen.

'That's what military service is for them,' mother said about air force pilots. 'Death follows at their heels.'

'Well, what do you say?' Father looked at me with unseeing eyes. 'Do you still want to become a pilot?'

'No,' I answered at the time. 'It's terrible to be a pilot.'

But then came the time of the *Chelyuskin* epic. The whole country was talking about the brave seven: Vodopyanov, Doronin, Kamanin, Levanyevsky, Lyapidyevsky, Molokov and Slepnyev. These men saved the crew of the steamship *Chelyuskin*, trapped in the Arctic ice. The whole world admired the feat of these heroes.

'No, mother, I've changed my mind. I want to train as a pilot very much,' I would say at that time. 'Look what a hero Vodopyanov is. Oh, how I'd like to become like him!'

The portrait of Vodopyanov, cut from a newspaper, lay with my pioneer's card. In the house, the model of an aircraft I had built hung from the ceiling. Along the wings, printed in large letters, the name Mikhail Vodopyanov was written. I climbed on to the roof of our house, perched on the chimney, released the model into the air and followed its flight with my heart in my mouth. . . .

But didn't this all begin with the circus? It stood on the bank of the River Vologda. The circular construction of wooden planks with its canvas marquee for a roof was for me like a second home. Our neighbour, Yevstoliya Ivanovna Bogoslovskaya, worked as an animal trainer on the staff there. She it was who took us children to this fabulous world of wonders.

The Manion acrobats were my favourite performers. Flying from trapeze to trapeze at a great height, they twisted in the air, caught one another by the hands and feet, swung to and fro, flew again and catching the trapeze, returned to the platform. I followed their work with a sinking heart. Only brave and very agile people could do this. The thought of becoming a circus artist like these flying acrobats would not leave me.

The sons of the horse trainer were about my age and we became friends. They showed me how to do various acrobatic tricks and I would steal away to the arena. Soon I was noticed. My parents did not discourage me in my enthusiasm for the circus and with their blessing I went away to the distant town of Nadyezhdinsky Zavod (now Serov) in the Urals with the '5 Borkis' jugglers. There I continued to attend school and at the same time trained with the circus. After six months, I could already juggle and perform acrobatics on the horses. But I longed to be an acrobat. When Borisov, my boss, found out about this, he took a dislike to me. Somehow at rehearsal, finding fault with something, he hit me hard on the cheek. Stunned, at first I didn't understand what it was all about. Out of shame and annoyance, I threw my oak juggler's clubs at him and walked out of the rehearsal. Then it happened that I was late lighting the torches, and, at the moment when the '5 Borkis' entered the arena, there was a hitch. In the circus at that time, the old strict traditions still persisted. For this negligence, Borisov beat me with a whip in the stables. I couldn't perform in the circus for a week. All this filled me with indignation. I wrote to my parents and, when I received a letter in reply, returned home, leaving the circus forever.

I had left the circus but still dreamed of flying high – a dream that was still deeply imprinted on my mind. It led me to aviation. I began to build model aircraft, to read books about aviators and to jump from the roof of my house clutching a large umbrella. Then the gliding club attracted my interest. When Sasha Rusinov went away to retrain at the Duderhoff school for glider pilots, he spoke for me and sent me an application form.

In Duderhoff, I had first of all to pass an examination – a flight from a high mountain with the head of the flying school in a two-seater US 6 glider. The glider was torn from its place and, lifting its nose high, was carried away into the sky. It took my breath away. Far below, the tiny little houses of Duderhoff were left behind. But I felt no fear. I made a turn, another, a third and came in to land.

'Well done!' said the examiner. 'Tomorrow you will have your medical and you will become a student at the school. Good luck!' My heart was ready to leap from my breast. I would be a student here!

But the medical board rejected me. My height was the minimum permitted for an aviator – 154 centimetres. In addition, the aged surgeon found that I was badly proportioned. He said that my legs were shorter than my body by 3 centimetres and therefore it was impossible to allow me to fly.

My mother threw up her arms for joy when I returned home. 'Yes, yes, mother, they wouldn't accept me. The doctors discovered disproportion.'

'Well, that's all right.' She gave a sigh of relief. 'Get undressed. You must be tired. We can soon do something about the disproportion. Auntie Anyuta can cure any illness.'

'No, mother, it can't be cured.' I began to tell them about my setback. 'They say I'm small, small and ungainly.'

Mother sighed. 'It's because you were born at a bad time. The war was on. The countryside was without food. We hadn't any firewood in the house. And then you developed rickets. I was pleased you even survived.'

'Don't grieve,' father said to me. 'There are many doctors. The main thing is: don't hang your head. Where there's a will, there's a way.'

'That's enough, old feller,' mother mimicked him. 'A way, indeed! With your instruction, he'll find a way to screw his head off.' Father was silenced.

Complications beset mother's life. Having lost his sight, father acquired a liking for the demon drink and often treated her roughly. It left its mark on her character. Mother loved us children very much but brought us up simply without being too kind. An ordinary besom broom helped her to solve difficult problems. I had caused my mother much anxiety by my trip to Duderhoff. Had it been a year or two earlier, she would have taken it out on me with the broom. Even then, mother looked several times at the corner where the uncomplicated implement for our upbringing stood. She looked but declined to use it.

The year of call-up approached. Once again, the medical board had to decide whether I was fit to fly. The surgeon had the last word. I was a centimetre over the minimum height. The doctor wrote 'Fit'. I jumped for joy and ran to get dressed.

'Well, well, what's wrong with your feet?' The surgeon walked up to me. 'There's almost no arch.'

'What arch?' I was on my guard, sensing misfortune. The nurse brought a bowl of water.

'Make a footprint on the floor. You see, you have a "bear's paw",' the doctor explained to me. 'They won't accept you in the infantry. Yours is a clear case of flat feet.'

Again the terrible conclusion: 'Unfit'.

For a long time that evening, I wandered about the streets of the town puzzling what I must do now and firmly resolved that flying for me was out of the question. And that is how things would have been had events not taken place which gave me new hope. Returning from the Arctic to Moscow in their four-engined aircraft, the aviation heroes, who had once saved the lives of the crew of the *Chelyuskin*, landed at Vologda. In the evening, the whole town, from the youngest to the oldest, gathered on the square to welcome these brave men. Fighting my way through to the platform, I caught sight of Vodopyanov among the guests. A big, broad-shouldered man in a fur jacket, just as I knew him from the newspaper photograph that I kept in my young communist's membership card, Mikhail Vasilyevich, by comparison with Molokov, who stood next to him, seemed like a fabulous warrior of old. Also there, were the polar flyers Alekseyev and Mazuruk. Smiling shyly, a little embarrassed by the noisy meeting, they won the hearts of the people of Vologda with the tales of their flights. From that day, my peace was finally lost. What steps I took to get into aviation! Where did I not apply by letter or enquiry? Then, suddenly . . . .

The timekeeper on our shop floor came to me. 'Telephone for you. It's the town council.'

I switched off the lathe and ran excitedly to the office. Who could it be, and why? What's more, it was from the council! I picked up the receiver.

'Hallo, it's Sasha here. Yes, I'm ringing from the town hall. There's a telegram. It says, "Send immediately one glider pilot to Koktebel for retraining." Will you go?'

My heart began to beat faster. Koktebel – the main gliding school! 'Of course I'll go, Sasha. Wild horses wouldn't stop me.'

The next day, with all my papers in order, I was at the station. Sasha and his wife, Vera, came to see me off. Panting, they ran up to my carriage just before the train departed.

'It's puzzling.' Sasha regained his breath with difficulty. 'It's as you predicted. The telegram was wrong. There is no longer a gliding school at Koktebel; it's a flying school. They train flying instructors and need a reserve pilot who has finished a flying-club course.'

I almost shrieked with resentment.

'But don't be upset,' said Sasha. 'Vera and I have been thinking. You have an official document and a telegram. You haven't seen the second telegram. Do you understand? Well, when you are there, act according to the circumstances. In Feodosiya take a bus marked with wings from the bazaar. The school is on the mountain. Oh, and I nearly forgot, here's your booklet about the school. Read it on the way. Here's Vera's sister Nadya's address. Call on her when you are free. Good luck!'

The train arrived at Feodosiya in the morning and, an hour later, the bus with wings painted on it delivered me to the Uzur-Sirt mountain, where the school was located. 'We cannot admit you,' said the headquarters officer when he took my papers. 'There's some kind of a misunderstanding. The commission will sit this evening. They will decide.' Satisfied that at least the commission would consider my case, I went out.

At dispersal, I could see gliders and aeroplanes. I set off to take a look at them. A tall sunburnt technician stopped me there. Recognizing that I had come to join the school, he gave me a can and asked me to fill up aircraft R 5 with oil.

'Take the funnel in the cowling,' said the technician. 'And the barrels are there in the corner of the hangar.'

Flattered by the confidence he showed in me, to be so entrusted with a task, I joyfully rushed to carry out the order and did everything as I was told.

'Well done!' said the technician. 'Let me introduce myself. My name is Prikhodko. Now bring some water. We must wash the wheels.' I ran for the water.

'Hey, laddie, come here!' the technician called me again. I walked up to him. He was holding the funnel, black with oil.

'Where did you get the oil?'

'There, in the barrel, the second on the left.'

'You cabbage-head! What have you done?' Technicians gathered round. One of them took the funnel from Prikhodko and asked me to smell it.

'It's waste. Couldn't you tell?'

'Mother of God! What's more, he's poured it into the petrol tank!' Prikhodko shouted in horror.

'What? I poured it into the yellow tank where the oil is.'

'Into the yellow tank, the devil take you!' thundered the technician. 'Have you just arrived from the moon? Don't you know that the fuel system is painted yellow?'

The engineer ran to see what the noise was all about. He listened to the technician who had started to stutter with excitement as he spoke, then looked me up and down.

'Have you never seen an aircraft before?'

'In the air, but this is the first time on the ground.' Everyone fell silent.

I thought all day about what had happened. The commission gathered in the evening. They called me last. It was already midnight. I solved the problem they set me about similar triangles, answered questions on aerodynamics, and explained Lilienthal's curve. At that moment, the engineer whom I had met came into the room where the commission was sitting. He looked at me, said something to a slim soldier who was sitting on the window sill and sat at the table. I stood expectantly, not saying a word.

'Fine,' said the slim man. 'You show some knowledge, but how did you manage to pour oil into the petrol tank, and waste oil at that?' All the members of the commission sat up. The soldier carried on: 'Do you know what you've done? Now this aircraft's flight to Kharkov must be delayed by three days. And today it had to deliver three gliders there for a competition.'

I told them how it had happened, then took from my pocket the booklet which Sasha had given me, opened it at the page where there was a portrait of Leonid Minov, master of sport in parachuting, and looked at the man seated on the window sill. 'I know you, Comrade Minov. I've read about you. They've written about your school here.'

The members of the commission were tired of asking questions. They were prepared to listen to me. I started to tell them about Sasha Rusinov, my instructor, who recently had worked at the school as a technician.

'Rusinov?' The engineer was surprised. 'He retrained here. An outstanding technician. Unfortunately, you are only his pupil.' Everyone laughed.

'You shouldn't laugh,' I said, offended. 'I'll do as well myself. Just help me to learn. Take me into the school. If you do I can play the accordion.' This statement about the accordion was quite unexpected and the members of the commission laughed even louder. This prompted me to go on.

'I can compile a camp news-sheet, draw, write verses,' I said.

'He's certainly a comic,' said someone good-naturedly, when everyone had stopped laughing.

'You've never flown in an aircraft, but this year we are training flying instructors,' objected Minov, becoming serious.

'But you could try. I'm quick on the uptake and learn fast.'

'You know what,' Instructor Yeremeyev stood up, 'enlist this lad in my group. I'll make a pilot of him.'

But they didn't give me to Yeremeyev. Minov, the head of the school, decided my fate another way. 'You're a cheerful chap,' he said. 'We'll admit you, but give you a reserve pilot's course of training as you might follow in a flying club. Then you will go home to Vologda. Lisyetsky will be your instructor. He has a group of youngsters.'

The commission brought its work to a close.

'So you play the accordion. That's fine,' Yeremeyev came up to me, 'we'll be able to dance.'

At two o'clock in the morning, they brought us to Feodisiya, to the medical board. 'You should have come in the morning,' grumbled the sleepy surgeon. 'Get undressed.'

While he was examining the others, I ran out into the corridor, took off my boots and socks, then, using the bottle of water which I had packed in advance, carefully moistened the soles of my feet, so that they gave the correct print, and walked into the corners to pick up dust. This I had thought up in Vologda after the commission discovered that I have flat feet.

'Do you ever wash your feet?' the surgeon asked me during the medical examination. 'Well, stand up. . . . So, once more, you must wash more often,' he grumbled. 'Get dressed!' Then he wrote 'Fit' on the card.

The next day, I was taking off in a U 2 aircraft into the Crimean sky and even tried to fly the plane. After landing, I reported to the instructor in the proper manner: 'Student Kaberov has completed a flight to acquaint himself with the area. May he receive your criticism?'

'Not bad for the first time. You understand what you are doing. That means that you will fly.' Lisyetsky smiled. 'And now set about your studies.'

The clouds were moving and gathering. I looked at them and in my imagination drew a picture of Koktebel again. I recalled the instructor, Alexander Andreyevich Batizat, who led our group up to the time when we left. I, like all the others, became a flying instructor. I could see the old fur cap, from which I was invited to pick the scrap of paper on which was written the place where I would be posted. What would be my luck? For a long time, I blindly sorted through the papers before I took one of them. I unfolded it. Well, not bad: Novgorod on the Volkhov. My friends chose other towns: Perm, Cheboksary, Leningrad, Moscow.

In the Novgorod flying club, there was one more happiness – Valya. 'I picked you out of a hat,' I told her in jest. That's how it was, in fact. Soon I went away to train in the Eysk military aviation school. After a little while, Valyusha joined me. And there – a new happiness - a little daughter, Ninochka. With what trepidation I first took her in my arms. By that time I was a mariner and wore a sailor hat with the inscription: Fleet Aviation School.

Clouds, clouds . . . . Fields of daisies amid the blue expanse of the sky. How many happy memories you bring me of childhood and youth! It seems that thoughts can carry a person far, far away for half an hour of peaceful rest on the bank of a river. But from the past it was time to return to the present. Soon I would have to fly away on reconnaissance. I dressed hastily and hurried to my aircraft.

Foreign Wings Above The Aerodrome

The Fascist High Command conducted an intense reconnaissance of our airfields, and had already delivered a series of bombing raids on them. The airfield at Kotly suffered and a unit based at Koporye aerodrome also had losses. Enemy bombers made a raid on our airfield as well, but there, warnings by intelligence were not bad and fighters succeeded in taking off to meet the enemy and give fierce opposition. The raid was not a success for the Fascists.

The remains of our aerial regiments and divisions, which had been depleted in fierce battles, flew to Leningrad. On the southern shore of the

Finnish Gulf, we maintained only naval airfields to the east and west of Peterhoff. Several army airfields remained active near Leningrad. In places, our bases were very close to one another.

We had just returned from duty, covering the attack bombers, which had delivered a blow on the enemy to the west of Begunitsy. Passing at low level over some of the populated areas, every one of us saw with his own eyes how these formerly flourishing villages had been transformed by the Fascists. There remained only the chimneys, which showed white against the ashes.

We flew out a second time, thirsting for a fight with Fascist fighters, but for some reason they didn't come to meet us. 'It means that the Fascist gentlemen are cooking something up,' said Novikov thoughtfully when we reported this to him. Straight away, he ordered Bagryantsev and Tenyugin to 'Stand ready'.

'Kaberov!' he called me. 'Gritsayenko has come. Your machine has been repaired. Give it a test flight. And be careful. There's something I don't like about the present situation.'

The CO started to ring the Commander at regimental headquarters, and I took my flying helmet and left the dug-out.

It was quiet and there wasn't a cloud in the sky. Having pulled on the white silk headgear, worn under the helmet, I made for my aircraft. Suddenly a strange noise reached me from a southerly direction. It grew louder. I stopped. Then I picked up the roar of aircraft engines, but I still hadn't become fully aware of the danger when an armada of aircraft, flying at low level, leapt from behind the hangars and obscured the sun. The whistle of bullets and the din of exploding bombs deafened me. I fell to the ground. Twin-engined Messerschmitts swept over dispersal. Choosing the right moment, I got up and ran to the dug-out at full speed. Having almost torn the door from its hinges, I rushed inside, stumbled over the step and sprawled on the floor. Someone dragged me further into the dug-out. The next moment, bullets penetrated the door in several places and the floorboards beside it. The whole of our living quarters, now plunged in darkness, shook. Outside could be heard the constant rattle of machine-gun fire. Anti-aircraft guns fired, bombs screamed and exploded, aircraft engines roared.

'Don't go near the doors!' shouted the CO 'Sosyedin, do you hear? Get away from the door.'

I pulled Nikolay towards me. 'What are you doing? Have you gone out of your mind?'

A bomb bursting close to the dug-out deafened us. Sand poured down from the ceiling. Three roof beams moved together and the roof threatened to collapse. But it was impossible to go outside. There, as before, were explosions and the whine of bullets. It was as much as we could do not to choke from the acrid smell of burning.

'This is the price we pay for being slack!' shouted Sosyedin, and with a crash threw open the door of the dug-out and leapt outside.

'Nikolay, come back!' I shouted, throwing myself after him.

Novikov's strong arms grasped me and flung me like a kitten into the corner of the dug-out. Unable to stop Sosyedin, he made do with me. At that moment, there were two more powerful explosions, one after the other, somewhere nearby. These so shook the ground that our living quarters seemed to move from their place. And again sand poured down the back of our necks. There was only one thought in my mind: 'Where was Sosyedin? Where had he run to? Was he alive?'

About thirty enemy aircraft attacked the airfield for half an hour. Gradually, the rumbling and din grew weaker and we jumped out of the dug-out. I rushed to Sosyedin's fighter but Nikolay had already started the engine, taken off and was speeding to catch up with the retreating enemy aircraft.

The airfield was enveloped in fire. The attack bombers, the reconnaissance float planes, the MiGs from a neighbouring squadron and our I 16s were burning. Beside the dug-out, Bagryantsev's duty aircraft was blazing. Mikhail was lying face down on the earth, his hands grasping his head. His boots and the lower part of his trousers were on fire.

'Misha, are you alive?' I grabbed his naval jacket and dragged him from the fire.

'Alive.' His voice sounded as if he were waking up but he suddenly leaped to his feet. 'Who is it? You, Igor? Well, what now? Seems it's over. They've gone, the swine.'

I looked at the flaps of his unbuttoned jacket. In several places there were holes.

'Are they really bullet holes?' Astonished, he counted them. 'Five! The jacket was hit but I wasn't touched!'

'Yes, Misha, you can count yourself lucky.'

At that moment, the engine fell off the aircraft. It burnt like a blazing bonfire in a pool of petrol next to the burning machine. People who had emerged from shelter made themselves busy at dispersal. Tenyugin ran past us. 'The hangars are burning! Hurry!'

I rushed after Tenyugin. We clambered on to the roof of one of the hangars. The camouflage netting was on fire. Tongues of flame crept across the mesh, swallowing it piece by piece. Tenyugin and I threw the netting from the roof. Bagryantsev and several technicians, who swiftly followed him, extinguished it on the ground. People were also working feverishly beside the second hangar. On the western side of the aerodrome, attack bombers were burning.

At that moment, Sosyedin's aircraft appeared above the airfield. Unable to catch the enemy planes, he had returned and started to make his landing directly above the burning bombers. It was dangerous and the duty officer fired a red rocket. Sosyedin made another circuit and again the same approach. He was coming in low above the burning aircraft when several explosions shook the air. An enormous column of smoke and flame was thrown into the sky. Nikolay Sosyedin's aircraft turned over and disappeared in a spinning ball of fire. We ran to the place where the fighter had fallen. It lay on the very edge of the marsh. Sosyedin was brought out from under the wreckage with hardly any signs of being alive.

Novikov, the squadron CO, shaken by what had happened, stood beside the U 2 ambulance plane, which was flown from Leningrad specially, and time and again asked the doctor if Sosyedin would live.

The doctor shrugged his shoulders. 'Everything depends on his state of health.'

Intently, Novikov watched how Sosyedin was stretchered on to the plane and observed everything that was going on nearby. Could any one of us, standing nearby the CO, have thought that the next day Sosyedin would no longer be alive? But that's how it was. A ridiculous misadventure had torn from our ranks a wonderful man, a master of his art. Novikov decided to fly the LaGG 3 fighter after it had been repaired.

To return to the events of that day: as a result of the enemy raid, we lost seventeen aircraft: six MiG 3 fighters and three I 16s, including Sosyedin's. Those whom we jokingly called our guests, and whose aircraft were not camouflaged, lost three attack Il 2 bombers and one reconnaissance float-plane. Two Yak 1 fighters, which had landed on the aerodrome just before the raid, were burnt. Also destroyed were our ageing Il 2 and the two-seater fighter trainer UTI 4. A few aircraft were undamaged.

Among the members of our regiment, Nikolay Sosyedin was the only casualty. At dispersal, where the attack bombers were packed, six sailors were killed. Trying to save the burning aircraft, they had rushed to the cockpits, which were engulfed in flames, and fired the rockets into the air. These brave men wanted to remove the 100 kilogramme bombs hanging from racks under the wings of the bombers. But flames blazed all around and there was an explosion in one of the machines. The bombs in the other aircraft detonated. In this gigantic explosion, the blast from which turned Sosyedin's aircraft over, the heroes were killed. It is known that there were six of these courageous lads, but unfortunately who they were I have not been able to establish.

In our squadron, during the attack, WO Korovin and Sgt Bokov fought the fire and saved their fighter. Technician Gritsayenko and engine fitter Alferov put out the flames which had already started to burn my aircraft.

The Regimental Armaments Engineer, Potapyenko, displayed unprecedented bravery and soldierly skill during the enemy attack. Not long before, he had found an opportunity to test a rocket launcher he had invented. Its base was a girder which is normally fixed under an aircraft's wing. Potapyenko made a gun stock and a firing mechanism and attached to it two wires leading to an accumulator. Loaded with an 82 millimetre rocket, the weapon was fastened to a stanchion.

Capt Potapyenko, scorning danger, set up his rocket launcher and opened fire on the enemy aircraft. One of his missiles hit a Fascist plane. The pilot of the damaged machine swung it sharply to one side and collided with the next aircraft. Enveloped in flames, the two fell to earth. Potapyenko didn't know whether to believe his luck. Afterwards he said: 'The Messerschmitts crashed into one another.' But the technicians who had seen all this accused the engineer of false modesty.

On 21 August 1941, the day after the enemy raid, it was announced that we would fly to collect new aircraft.

CHAPTER FOUR

LaGG 3 Fighters For The Squadron

Visiting Lavochkin

The twin-engined transport aircraft was carrying us further away from Leningrad. The engines droned steadily. The capacious interior of the Li 2 quivered gently. We were flying to the aircraft factory for our fighters. The new CO, Capt Umansky, led our group. There were places in the plane for everyone. Some arranged themselves on folding seats, others like myself sat on our parachutes, which we had brought with us for the return flight in our fighters. It was the first time I had flown in a passenger aircraft. The door of the cockpit was open, and I could see the captain piloting the plane. To his right was a co-pilot. Without hurrying, the captain lit a cigarette then handed over the controls to his partner and came through to us. Once he had asked how we felt, he returned to the pilot's cabin, sat in his chair and opened a newspaper. How strange this seemed! Nothing in common with piloting a fighter aircraft; there was an atmosphere of complete and unhurried calm.

They say that fighter pilots are nervous, energetic people, quick at making decisions. You could do nothing without such a character. You couldn't sit doing nothing and what's more there was no one to work out the course for us. You must do everything. You are pilot, navigator, gunner, radio operator and flight engineer. And if you want to relieve yourself, you must wait until you land. Yet here the designer had provided for everything, even a toilet. A sign had been drawn on the door.

I turned to Bagryantsev. 'Mikhail Ivanovich, how do you like this aircraft?'

'It's a bit old, but not bad,' he said, casting a glance around the passenger compartment.

'Would you like to fly one of these?'

He smiled. 'No, I prefer a fighter.'

'Neither would I exchange a fighter for another, not even for the most comfortable plane,' I said. 'You see, in a fighter, you are free like a bird. If a Messerschmitt attacked a plane like this, what could you do? But if it caught you or me in a fighter, we'd destroy it in no time.'

Bagryantsev agreed. 'That's true, but,' he nodded towards the pilot's cabin, 'they experience an adventurous life. They deliver urgently needed supplies, they evacuate the wounded from the front. They fly in bad weather and at night. It's not easy for them either.'

They were already waiting for us at the appointed destination. We rested and in the morning arrived at the factory. Its gigantic shop floors, conveyor belts, the whole process of aircraft manufacture, made an enormous impression on us. New LaGG 3 fighters were constantly coming off the production line.

The days spent in training flew past imperceptibly. After the tests, the chief designer of the aircraft, Semyon Alekseyevich Lavochkin, invited us to his home. This understanding and cheerful man greeted us warmly and sincerely. He shook each one of us by the hand, invited us to sit down and then produced a packet of Kazbek cigarettes. 'Help yourselves, sailors!'

Semyon Alekseyevich spent a long time asking us about every detail of the situation around Leningrad. The designer told us that the LaGG 3 aircraft had been tested in battle and the factory had received good reports about the new machine. He also informed us that successful work was going on in the construction of a new fighter with an air-cooled engine with qualities far exceeding the existing machine.

Lavochkin asked us to tell him about the tactics of Fascist fighters and bombers and about the performance of enemy anti-aircraft guns. He listened to us attentively and made notes on his writing pad. Despite the serious nature of the matters under discussion, Semyon Alekseyevich found time to joke. Almost three hours of conversation passed imperceptibly.

After leaving Lavochkin, we were detained in one of the workshops where we discussed the quality of the machines. The factory engineer who accompanied us said: 'Basically, the machine is well made, but unfortunately there are some faults which we've come across. Come and see who is assembling the aircraft for us.' Standing behind the lathes, at the benches, on the conveyor belts – almost all the workers were elderly, or young women; and in places, many teenagers were working. 'The men have gone to the front,' the engineer continued. 'We already have many widows and orphans.'

In the morning, we drove to the aerodrome. Each one of us had to fly a circuit with the undercarriage retracted. When it was my turn to fly, I took my place in the spacious cockpit. I was especially pleased that the rudder pedals were conveniently positioned. No need to say anything about the radio; it had been our dream for some time.

'Have I permission to taxi for take-off?' I asked from the cockpit.

In the headphones, the reply came immediately. 'Permission granted!'

I taxied and asked permission to take off. The aircraft lifted gently from the ground. I pressed the red button. Then somewhere below there was a gentle slap and two red lights lit up – the undercarriage had retracted. After the I 16, in which it was necessary to turn the handle to wind a hoisting cable forty-four times, it seemed a miracle. The machine gained height. I could feel the power of the engine. I had a new aircraft in my hands. It was great!

We returned to our quarters in high spirits, as if we had accomplished something extremely important. There, at the factory aerodrome, were so many aircraft that you couldn't drop an apple between them. I looked at them and my soul rejoiced. Among those people accompanying us was one of the engineers from the factory. We stopped beside an incomplete row of aircraft.

'A group of army pilots has already taken nine aircraft,' said the engineer. 'You have been allotted the numbers from eleven to twenty. Write the numbers on the sides, and may a favourable wind follow you, sailors!'

Soon we took off into the air. Ten LaGG 3 fighters led by a Pe 2 twin-engined dive bomber formed up and followed the planned course. The weather was sunny and clear. Visibility seemed unlimited.

After some time we landed at one of the intervening aerodromes and started to refuel the aircraft. It became clear that Volodya Khaldeyev had been delayed on the flight by a failure in the mechanism regulating the airscrew. At this moment, the airfield Orderly Officer came up to us. On his tabs were the three pips of a senior technical lieutenant.

'Who is the senior officer in the group?' he asked Bagryantsev.

I looked at the orderly and could not believe my eyes. 'Kargashov, Aleksandr Fyodorovich! Fancy meeting you!'

'Kaberov! I never expected to see you! Where are you from?'

'We're taking our aircraft to the Baltic. But how did you come to be here?'

'We are forming a unit. Soon we shall also be at the front.'

We shook hands firmly and began to talk about Novgorod and the friends and relations we had left behind. Kargashov, at one time, had been the engineer at the Novgorod aeroclub when I was a pilot instructor. Aleksandr Fyodorovich and his comrades were making serious efforts to prepare for their departure to the front. Both Kargashov and I were very alarmed by the fact that Novgorod was already in German hands. We did not know what had happened to our families. We could have talked on endlessly but Kargashov was busy being airfield duty officer.

'I almost forgot,' Aleksandr Fyodorovich suddenly remembered. 'I should have told your senior officer. While the weather is good, you must take off. All the best, my friend. Until we meet in Novgorod!'

We bid farewell and I ran to my fighter.

I wanted to say earlier that Kargashov and I actually met in Novgorod after the war. Aleksandr Fyodorovich followed a long and difficult path from Moscow to Berlin. After the war, he was demobilized and, for a long time, worked in one of the Novgorod factories as an engineer, and now has already retired. Sometimes I see him walking with his wife along the embankment of the Volkhov. As soon as the sound of an aircraft is heard, Kargashov stops and follows the flight of the aircraft with his eyes.

However, to return to our flight from the aircraft factory to Leningrad.

. . . The aircraft rocked, as if on waves, flashing the bright discs of their airscrews in the sunlight. More and more, I was pleased with my new machine. How would it prove itself when we met the Junkers and Messerschmitts? These were the first LaGG 3s in Leningrad. The armament on them was excellent: a cannon and four machine-guns (two heavy calibre and two ordinary calibre weapons).

We arrived at Nizino, circled the aerodrome and landed. Tenyugin got out of his cockpit and exercised his tired legs after the long flight.

'Well done, Igor. Welcome to your native soil at Nizino.'

'The same to you, Volodya!' I shouted at him.

We made for the CO's aircraft. 'Well, at last we've reached home,' said Capt Umansky. 'It seems that everything's in order apart from Khaldeyev's plane. They will remove the defect and evidently he will fly home tomorrow.'

Umansky looked at both of us: 'A fierce struggle lies ahead, comrades!'

Do Pilots Need Trenches?

Heavy rain lashed down all day but stopped by evening. In the morning, a dense fog covered the aerodrome. It was still only 7 September, but autumn had already set in.

During the two weeks of our absence, the front had moved 25 kilometres closer to Leningrad. After taking Novgorod, the Fascist forces had seized Chudovo and now surrounded Leningrad and were advancing on the Neva and Lake Ladoga. Tosno was already occupied. Battles were going on for the Mga station. In all, 6 kilometres separated our aerodrome from the enemy's trenches in the region of Ropsha, now seized by the Fascists. Since morning, Capt Umansky had been moving about dispersal, looking at everything there with a master's eye. Then he summoned engineer Sergeyev.

'Do you know that there are only a few kilometres between our aerodrome and the front line?'

'I do.'

'Well then, I'm asking you to clear away everything you don't need from dispersal, camouflage the armourers' tent and make the slit trenches around the aircraft deeper.'

'We'll need time to do that,' muttered Sergeyev timidly.

The Squadron Commander seemed to ignore the remark. 'Report in two hours. And this evening, remember, this evening, engineer, you and I and the Commissar will make an inspection of small arms held by the junior aircrews and the ground staff.'

'I don't know,' Sergeyev shrugged his shoulders in confusion, 'there's the servicing of aircraft . . . and all this. . . . I don't know. . . . We won't have the time.'

'Then what are you doing here, engineer?' said Umansky sharply. Repeating once more all his demands, he finished the conversation with: 'Get on with it!'

The engineer moved away. In the dug-out it was so quiet, as if not a soul remained. I drew up the next number of the camp news-sheet and thought about Sergeyev. There was no doubt that he would grumble but do everything that was ordered. I ran to dispersal to display the news-sheet and there work was already in full swing. Gritsayenko and Alferov were standing waist-deep in the trench and digging with shovels.

'Never fear, everything's going well, Comrade Commander. Who knows – maybe tomorrow we shall have to open fire from these trenches.'

The engineer was nowhere to be seen. I found him in the aircraft container which served as the hut for Bagryantsev's flight. Mikhail Ivanovich was sewing on a clean undercollar and Sergeyev a button on his overalls. I sat down next to them, pulled my weapon from its holster and began to examine it.

'Yes, I almost forgot!' Sergeyev said suddenly. 'I must inspect my weapon too. It will be too late this evening.' He spun the cylinder of his revolver, removed the cartridges and, holding the barrel to the light, examined it. 'He'll hang me. They hang people for less.'

The engineer hurried to the armourers to organize inspection and cleaning of the weaponry and in exactly two hours, he reported to the CO.

'Comrade Captain, all your instructions have been carried out. The weapon is in perfect condition.'

'But you said you wouldn't be able to cope.' Umansky looked at the engineer with eyes which had become kinder. 'Thank you, Vladimir Andreyevich.'

By noon the fog had lifted and in the clear space which had formed above the aerodrome, the blue sky peeped through. The CO summoned Bagryantsev, Semyonov and me. Before the Captain lay a chart with a route marked on it.

'Reconnoitre the road from Chernishov to Koskolov,' said Umansky, turning to Bagryantsev. 'Pay particular attention to the shore of Luga Bay. Find out whether or not the enemy forces are gathering there. Take off immediately.'

Over Ropsha, our aircraft ran into flak. Bluish shell bursts, diffuse like jellyfish, rose before us. Below, the fog persisted and only through rare openings, like separate islands, was the earth visible. It was useless to circle there, so we turned back. Ahead and a little to one side, the curtain of fog parted, revealing a small strip of land.

'Follow me!' I heard Bagryantsev's voice over the radio. His aircraft plunged down. I removed the safety catch from the trigger and quickly followed him. A road stretched beneath us. It was filled with enemy troops moving towards Leningrad. From time to time, vehicles overtook the infantry. Taking advantage of the foggy conditions, Hitler's troops were moving up to the front in daylight. Clearly they did not expect us to appear and did not manage to disperse. The machine-guns and cannon of the LaGG 3 did their work. At least a hundred enemy corpses remained on the road after our attack. Bagryantsev even managed to set on fire a light vehicle.

Breaking through the layer of fog, we soared upwards. Blinking in sunlight still as bright as summer, we set course for Nizino. Back at the aerodrome, when Umansky had heard Bagryantsev's report, he asked us to point out as accurately as possible on the map the place where we had attacked the infantry. The CO was interested to know how many Fascist troops there were, how many vehicles and of what kind.

'But tell me, Comrade Bagryantsev,' he said a moment later, 'what conclusions do you yourself draw from this flight?'

'To me, the conclusion is clear. From Ropsha to the shore of the Finnish Gulf is not far – something like 15 to 18 kilometres. The Germans are gathering their forces near Ropsha. That means they are preparing to make a breakthrough to Peterhoff. Our aerodrome is in their path. It will impede them.'

'Of course, you are right, Mikhail Ivanovich,' said Umansky thoughtfully, 'and I'm pleased that we agree on this. I must admit that the problem of guarding the aerodrome has been troubling me. . . .'

Soon after our conversation with the CO, four Me 109s appeared above the aerodrome. Like black kites looking for prey, the enemy aircraft made one circle after another. Without doubt they were reconnaissance aircraft. They made for home without accepting battle with our fighters, which hurriedly took off in pursuit.

It was clear that Hitler's aviators had become interested in our new technology. The next day, a small single-engined German Henschel 126, accompanied by six fighters, appeared over Ropsha. Evidently, its duties included the correction of fire from a German artillery battery, aimed at our dispersal area. Delay was out of the question. A rocket went up and our duty flight (Kostilyev, Kirov and I) took off.

The battle didn't take long, but was fierce. The Henschel took refuge in the clouds and didn't appear again. The fighters, sensing their numerical superiority, accepted our challenge; but in only fifteen minutes, two of them were shot down. The rest, taking advantage of cloud cover, withdrew from the conflict.

When we landed, the Adjutant informed Kirov and me that, after the aircraft had been refuelled, we would be on duty covering the airspace above the airfield. Bagryantsev, Kostilyev, Soldatov, Tenyugin, Shirobokov and Semyonov were summoned by the CO. Later, in the headquarters dug-out, these comrades told us what the meeting had been about.

First of all, the CO gave them information about the situation which had developed on our part of the front. The Germans were throwing in even more fresh troops. Sensing that our air power was weakening, tanks, self-propelled weapons and columns of enemy soldiers were moving in the open even by day. Our strike aircraft and bombers, operating from aerodromes on the Karelian Isthmus, did not remain on the ground for a moment longer than necessary. But their efforts were not enough. So the problem of destroying the enemy tanks also fell to LaGG 3 fighters.

Hearing this, Bagryantsev was astonished: 'I don't understand. What harm can a 20 mm missile from an aircraft cannon do to a modern tank? It's like a pellet against an elephant! We don't have anti-tank weapons. . . .'

Capt Umansky let Bagryantsev finish, then he stood up:

'It's an order and we do not have the right to ignore it.'

And so, seven LaGG 3s, led by Capt Umansky, took off. Their target – a German tank column on the road to the Ropsha region. After forty minutes, the fighters returned. But only Bagryantsev, Kostilyev, Semyonov and Shirobokov returned. Capt Umansky, 2/Lt Soldatov, and 1/Lt Tenyugin were missing.

The tank column, which the seven Soviet aircraft attacked, was given air cover by a large group of enemy fighters. Our comrades could only break through this cover with great difficulty. Firing along the column from cannons and machine-guns, they made only one run over the target, and that without the whole group. 2/Lt Soldatov's aircraft, hit by anti-aircraft fire, did not reach the target and flew away towards the front line.

The Fascist pilots had a numerical advantage and the advantage of altitude. They threw themselves at our six from all sides. Damaged during the strike by anti-aircraft fire, Umansky's and Tenyugin's aircraft could not sustain a long attack. Capt Umansky soon baled out over territory occupied by the enemy. Tenyugin still fought alongside his comrades for some time. Five against eighteen! Unable to attack the tanks any longer, Bagryantsev, who was leading the group, gave the signal to our fighters to move away towards the front line. Tenyugin gained height so that he could glide home if his engine failed. Four Messerschmitts attacked him. The brave pilot engaged them in an unequal battle and, within only a few seconds, one of them was in flames. The others attacked Vladimir Tenyugin furiously. The engine of his machine had been damaged by anti-aircraft fire and when it stopped, Tenyugin baled out. Enraged by their failure, the Fascists shot him as he hung in the air, each of them making two attacks. It was a bitter experience for his friends too, who, being engaged in conflict with the other Messerschmitts, could not help Tenyugin.

Back at the aerodrome, we found out that Aleksey Soldatov was wounded, but had reached the front line and made a belly landing in the vicinity of our forces.

In the evening, the pilots assembled in order to mark the bitter loss of our fallen comrades with a traditional drink. Losing three at once was something which hadn't happened to us before. The cruelty which the Fascist pilots had displayed in shooting Tenyugin made us all think deeply.

'I never did like Mondays,' said Bagryantsev suddenly. 'They're never easy. But this morning I didn't think it would be like this.'

But of course, the cause of our misfortune was not Monday. As I saw it, the group, having lost its leader, was not sufficiently united, even though all my comrades fought courageously. Who could know whether the next day, Tuesday, would not be unusually difficult? And who could know whether at dinner once again we would not be silent and, like the evening before, would drink our hundred grammes in sorrow as a mark of respect to Mikhail

Ivanovich Bagryantsev himself? Nobody could foresee everything that the approaching day had prepared for us.

Meanwhile, the car transported us to Nizino. Each one of us was tired and longed for rest. That night, Umansky's, Tenyugin's and Soldatov's beds remained untouched. Volodya's bunk was next to mine and that evening I felt the loss of a friend particularly keenly. He was a taciturn person but, the evening before as he lay down to sleep, he had suddenly become talkative, not excitedly, of course, but thoughtfully, as the mood took him, as we say. The lights had gone out and our comrades were sleeping but Volodya Tenyugin still spoke to me in whispers about his Ostashkov, about Seliger, recalling his mother, Yelizavyeta Fyodorovna, and his father.

I slept little that night. I thought of Volodya and about Umansky. Isaak Markovich, I knew, had a family somewhere – a wife and a little daughter. What else did I know about Umansky? I knew that before he came to us, he commanded the second squadron in our regiment which was equipped with MiG 3 fighters. I knew that Isaak Markovich graduated from the Odessa school for military pilots in 1930. A former fitter in the Kharkov factory 'Hammer and Sickle', he became a pilot and an experienced commanding officer. Umansky had already been awarded a military decoration during the conflict with Finland. The memory of the day when he joined our squadron rose in my mind. He had arrived at the official meeting and was about to speak when, at that moment, I asked Kostilyev something. He didn't even have the chance to reply before I heard:

'Comrade Kaberov, when the CO speaks, subordinates pay attention.' I stood up.

'Sit down,' said the Captain.

The meeting continued. Meanwhile, ruffled, I looked the new CO over with the clear wish to find something negative about him. But I didn't succeed. Even then, he gave me the impression of being a very reserved, conscientious person whom experience had matured. His narrowed eyes cast a strict glance. His cheeks and chin were clean shaven. The buttons on his naval jacket shone. A fresh undercollar surrounded his strong neck in an even band. Medals glittered on his chest. I looked at him fixedly and suddenly caught myself feeling my chin with the palm of my hand. (Was it clean shaven?) I calmed down; it wasn't bad. Then, inconspicuously, I wiped the buttons on my tunic with my sleeve. Meanwhile the meeting came to an end. The CO looked at his watch.

'I ask you all to synchronize your watches. The CO's time is precisely sixteen hours and twenty-one minutes.'

I must confess, this was the first time I had heard of CO's time. It rather astonished me that Umansky considered his watch the most accurate in the squadron. I had no chance to check whether this was so. But he himself was an exceptionally punctual person – that I was able to confirm. And, moreover, I wanted to emulate him. It was then, after the first meeting which he conducted, that I put my equipment in order with particular thoroughness. Nor was I alone in this. It began with little things, but even this was important. We began to adopt all that was best about the CO, all that was characteristic of him: the fighting ability, punctiliousness, resoluteness and discipline of Capt Umansky became our features. And now he was no longer with us. No one had seen where the CO had landed. We wanted to believe that he was not dead.

In the morning, we were woken early. Again the first thought was: 'Tenyugin . . . Umansky . . . .' We washed and hurried to our transport.

We had hardly arrived at the aerodrome dug-out and jumped from the transport, when two Fascist Me 109s flew at great speed and fairly low altitude over our dispersal. Then they gained height and began to circle overhead. Bagryantsev hurried to his aircraft and took off. Shirobokov followed him. Kostilyev and I were ordered to remain on the ground. Bagryantsev and Shirobokov hadn't managed to gain enough height before the Fascists attacked them from above. A bitter battle started. A neighbouring squadron sent two MiG 3 fighters to help our comrades. But they had hardly reached the fight before a second pair of German fighters appeared. Attacking one of the Fascists, Mikhail Ivanovich came under fire from the leader of the second pair. Bagryantsev's plane burst into flames; spinning, it fell to earth. The technicians and the doctor hurried to the place where it fell. Soon they returned. The doctor had recovered something in a burnt flying suit. We uncovered the head . . . .

In the evening, I walked past the aircrew's quarters. On the door, written in small letters, was the following notice: 'Here from 22 June until 9 September 1941 lived Second Lieutenant Bagryantsev's flight. All have perished.'

Battles From Dawn Till Dusk

At dawn on 10 September 1941, a car rushed us to the aerodrome. The sky in the region of Ropsha and Gatchina was illuminated by the red flashes of enemy artillery fire. Flashes from nearby gunshots (something like a Morse code) – sometimes lasting a moment, sometimes for several seconds – lit up the tops of the fir trees. Eventually Lt Khaldeyev (on the previous evening, he had flown in to us and taken over the squadron), who was sitting next to the driver, stopped the car, got out and listened. The rumble of the distant artillery cannonades and the thunder of nearby gunfire did not cease. There was no doubt that Hitler's troops had undertaken a new attack on Leningrad. Shells burst somewhere beyond the aerodrome. Khaldeyev got back in beside the driver and the car, bouncing over the pot-holes, sped on.

'We'll certainly be busy today!'

We soon arrived at the aerodrome which was on our front line. The new squadron CO, Volodya Khaldeyev, calmly carried out his duties in a businesslike manner. It seemed as if he had always been our CO. Commissar Isakovich helped him. The serious political officer, a short, lively, energetic man, not being a pilot, did a great deal to raise the military preparedness of the squadron. Volodya had someone he could rely on in any eventuality. The problem before us, that September day, was formulated thus: give cover to the forces in the region between Gatchina and Krasnoye Selo.

Six MiG 3 fighters from a neighbouring squadron were the first to take off. Only four returned to their own aerodrome. Then it was our turn. Khaldeyev, Shirobokov, Kirov and the new pilot, Myasnikov, went off on patrol. It fell to the lot of Kostilyev and me to carry out our duty by sitting in our aircraft. I had hardly taken my place in the cockpit when Gritsayenko came up to me.

'What do you think happened to those two?'

How could I answer? Aleksandr Nikolayevich lowered his eyes and fell silent. Then he took a clean handkerchief from the pocket of his overalls, wiped the glass of the gunsight, which was clean enough anyway, and the cockpit hood, then, patting the engine cowling, said:

'The machine won't let you down, comrade.'

I was about to thank the technician, but at that moment the increasing roar of engines reached us.

'Messerschmitts!' shouted Gritsayenko and for some reason squatted down. At enormous speed, four Fascist fighters passed above our heads. Without waiting for orders, Yegor and I started our engines and took off into the air.

For some reason, Hitler's pilots did not touch us on take-off. Maybe it was conceit. It might be said that four against two is easy to cope with; but twenty minutes of heavy fighting did not bring the Fascist pilots victory. We were tired but we made them sweat. No matter how experienced or strong these Fascist warriors were, there was nothing they could do but go away, having achieved nothing for their pains.

Yegor and I landed our aircraft and found it difficult to get out of our cockpits. Every muscle ached. Then all our four fighters landed (three LaGGs and a Yak). The lads had been engaged in a battle with ten enemy fighters. Shirobokov had shot down an Me 109. On the ground, he immediately and excitedly started to tell the group, led by Volodya Khaldeyev, what had happened.

In order to make it easier for the pilots, Anikanov, the Adjutant of the squadron, brought the operational record book from the dug-out, opened it on the wing of a fighter, as if it were a table, and started to write down the results of the fight. Without a clerk, the Adjutant's troubles multiplied. This was because Zhenya Duk was suffering serious concussion as a result of an injury sustained during an enemy raid on Nizino. He had been admitted to hospital.

Again the signal rocket shot into the sky. I took off after Kostilyev and Khaldeyev. Krasnoye Selo and Pushkin were beneath us. A battle was going on on the outskirts of Pushkin. From there it was only 20 kilometres to Leningrad. A dogfight was raging over Gatchina. Our army fighters had intercepted a group of Ju 87 dive-bombers. We watched the battle attentively, but it was strictly forbidden to be diverted from our own objective.

Then suddenly from nowhere the reconnaissance and spotter plane, the Henschel 126, appeared. Our old friend! Khaldeyev prepared to attack it but was himself the object of an attack by a pair of Messerschmitts. I wanted to help him but it was impossible to turn, so I threw my fighter between Khaldeyev's plane and the Messerschmitts. A burst of machine-gun fire, intended for Khaldeyev, struck the tail of my aircraft. The machine shuddered but responded to the controls as before. The Henschel managed to avoid the attack and Khaldeyev pulled up above it in a steep climb. Neither did an attempt by Kostilyev to attack the Henschel prove successful. He was compelled to do battle with a second pair of Messerschmitts.

Meanwhile, over the radio we heard an appeal: destroy the spotter plane! But the Henschel was very manoeuvrable and it was not easy to hit it. A further four Fascist fighters came at us out of the sun. Already there were now eight of them and only three of us. Khaldeyev flew away. A black trail of smoke stretched behind his plane.

'What's the matter, Volodya?' Yegor shouted.

'I'm all right, I'll reach the airfield,' Khaldeyev replied.

But his machine, for some reason, turned over and, twisting into a spin with smoke trailing behind, made for the spotter aircraft surrounded by Messerschmitts. It looked as if Khaldeyev had been hit, but he made an unexpected manoeuvre. Tracer fire penetrated the Henschel. The enemy plane burst into flames and fell to earth like a charred and smoking log. The Fascists were gripped by confusion. For some reason, the Messerschmitts took to the skies. Khaldeyev vanished against the background of smoke covering Leningrad. Only the burning remains of the Henschel were still visible.

Our mission completed, we made for home. Having landed, we taxied to a halt, climbed from our cockpits and saw Khaldeyev. It turned out that he was already home.

Yegor walked up to him. 'Well, how are you? Aren't you wounded?'

'No.'

'And the aircraft?'

'Nothing that can't be put right in an hour.'

We congratulated him on his victory, but this he brushed aside. 'Yes, but it was nothing! I finished off an already damaged enemy aircraft. All three of us played a part in this.'

'Don't be so modest,' said Yegor and suddenly turned to me. 'I'd like to tear off this lad's ears.'

'What for?'

'For creeping into my cone of fire.'

'I did no such thing.'

'Well then,' he turned to my aircraft. 'How many bullet holes in it?'

'Four!' said Gritsayenko.

'Your lunch is getting cold, lads!' Suddenly a girl's clear voice sounded above the noise at dispersal.

'Well, it certainly wouldn't be wrong to have a bite,' agreed Khaldeyev and looked at his watch. 'It's rather early, but if Shurochka has arrived . . . .'

We ducked under the tent canvas and there a pleasant surprise awaited us: the smell of mushrooms. Where could they have got them? It was a long way from there to the forest, almost to the front line. But this hadn't frightened Shurochka. It turned out that she had been in the wood that morning and now, if you please, mushroom soup!

Yegor took a sip. 'That a front line soldier should have such mushrooms!'

But at that moment my mechanic, Gritseyenko, poked his head into the tent. 'Commander, three Junkers, without fighter escort, have dropped their bombs on Strelna and turned in our direction.'

The mushroom soup remained on the table. We were in the air again. Khaldeyev's aircraft was being repaired, so Kirov flew with us to make a third.

We gained height. The Fascist pilots probably saw us. Not by chance did the Junkers turn away from the aerodrome and make for Gatchina. Two of them descended, but one gained height, clearly intending to enter a storm cloud: a gigantic fluffy cap hanging above the southern border of our aerodrome. Kostilyev ordered me to intercept this Junkers and he, together with Kirov, flew off in pursuit of the other two.

The enemy bomber was already at the very edge of the cloud. I caught up with it and found it in my sights; but then a dark, swirling storm cloud swallowed up the Junkers and, a moment later, me. My machine shook severely, and was tossed about. Damp snow stuck to the cockpit cover. Neither earth nor sky was visible. It became as dark as night and I had to fly on instruments.

I held the aircraft on its course with difficulty: fear seized me. My plane moved quicker than the Junkers. That meant that the enemy bomber must be somewhere near. Striving to avoid a collision, I throttled back and, with an effort, tried to peer into the impenetrable space. Suddenly, the fire of tracer bullets cut the gloom ahead of, and a little to the left of, my plane. I threw my machine sharply to one side. Now I could see where the enemy fire was coming from. The dim outline of the huge bomber was visible. It was no more than 30 metres away.

The air currents became rougher. The Fascist gunner had evidently lost me, but he continued to fire at random. He was playing into my hands. I had him in my sights and was sure to hit him.

The Junkers burst into flames and started to fall. First holding back in order to avoid collision, I then went into a dive. Soon bright daylight struck my eyes. I looked around. The bomber plunged to earth out of control. Another few seconds and it fell right on the road between Strelna and Ropsha. A huge column of smoke and flame rose high above the earth.

'That's the way for Fascists!' I shouted from the cockpit. 'Greetings from Nizino!'

I was seized by an inexpressible joy. Oh, how I wished that one of my friends could have seen the burning Junkers which I had brought down! But neither Kostilyev nor Kirov was in the vicinity. I consoled myself with the fact that, during the dogfight, others could have followed the aerial battle from the aerodrome. The burning bomber had fallen some 2 or 3 kilometres from Nizino.

I circled, looked for my comrades, but still couldn't see them. To be sure, I gained height. Krasnoye Selo, Pushkin, Krasniy Bor; there everything was burning, covered with smoke. And there was the front. . . .

On the aerodrome, the technicians gathered round and began telling us what the aerial battle had looked like from the ground and how the burning Junkers had crashed. Yegor went off to make his report to the CO and the smiles of our friends and the warm handshakes came only to Kirov and me. As always, my comrade was silent. But Fyodor Ivanovich (everyone in the squadron addressed him by his forename and patronymic) did not like boasting. Making the excuse that he had to go to the dug-out, he left. The technicians turned to me alone.

'How did you shoot him down in the cloud? You couldn't have seen anything there.'

'Well then, he was visible,' said Gritsayenko with pride as he refuelled the aircraft.

'Since childhood, the Lieutenant has adored carrots, and, as a result, they say a man can see in the dark like a cat,' joked Alferov the fitter.

Isakovich, the commissar, and Myasnikov, the new pilot, arrived. We heard Shurochka's voice: 'Lieutenant, where is Fyodor Ivanovich? The mushrooms are cold.'

After lunch, the CO ordered Kostilyev, Kirov, Semyonov and me to take off and cover the troops near Krasnoye Selo. We did so without delay, gained height and reached the prescribed area: there were swarms of Fascist fighters. Covering their forces, they were following the line of the front in two groups, one above, the other lower. They had a score of planes; we had only four. The very fierce, uneven struggle lasted almost forty minutes. Only with the help of army fighters, which arrived to relieve us, were our four able to break away from this pack of Fascist wolves.

On the ground, I felt devilishly tired when I got out of my cockpit. The earth swayed beneath my feet as if I was on the deck of a ship in a storm. My comrades were also shaken. Kostilyev and Kirov adopted a 'horizontal position', on jackets which Linnik, the technician, spread for them, and fell asleep. I had to report the result of the dogfight to headquarters, instead of Kostilyev. Soon I returned to the aircraft. Boris Semyonov was sitting beside his sleeping comrades. Diffidently turning away from me, he rubbed his glass eye. Again, involuntarily, I thought how difficult it must be for him to fight – difficult, but he didn't complain. We tried to protect him in battle. He knew this and worried as if he were in some way to blame.

Boris lit up a cigarette. I sat beside him. We remained silent and lay back on the grass. I can't remember dropping off, but in my sleep I heard a shout.

'Junkers, Commander, Junkers!' Opening my eyes, I threw off the jacket which Alferov had placed over me.

'What's that?'

'A Junkers over the airfield, Comrade Commander!'

I rushed to my aircraft. Gritsayenko was fastening the last clasps on the top of the cowling, but for some reason they didn't fit.

'Hurry, Sasha!' I urged the technician. 'Or the Junkers will get away.'

Having secured the last bolt, he patted the cowling and jumped down from the steps. I swept from the ground, quickly gaining height. Myasnikov in his Yak took off behind me. Meanwhile, the Junkers made off.

'Chase him or he'll get away,' shouted Myasnikov.

'No, he won't . . . !'

A few moments more and the Junkers would have been hit, but then something happened which I didn't understand. My aircraft shook from an unexpected blow. I had the impression that something had fallen on it. Instinctively, I ducked inside the cockpit. My field of vision was restricted. Nothing was visible ahead or above. I could make out a little to the right and left, but the wings obliterated all else. It turned out that I had hurried the technician and brought things on myself. I banked away and explained to Myasnikov over the radio what had happened to me.

In reply I heard: 'Go in to land. I'll cover you. The Junkers has gone. I'm fighting four Messerschmitts.' I tried to raise the displaced cowling but without success. Under the pressure of the slipstream, it held the cockpit firmly closed. I couldn't even move it. I saw through a narrow slit to the left how a Messerschmitt flew past me. I threw the fighter to one side and dived. For a moment, I saw Peterhoff Park. As I turned I caught a glimpse of part of the Finnish Gulf – the aerodrome had to be ahead. I lowered the undercarriage, and flew almost blind. Messerschmitts were somewhere nearby; so was Myasnikov – one against four of them.

To reduce speed, I lowered my flaps. I saw our hangars to one side. I turned and went into a glide. I twisted my head to left and right. Every nerve, every muscle was strained to the very limit. I lost height. The ground was near. The water-tower flashed past on my left. It turned out that I had come in at an angle to the runway. The dispersal area for No. 1 Squadron was ahead but it was impossible to correct things now, so I cut the engine. The aircraft was nearly down and I could hear Myasnikov's voice in the headphones: 'Get down quickly, Kaberov, quickly. They're diving; there's nothing I can do!'

The slightest mistake and it would have been the end. But the aircraft struck the ground with its wheels and rebounded. I wrestled blindly with the controls. Another rebound, but weaker. And then the plane rolled along the ground, but where – I couldn't see. I applied the brakes again and again. I didn't want to run into anything. Finally the plane stopped. Quickly I undid the harness, threw off the damned cowling and in one go, leaped from the cockpit. Meanwhile, the Messerschmitt was already diving towards my machine. I ran aside and fell on the grass. The enemy fighter fired a burst and the bullets lifted the earth in front of the plane.

'You missed!' I shouted maliciously. 'You need to learn how to shoot.'

But a second fighter dived, and after it a third. I crawled aside. The second, to my astonishment, fired a burst at the first. It was Myasnikov firing at the Fascist. But Myasnikov, in his turn, was being attacked by another Messerschmitt. I jumped up from the ground, shot like a bullet to the cockpit and switched on the transmitter.

'Myasnikov, a 109 behind you.'

The Yak turned in a flash, and so sharply that the Fascist fighter had no time to open fire but climbed away into the sky. The Messerschmitt, which Myasnikov had already hit, started to smoke and made for home.

The fight was over. The skies were clear. The Yak lowered its undercarriage and came in to land. I taxied to dispersal and my aircraft was surrounded by technicians. Engineer Sergeyev came up. His face was as dark as a storm cloud. He raised the cowling in silence, and tried to look under it as he sat in the cockpit.

'Gritsayenko should be made to sit in the aircraft and experience a blind landing,' Sergeyev said to me.

'In this case, it was my fault, comrade. I hurried the technician.'

Sergeyev suddenly knitted the prickly tufts of his whitish eyebrows. 'For such disgraceful practices, Comrade Kaberov, we, the technicians, are responsible. As things turned out, mistakes were made.' He turned to Gritsayenko: 'The aircraft must be airworthy in twenty minutes! See to it!'

Having landed his Yak, a tired Myasnikov climbed from the cockpit, removed his flying helmet, smoothed his hair, wiped the sweat from his face with his sleeve and came up to us. Looking over the cowling, thrown across the cockpit, he shook his head:

'Well, such things do happen! How did you manage to land?'

'With your help, Comrade Lieutenant. All thanks to you. But the aircraft was not damaged because its construction is reliable. Such a landing in an I 16 would not have been so easy.'

'Yes, "Ishachok" [I 16] is a strict machine,' agreed Aleksandr Fyodorovich. 'But have you never flown in a Yak? Exceptionally easy to fly. Easier than an LaGG.'

I looked at Myasnikov and thought: what a good, kind person you are!

'How did you manage alone to keep four Messerschmitts away?' I asked him. 'Yes, and give me cover?'

'It's my little "Yak" which is so frisky,' he said, glancing at the aircraft. 'Before this, we flew in "Chaykas". In such a kite I couldn't have done it. If somehow you can take a flip in a "Yak", you'll say: It's not an aircraft – it's a dream!'

Myasnikov, without realizing it, had started speaking to me in affectionate terms. Now he and I were at ease with one another. He offered me his hand.

'Let's be friends. And thank you for your help. I really didn't see that second Messerschmitt.'

We entered the dug-out. It was noisy there. Khaldeyev, a usually taciturn and even-tempered person, was railing at someone on the telephone.

'Yes, in all I have seven pilots on duty. Is that clear? Three on patrol, four on the ground, refuelling. What? The ones being refuelled, are they ready for action? What are you saying? . . . Have you gone out of your mind?!' Khaldeyev's face turned red; he raised his eyebrows and his eyes seemed to flash like lightning. 'What sort of Stormoviks? Where? Escorting? Six? And two more in the air? Have you got your arithmetic right?'

He threw down the receiver and went out of the dug-out. We followed him. Another dogfight was going on above the airfield. Four I 16s were fighting four Me 109s. Two MiGs slowly took off. Apart from that, our trio – Kostilyev, Kirov and Shirobokov – on their return from patrol decided to help the I 16s. The Fascists left the battle straight away.

Khaldeyev, Myasnikov and I were again sitting in our cockpits. The usual duty inspection had begun. The cowling was still removed from Myasnikov's 'Yak', the ammunition was being replaced and they were repairing something that was faulty. Anikanov unexpectedly ran up to Khaldeyev's aircraft.

'There they are, comrade. They're coming in over the Gulf!'

'Who?'

'Stormoviks. You, Myasnikov and Kaberov – go and escort them.'

'How about covering the airfield?'

'It's no longer necessary. . . . Start up – quickly!' Khaldeyev and I took off. Myasnikov remained on the ground because his aircraft had developed a fault.

We caught up with the assault aircraft and got into formation. Seven Il 2s were flying with an escort of four I 16s and two Yak 1s. We could see from the numbers on the fuselages that they were army aircraft. Where they were going, we didn't know.

In the region of Krasnoye Selo, twelve Me 109 fighters fell on us. The assault aircraft flew on to the target; the I 16s followed them, but we were again in a fight. There were four of us: two army Yaks, Khaldeyev and me. We had no radio contact with the other two. Fires were blazing on the ground. Where were the assault aircraft and what were they doing? We didn't see. Four of the Messerschmitts went after them; eight took us on.

After twenty minutes of fighting, which produced no result, the Yaks started to break away and make for Leningrad. We followed them. The Messerschmitts, like wasps, wouldn't leave us. Gorelovo was beneath us, only a stone's throw from Leningrad. Here, one of the Yaks burst into flames and fell to earth. I couldn't see if the pilot managed to bale out. Then from out of the blue, the 'kings of the air' (I 15b fighters) with their rockets again came to our aid. The Messerschmitts retired from the battle. We made course for our aerodrome. My mouth was dry – I couldn't breathe – I could hardly wait to land. Staggering, I walked to the dug-out. Just as tired, Khaldeyev walked with me.

'What a day!' he said, dropping on to his bunk. 'I feel as if I'm going out of my mind. Exhausting battles.'

For some time, Khaldeyev lay silent, then spoke again. 'It was the kind of situation when pilots say: if you want to live, land.'

'We should find out whether the assault aircraft have returned to base.' My words must have reached Anikanov's ears.

'I can report,' he announced triumphantly, 'that a message has been received to say that the assault aircraft pilots thank the naval fighter pilots for their help.'

Then he added somewhat quieter: 'They all returned. The pilot from the Yak is alive but suffered some burns.'

I felt calmer and fell asleep. But soon someone started to shake me by the shoulder. A naval messenger told me that some pilot wanted to see me urgently. I jumped up, looked at my watch and asked Anikanov whether there would be any more flights that day.

'Hardly. You've taken off six times each. What more could you do? An order has been received from regimental headquarters: let the pilots rest!'

I went out of the dug-out. A quarter of an hour's sleep had removed some of my tiredness. I could find no one at dispersal. Gritsayenko said that two people had been asking for me but had gone away somewhere. But no, there they were, hurrying to meet me.

'Comrade Instructor, good to see you!'

'Baranovsky! How did you get here?' We embraced.

'They told me, Comrade Instructor, that you were in Nizino. My friend and I didn't think twice. We took a boat and came to Oranienbaum. Now we are here.'

Baranovsky's smiling, pock-marked face shone with joy.

'This is the man I told you about,' he said to his companion.

Aleksey informed me with pride that he and his comrade were flying in I 15b fighters, and that their programme of military flying was completed. The next day they hoped to carry out their first operational flight.

Alyoshka! Before me sat Alyoshka Baranovsky who made his first solo flight in the aeroclub as part of my examination for my flying instructor's certificate. Now he was no longer a student but a fighter pilot. The next day he would go into battle.

'Well, what next?' He suddenly became excited. 'Maybe tomorrow, together we shall strike the Fascists. I am angry with them, Comrade Instructor, oh so angry. There are so many of our towns and villages under the jackboot; and my native village of Bor as well. It's beyond Staraya Russa in the Zaluchsky region. Is there anything left of it? And what has happened to the older members of my family, to my brother and sisters? I don't know.'

He took a long drag on his cigarette to control his agitation.

'Alyosha,' I said, 'all my family were in Novgorod and there is no news from there either. Can they get away or can they not? Where are my parents? Where is Valya? I don't know.'

'And the Messerschmitts, are they powerful machines?' said Baranovsky, turning to practical matters. 'How do the Fascists fight in them?' But suddenly, aircraft flew right over the tent and drowned Aleksey's last words. I ran outside. A pair of Me 109s were gaining height in a steep climb.

'You can look at Messerschmitts for yourself,' I said to Baranovsky, who had also run from the tent. We both craned our necks skywards. On one side, I heard someone starting an aero-engine. The next moment Alferov appeared in front of me. 'Kostilyev and you are to scramble, Comrade Lieutenant!'

I hurriedly shook Baranovsky's hand, waved to his comrade and dashed through the bushes to my aircraft.

'Goodbye, Alyosha.'

'See you soon, comrade. Good luck!' Baranovsky shouted after me.

'See you, Alyosha!' I shouted back as I ran.

Kostilyev was already up. I flew after him, buttoning my flying helmet as I went. I was probably nervous: how would things turn out? But the Fascists – there they were ahead – four of them. 'There won't be any more flights today,' – I remembered the adjutant's reassurances. Where the devil did these four come from at this time in the evening then? It was evident from their movements that these pilots were old hands. A carousel of fighting planes revolved above the aerodrome.

'Watch out – they'll catch you in crossfire!' I shouted at Kostilyev.

'Keep calm, Igor, keep calm!' I heard Yegor's voice.

Calm, what sort of calm! Enemy fighters were so close that a second later I would have found myself under fire. I climbed and rolled. The LaGG 3 shuddered but obediently turned over. Tracer bullets flashed past. Yegor turned sharply and shot upwards. I kept close to him. Two Messerschmitts happened to be beneath us. Yegor quickly closed on them and, as he did so, fired at the leader. Something flew off the enemy machine, which went into a spin, immediately came out of it and then, as we say, took to its heels.

'That'll teach you!' Yegor shouted joyfully over the radio.

Yegor and I tried not to lose sight of one another. Kostilyev got on the tail of a Messerschmitt, but at the same time another enemy fighter fell on Kostilyev's plane. I threw my machine into a steep turn and, gaining height, succeeded in firing a burst at the second Messerschmitt. It turned over completely, lost height and went away, leaving behind a trail of smoke. Once they had circled above the aerodrome, the last pair of Fascist aircraft followed after it.

What a day! Seven operational flights, one after the other. And what sorties! If I had any strength left, then it was only enough for a landing. I had one desire – to land, taxi and sleep. . . . However, to land in the twilight was not so easy. I made a mental check: had I done everything that was needed? I lowered the undercarriage, also the flaps. Straining to see, I guided my aircraft to land. How pleasant to hear the hissing of the brakes! The plane came to a halt and I was so relieved. It was as if there had been no fighting. Working on low throttle, the engine gently turned over. And then everything dissolved in the half light of the approaching evening.

I came to on hearing a strange noise. Someone was pushing me to one side, shaking my shoulder, shouting noisily right in my ear. I opened my eyes and saw the anxious face of Gritsayenko, my mechanic.

'What happened, Comrade Lieutenant? You aren't wounded?

Not being in a condition to understand where I was or what I was doing, I blinked. No, it seemed that everything was all right. The aircraft stood at the end of the airfield. The engine was running. I was sitting in the cockpit. In front of me was Gritsayenko with his copper-coloured, unshaven, bristly beard.

'I must have fallen asleep, Sasha,' I said guiltily to the technician. 'Let's taxi.'

He shook his head sadly and walked to dispersal.

Stand On The Threshold Then Enter

It seemed impossible to imagine a more difficult day than that Wednesday which had so enfeebled us. But the night passed and it was as if everything had started from the beginning again. Thursday 11 September was in no way easier than Wednesday, perhaps even more difficult. Again we gave cover to our forces in the area of Pushkin, Krasnoye Selo and Krasniy Bor. Again armadas of Junkers flew towards the front lines to bomb our forces. The breaks between sorties were short, very short. During these minutes, every one of us felt one desire – to lie under the wing of a fighter and gather strength for the next fight.

Each of our fighters made between five and seven flights that day. But we only managed to shoot down two enemy aircraft, a Ju 87 and a Henschel 126 (it was directing artillery fire in the region of Krasnoye Selo). Our CO, Vladimir Khaldeyev, shot down the Ju 87 and the Henschel was shot down by Kostilyev and me.

The Germans lost an Me 109 fighter in extremely mysterious circumstances. In the course of battle, and without any of us attacking him, the enemy pilot unexpectedly jumped from the cockpit of his fighter and opened his parachute. The aircraft spun to earth and fell on our territory. Most likely it had been hit and was uncontrollable. The other Me 109s left the battle (evidently they had run out of fuel). Taking advantage of the pause, Kostilyev and I decided to turn our attention to the parachutist and see if he was alive. Kostilyev, reducing speed, flew right past him. Following Yegor, I saw how the Fascist suddenly threw up his arm. This gesture reminded me of the Fascist salute. 'How well drilled the scoundrel is!' I thought. 'In a few minutes, he'll be a prisoner, yet he still gives himself airs; what's more he's probably foolishly shouting "Heil Hitler"'.

But no, I was mistaken. It was much more serious than that. Kostilyev suddenly turned his machine sharply aside.

'He's shooting,' Yegor shouted to me over the radio. 'Keep clear! I've already got a hole in my cockpit. Yes, and what's more, he hit my hand, the skunk. . . .'

Our indignation knew no bounds. Here was an armed Fascist. How would he conduct himself on the ground when our soldiers tried to approach him? How many would remain alive in such an attempt? No, better the Fascist should depart this life. In the twinkling of an eye, we tore his parachute to shreds.

It was already ten o'clock in the evening, when an unshaven and extremely exhausted man walked into the dug-out. Tall, with the eyes of a hawk, he was like Zaur from the pre-war film of the same name.

'Capt Umansky!'

We rushed at him, his unexpected arrival sending us crazy. Yes, it really was Umansky. Somewhere in the region of the enormous Porsolov marsh, he had cut through the front line and arrived at his aerodrome. Our CO had experienced much. He had dropped by parachute behind enemy lines. By day, Umansky had hidden in the forest or the thickets and bushes; by night he had walked, avoiding populated places, following a course to the north of the front line. Sixteen kilometres separated the place where he came down from territory not occupied by the enemy, but it had taken him three days to cover the distance. Then, there it was – his own aerodrome, the dug-out and the guard at the entrance to it! Later, Umansky told us how disturbed he felt at that moment.

'I stood, listening. The aerodrome was quiet,' he said. 'My heart beat with joy. I asked the sentry for a light, sheltered the cigarette in my sleeve and greedily inhaled the smoke. Home! From joy, I wanted to embrace the reserved young lad on guard duty and everything else about me – the earth, the trees, the sky. I stood by the door, stroked the thick bristle of my beard with the palm of my hand and thought: will they recognize me? They did . . . .'

The news of Umansky's return spread with the speed of lightning through the squadron. One after another, people came into the dug-out. Yet he still could not believe that he had finally returned home.

'Take off your coat, Comrade Commander. They'll bring you something to eat presently.'

'But I'm not hungry,' he said. 'Don't put yourselves to any trouble. I've rations still untouched.'

Umansky drew from his pocket and poured out on the table a handful of rye grains, cranberries, whortleberries; 'and look here' – he placed the well-thumbed remains of a swede on the paper tablecloth, blew from it the tobacco dust – 'there's vitamins for you.'

'Yes, and with grub like that, Comrade Captain, your legs would soon give out.'

'Quite the contrary; without them you'd soon give up the ghost.'

The CO recovered his strength, shaved, checked his watch against ours, reported his arrival to regimental headquarters and began to ask us how things were going in the squadron. We talked and grieved for our dead comrades. Then Umansky started to tell us about everything that had happened to him after the loss of his aircraft.

'I came to earth in a forest, took down my parachute from a tree, hid it in the bushes and set off northwards. I destroyed all my documents apart from my party membership card – here it is. I thought of hiding it, but where? The forest was surrounded by marshland. Moreover the Fascists were nearby. When it became dark, I went out on to the road. I wanted to run across it but suddenly heard 'Halt'. Then a rifle bolt clicked. I stayed still, then quietly crawled back. I hid almost three days in a ditch covered with leaves. Along the road, cars and troops moved in an endless stream. Hitler's troops, armed with automatic rifles, combed the woods. Only last night did I succeed in crossing the road. I quenched my thirst in the swamp and walked and walked. I met a forester; he gave me refreshment at his house. In the evening, a little boy, the grandson of this good man, led me to the aerodrome.'

CHAPTER FIVE

Retreat From Nizino

The Hard-Won Gold Of Courage

Returning from a military exercise, I noticed from the air an I 16 aircraft on the ground beside the dispersal area. Who was visiting us? Gliding in, I saw on the fuselage of the plane the number '41'. A familiar aircraft; I had seen it before somewhere. I landed, still puzzling over where I'd met that aircraft before . . .' And suddenly, I remembered a photograph printed in one of the naval newspapers. In the photo, I had seen I 16 No. 41. Brinko it was who had flown in! A pilot from Khanko – Hero of the Soviet Union, 1/Lt Brinko! However, they were saying he was already a captain.

I switched off the engine, jumped out of the cockpit, reported the results of the flight to the CO and ran to the I 16. People had gathered beside the machine. I saw 1/Lt Alekseyev, one of the pilots from 3rd Squadron and our technicians. Yegor Kostilyev followed me to the aircraft. Alekseyev, Brinko and Kostilyev were old friends.

'Long time, no see!' Yegor embraced our guest. 'Congratulations, my friend. Congratulations.'

Brinko, without removing his parachute, sat on the grass, grasping his knees. A conversation started about friends and comrades, about the days before the war. Unexpectedly, the conversation was interrupted by a heart-warming shout: 'Boys, the Fascists have put up a blimp.'

Everyone turned round. Yes, sure enough, above Ropsha the enemy was slowly raising, on flexible steel cables, an observation balloon. The gigantic German 'sausage' swayed on its pliable wire hawsers as it rose slowly. We watched it with interest. At the same time, we heard the roar of engines behind us. The I 16 raised a dust, sped across the airfield and quickly gained height. Meanwhile, in the gaps in the clouds, four enemy fighters flew past – cover for the balloon.

'Well,' shouted Yegor, 'we must help.'

We rushed to dispersal, but our aircraft were still not ready for action. However, Pyotr Brinko no longer needed help – he was attacking the balloon. Before our eyes, in a fraction of a second, all that remained of the balloon was the fabric and a dark cloud of smoke blown by the wind. The fabric and the basket plunged to earth. Brinko's aircraft was already speeding over the airfield and coming in to land.

'There you are, Igor,' Yegor said to me. 'Now you've seen how you must work. Fly over the target, knock it out and land. They don't make anyone a hero for nothing, brother!'

Having landed, Brinko taxied to the place where he'd been before, jumped nimbly from his cockpit, sent one of the fitters to find fuel and, folding the ear flaps of his flying helmet under the straps of his goggles, again sat down on his parachute.

'Well, Yegor, where were we before we stopped? Ah, now I remember!' he said cheerfully, and with a smile, took up the conversation where he had left off.

Everything which I have heard and read about this magnificent pilot will always remain in my memory. After the war, I obtained a little more precise information when talking to Mikhail Lvov, who is now Lieutenant Colonel in supplies. It's true we live in different towns (he in Moscow, I in Novgorod) but each year we meet in Leningrad, where, on 9 May, the veterans of the Baltic Air Forces assemble.

Brinko was serving in the Far East when the military conflict flared up on the Finnish–Soviet border. For courage and valour, displayed in the battles during the winter of 1940, the young pilot was awarded the Order of the Red Banner. From the beginning of the war, Brinko served under Maj Romanyenko, Hero of the Soviet Union, and defended the Khanko peninsula. It was here that the fighting character of the man, passionately in love with his difficult and dangerous profession, was revealed in full measure. On 3 July 1941, two Fascist fighters unexpectedly attacked the aerodrome. Under fire, Brinko was able to get his machine into the air and gain height. There and then, above the airfield, he shot down one of the enemy aircraft. The next day, he destroyed a Junkers. On 8 July, returning to the airfield after attacking enemy forces, Brinko met and attacked a Fascist bomber, which he could not identify from its construction. The engine nacelles reminded him of a Ju 88, but it had the twin-finned tail of an Me 110. Pyotr Brinko shot down this aerial hybrid at his second attempt and it plunged into the water. The aircrew were killed. The sunken aircraft was brought out of the water and displayed in Khanko's central square. It turned out to be a Ju 86.

Comrades admired Pyotr Brinko's bravery and fighting skill and studied his flying technique. But, as a rule, he was dissatisfied with himself.

'No, no. That time I took off late. I must be quicker. I must train harder!'

Everything was calculated to the second: what, in this or that event, must the mechanic do, what must the fitter do and what must he do himself? 'If I take off a second earlier,' Brinko would say, 'the enemy will die. If I delay for a second, I shall die myself.'

Once during lunch, Brinko, who had not finished his soup, jumped up and went out of the dug-out and rushed headlong to his aircraft. He thrust his arms into the straps of the parachute, conveniently hung on a bush, jumped into the cockpit, started the motor and looked at his watch. Returning to the dug-out, he waved his arm in annoyance.

'Yet again I didn't manage it . . . .'

Someone reproached Brinko: 'You're disturbing honest people. What do you want more than others?'

Brinko answered only with a brief, angry glance. Yes, when we are talking about the business of war, he did want more than everyone else. However, the same kind of restless brave person, Aleksey Antonyenko, was the leader of the pair and flew with Brinko from the first days of the war. On 14 July 1941, both of them received the distinguished title of Hero of the Soviet Union. Two days later, this memorable event was marked by a new victory over the enemy. At dawn on 16 July, an orderly ran into the dug-out where Antonyenko and Brinko were sleeping.

'Two Fiats over the aerodrome!' he shouted. Antonyenko and Brinko were in the air in a minute; and in another ten, both Fiats were burnt out on the ground.

On 23 July, Antonyenko and Brinko flew out on reconnaissance. Having completed their mission, they decided to take a look at the enemy's naval aerodrome. Fascist seaplanes were floating in the water there. Then they returned home, reported the results of their reconnaissance to the CO and in the evening, accompanied by two 'Chaykas', repeated their attack on the naval aerodrome. But this time six enemy aircraft met them and a fight began. Four of our fighters won a victory over five Fokkers. Brinko shot down two of them. So, in one day, he destroyed four enemy aircraft.

The fighting endeavour of this man was inexhaustible. On 2 August, a flight of Fokkers arrived to make a low-flying attack on the aerodrome. Again, the first aircraft to take off and come under enemy fire was Brinko's. Having gained height, he destroyed an enemy fighter with his first attack. And on 7 August, this courageous pilot shot down a Ju 88 bomber over the island of Dago.

There was also another truly unique incident. Brinko's machine needed repair. The CO ordered Pyotr to fly to Tallinn where there were aviation repair workshops. Having landed at Tallinn aerodrome, the First Lieutenant handed over the aircraft to the technician, who was about to go to the workshop. At that moment, the anti-aircraft guns opened up. A Ju 88 reconnaissance aircraft was passing over the town. Pyotr rushed to his aircraft, but as it turned out, the technician had already taken the parachute from the cockpit of the fighter. Should he sit straight on the low bucket-shaped seat? In such a position, he wouldn't be able to see anything. Moreover the gunsight would be above eye-level. What should he do? Brinko placed his feet in the pedals of the rudder bar and, with his back pressed against the back of the seat, took off. There is no need to say how dangerous this was. But Brinko thought only of shooting down the enemy reconnaissance aircraft, which had appeared over the town. And he shot it down before the eyes of the astonished people of Tallinn. One of the members of the aircrew died in the aircraft, but three baled out and were taken into captivity. They turned out to be experienced aviators: all of them had been awarded Hitler's Iron Cross. Brinko landed his plane safely.

'Well, there it is, now you can repair it!' he said quite seriously to the anxious technician.

I thought of asking Pyotr Antonovich to tell us something about his fighting experiences, but the noise of the rocket interrupted me. A shout reached me from dispersal.

'Kostilyev's flight – scramble!' Yegor and I hurried to our aircraft.

In the air, carefully following my leader's machine, I was still thinking about Brinko, this understanding person, a Hero of the Soviet Union. To have shot down fifteen enemy aircraft and an observation balloon – to do that you have to be a real ace.

Could I have known that I would never see Pyotr Brinko again. The next day, he was killed. When attacking yet another enemy balloon, he was mortally wounded by shrapnel from an anti-aircraft shell. Brinko's attempted landing didn't succeed. The damaged aircraft quickly lost height, struck a wing on a pylon supporting a high-voltage electric cable and crashed.

Friends buried Pyotr Brinko beside Hussein Aliyev in the shade of birch trees. But the next day, Fascist forces reached those parts. They destroyed our Nizino, demolished the aerodrome, cut down the birch trees and flattened the burial mounds. The vandals brought down their blind and thoughtless fury even on the dead.

Bomb Craters On The Airfield

The drizzling rain, as fine as if it had been passed through a sieve, irked us. A cold, gusty wind blew from the gulf. Maliciously, it tore the last leaves from the bushes and spread them across the aerodrome on the moist earth.

I climbed out of the cockpit and exercised my legs, which had become stiff during the flight. In such weather, I would rather be sitting at home beside a warm stove and reading an interesting book. But where was our home now? Perhaps the invaders had already moved in: a brand new house, still not three years since it was built. And the garden: was the garden still there? And where were you, my family, my wife and little daughter? Are you alive? Did they manage to evacuate you? And if not, what lies ahead for you?

I came into the dug-out. The lads were already asleep in their bunks. I took my place by Kostilyev's feet and, exhausted, closed my eyes. But my thoughts again returned to Novgorod. Our forces had already abandoned it by 15 August, and it was now 13 September! And since then, no news of my relatives. How quickly everything had changed! Not long before, we had been worried that we wouldn't have to take part in aerial combat. But now . . . .

That day, for example, many of us had already made five sorties, and every one of them with the same purpose – giving support to forces in the region of Pushkin and Pulkovo. There, on the ground, they were saying a cruel battle was going on. Troubled thoughts don't let you sleep.

'Why are you lying at our feet?' Kostilyev looked at me with sleepy eyes. 'Come on, kip down with us. There's room for everyone.'

'Thanks, Yegor, I'd better take a stroll.'

I went out cautiously, so as not to wake the lads, closed the door of the dug-out and, at that moment, a deafening sound like thunder rolled across the airfield. A column of flame and earth, as high as the roofs, rose beside the hangar. Hardly had ten seconds passed before a new explosion followed. Quick, to the aircraft!

'Take cover!' somebody shouted. 'Bombardment!'

'What bombardment? From where?' Gritsayenko asked.

'From Ropsha, probably, I imagine. From there to the forward positions is 6 kilometres. You must go quickly along the slit trenches. I must go to the dug-out.'

But I hadn't succeeded in running as far as the trench when a piercing whistle above my head made me throw myself to the ground. The shell exploded in the bushes beyond dispersal. I stood up. My hands and clothing were covered in sticky clay. Finally I made the dug-out. From the doorway, I could still hear the Adjutant's voice. He was acknowledging an order from the Regimental Commander:

'In twenty minutes, all aircrew personnel to leave the aerodrome. Land on the emergency airstrip. Take off independently, when you are ready.'

'What does this mean, Andreyich?' I said to Yefimov, who was standing next to me. 'If we leave, we shall abandon Nizino . . . .'

Two days before, Yefimov had flown in to join us from Ezel. He glanced at me pensively, then said in a low voice: 'They 'phoned from headquarters. . . . You are to receive your party membership card. . . . A representative is waiting in the "pillbox". Let's go quickly.'

Knowing that I could no longer return to the dug-out, I carried my accordion, put on my raglan coat and Yefimov and I left the dug-out. We had started to call the small shelter dug into the river bank the 'pillbox'. It was only a stone's throw away – in all, some 50 metres; but to cover this distance was not easy. Another explosion shook the earth. The shell exploded to our right, causing no damage. We dropped to the ground, got up and then above our heads there sounded the whistle of a shell. Again we had to bow down to this flying idol. Soaking wet, daubed with clay, we at last reached the 'pill-box'. The Regimental Commissar, Kozhemyako, met us at the door.

'Have you got a match? We've also suffered a little. The oil-lamp has gone out.'

Yefimov found some matches. Soon a dim flickering flame in the oil-lamp illuminated the cement walls. Glass which had fallen from the broken window crunched under our feet. The door had been torn from its upper hinge and hung askew from the lower one.

'The last shell did that,' said the Commissar, noticing that we were looking at the door. Bending down beside the table, he picked up documents which had been swept on to the floor by the blast. We helped him.

'So, as you see, sometimes this happens,' said Kozhemyako, wiping the table with a scrap of newspaper and blowing the dust from the papers. Then he became serious. We lapsed into silence. My party membership card was in the Commissar's hands. Giving it to me, somewhat ceremoniously, Kozhemyako said:

'Remember, Comrade Kaberov, how irreconcilable Lenin was to enemies of the revolution. The honour of fighting the enemies of our homeland falls to you under the banner of his party. Be worthy of this high honour!'

Having handed me the ticket, he warmly congratulated me as a comrade and addressed me as we parted:

'Fight, you understand, as Bolsheviks fight!'

Our aircraft left Nizino aerodrome under fire. I gave it full revs. The fighter moved straight from dispersal and crossed the airfield for take-off. Ahead, piles of upturned earth were visible. I tried to avoid a crater but it was too late. I pulled the stick towards me. The aircraft rose up and I, holding it in the air with difficulty, skipped across the crater. The powerful motor pulled the machine from the ground. But ahead was another obstacle – the aircraft of another squadron. I pressed the button to lift the undercarriage and my fighter, with wheels retracted, safely passed over their dispersal.

To the left was Ropsha – occupied by the enemy. I directed my machine towards the forest and, gaining speed, turned about. Three anti-aircraft shells burst in the air, just in front of my fighter's nose. I turned away towards the gulf. The city on the Neva was cloaked in dense smoke. It was almost invisible. 'Goodbye, Nizino! Forgive us, Leningrad! We, your defenders, are only leaving our military positions for a time. And we shall defend you, our heroic city, to the last breath!'

Our new aerodrome lay in the forest. It was large and as level as a table. A separate shelter, protecting each aircraft from bombs or artillery bombardment, had been built there. Kostilyev and I examined the timber walls, which had been set deeply in the earth, and the three layers of beams. The structure, which had been covered with earth above and at the sides, was turfed over – a real fortress. I had no idea that it had been built by women. But there they were, modest Leningrad workers, standing, smiling shyly and listening to our words of praise. Among them were many quite young girls.

Yegor climbed on to the roof of the shelter, admired the spruce trees planted there and jumped up and down to test the strength of the roof.

'Did you really build this yourselves?'

'Well, who else did it?' A young woman, dressed in a padded jacket, lifted her hands, soiled from work.

'What are these? Aren't they the same as men's?' There was resounding laughter from the girls.

I remembered that my things were in the aircraft, so I took out from the fuselage my case, wrapped in its cover, and my accordion with its three rows of keys. Everyone called it a bayan.[6] Well, it did look like a bayan. True, at that moment it did look unsightly for, during the bombardment, it had become dirty in the clay.

'Listen everyone, a bayanist!' A woman turned to me. 'At such a moment, you should play, shouldn't you?'

She quickly cleaned the dirt from the accordion, wiping it carefully with the sleeve of her padded jacket. 'Well, play something cheerful, comrade.'

She put her shovel aside, shook her shoulders like a gypsy, stamped her feet and waited in a motionless pose. The bass notes of the accordion and the voices resounded as smiles lit up the faces of the Leningrad girls.

'Oh, to the devil with grief!'

'Our hawks have flown in. Let's dance, girls!' The young woman moved in a circle and lumps of earth flew to all sides from her stamping boots. From near and far, people were attracted to our shelter. One girl enticed Kostilyev into the circle and they whirled in a dance. Yegor, tall and laughing, performed such tricks that, watching him, you could forget all your troubles. The dance and the music were cut short by a command:

'Aircrews to the CO!'

We went to a nearby shelter where technicians were wheeling in Kostilyev's aircraft. The Deputy Regimental Commander, Capt Koreshkov, informed us with regret that, when taking off from Nizino aerodrome, Senior Lieutenant Kirov ran into a bomb crater, crashed the aircraft and received serious injuries himself. 2/Lt Semyonov also suffered injuries. He had to ferry a UT 1 to the Karelian Isthmus. The blast from a German shell turned the aircraft over as it was taking off. He flew across a hangar and fell. Boris Semyonov, when extracted from the crash, was taken to hospital in a serious condition.

We dispersed, depressed by what had happened. Leningrad was in trouble and there were so few of us left to defend it from the air.

Two days later, news came that Boris Ivanovich Semyonov had died without recovering consciousness. War had deprived us of yet another remarkable pilot, a very brave man of great spirit.

Until The Letter Was Opened

The regimental headquarters' staff and the aircraft technicians arrived at the new aerodrome late at night. However, no break in military activity occurred.

Beneath us was the Finnish Gulf. At that early hour, not a single ship ploughed its waters. Leaden waves, driven by a north wind, broke on the shore, leaving a lace-like foam upon it. This white strip stretched along the whole of the southern shore.

I was surveying the troubled Leningrad sky attentively. From time to time, my glance involuntarily stretched to the Peterhoff side; to Nizino, which we had abandoned; and Ropsha, left ruined and burnt by the Fascists. On the northern side of it, a large fire blazed. One would have thought that there was nothing to burn, but just the same, something was burning. Fascist forces in the region of Ropsha had gone on the offensive and broken through to the Gulf. . . .

Five of us were in the air: Myasnikov, Khaldeyev, Shirobokov, Kostilyev and I. 1/Lt Myasnikov was leading the group. In his Yak, like Chapay on his valiant steed, he flew ahead. He made for Pulkovo and Pushkin. Decisive battles for Leningrad were raging and we had to protect the land forces from aerial attack by the enemy there. To the east of Pushkin, two centres of conflagration were growing. Something was also burning in Krasnoye Selo. A battle was raging near the Pulkovo Heights. From the cockpit of my plane I could easily see explosions caused by artillery shells. They were quite near to Leningrad.

We had gone out to meet them, but where were the Fascist aircraft? They usually hung about here from morn till night. The fact that this time they weren't there put us on our guard. I carefully searched the sky. But suddenly I remembered my wife's letter and my hand plunged into the breast pocket of my shirt. There it was, this long-awaited letter. Gritsayenko had brought it that night from Nizino and given it to me as I sat in my cockpit. On the envelope – the Vologda postmark. The address was written in Valya's handwriting. I had immediately transferred it to a secret pocket in order not to lose it. I was calmer in my mind because it had come from Vologda. That meant that my wife had managed to leave Novgorod and travel to my parents' home. Somehow they were now there.

I surveyed the railway line leading to Gatchina. I wanted to see Duderhoff and that upland from which in 1936 I had flown in a glider at the flying school. They hadn't admitted me there. 'Disproportion. Oh, yes!' The voice of the strict doctor echoed in my memory. How then he laughingly pointed at the ceiling, 'Aircraft there are all different. . . . But your body is out of proportion.'

Myasnikov's aircraft made a sharp turn to one side. Kostilyev and I followed him. A burst of fire cut across our formation. Four Messerschmitts attacked us ineffectively and in a steep climb flew away into the blue sky. I followed them with my eyes and for the first time I noticed how evil the Fascist aircraft seemed. Yellow tips to their wings and on them black crosses against a white background. There was something vile, serpent-like about them. A moment's inattention and they were ready to bite.

Another four enemy fighters appeared out of the sun. I immediately noticed them: we now had light-filtering sunglasses and the sun was no hindrance to us. I informed Myasnikov about the second group of Messerschmitts and he made for them straight away. Five of us and eight Fascist fighters circled in a whirlwind of aerial battle. Beneath us flew a group of dive-bombers escorted by our Chayka fighters. A pair of Messerschmitts tried to attack them.

'Igor!' Yegor managed to shout. I understood what he had in mind and made for the Messerschmitts. Meanwhile, the Chaykas were repulsing them. The leading Me 109 was falling in a spiral, trailing smoke. A second, seeing how things were going, tried to gain height but I was in time to catch him. Choosing a suitable moment, I fired a burst. The Fascist turned over and for some time flew upside down. Then he adopted a normal position and, suddenly turning the aircraft, fell into a spin. I followed him without firing. What would he do next? Possibly he was feigning. Yegor had told me that sometimes Germans resort to such tricks. And in fact, at an altitude of 500 metres, my opponent came out of his spin and, accelerating, flew close to the ground.

'Oh no, you won't escape, now that I have the upper hand!' I accelerated to full speed and went after the Messerschmitt. The Fascist put his plane into a sharp turn. I did the same. He climbed steeply. I only had to do likewise. I pressed the trigger and the Messerschmitt reeled from side to side for the last time and dropped its nose. Describing a curve, it struck the ground just below the Pulkovo ridge. A bright flame and dense black smoke rose into the sky. Oh, how I would like to show that to the officious doctor, who didn't want to pass me as fit for service in the air force! No doubt he wouldn't believe his eyes. No, you must have been in some way mistaken, doctor. Your 'disproportion', despite all that, is flying a military aircraft and defending Leningrad from the air. Oh, yes!

I swept at full speed over the battlefield below the Pulkovo Heights. The outline of the partially destroyed observatory was visible through the smoke. Was it occupied by the enemy? I felt that they would open fire on me from the hill. Just in case, I bent over the gunsight. Would I succeed in passing over unharmed? But I needn't have worried. In the blue smoke above the ruins of the main building, a red flag was visible. It fluttered in the wind like a flame from the crater of a volcano.

'Our Pulkovo Heights! Ours!' I shouted at the top of my voice. 'They shall not pass!' I yelled with all the strength of my lungs and, pulling the stick towards me, made for the sky where my friends were engaged in their unequal battle.

Ten minutes later and this battle had finished. Once they had reached a high altitude, the six Me 109s got into formation and turned towards Gatchina. For some time, we still gave cover to the area where our troops were fighting and only then, when we received special orders over the radio, did we return home.

After landing, I reported to Myasnikov about the flight and returned to my aircraft.

'Well, how are things in Vologda? What does your wife say?' Gritsayenko asked.

'I shall read the letter presently, Sasha.'

The technician finished his inspection of the aircraft, instructed Alferov to refuel the fighter and, wiping his hands with a rag, walked towards me. I was sitting on the edge of the wing, reading the letter, line by line. This was the accepted way of doing things. A letter from relatives brought pleasure to everyone. It was a sin not to share the news.

Dear Igor! (wrote my wife.) We have managed to get to your parents' home. We travelled from Tikhvin to Vologda in a goods van. It's quiet here and there's no war. It's strange. I didn't know that you have to get used to silence. Half of Novgorod has been destroyed and was burning like a bonfire when we left at night. The bridge over the Volkhov was still there but mined ready for destruction. As I ran with Ninochka in my arms, I could not believe my eyes. What have these barbarians done to our town? Only walls remained of the fourth school where I studied. My first school (we also ran past it) was also destroyed. Many houses had been burnt down. You couldn't walk through Leningrad Street. Rubble from the houses blocked the street. There were victims of war, people with injuries . . . I can't tell you everything.

Some kind driver took us to the van. He drove to Chudovo. The road was dry and by morning we had arrived. From Chudovo many people set off by barge to somewhere on the Volga. Mother, Ninochka and I went on foot via Budogosh to Tikhvin. Masha Ivanova and Pelageya Nikolayevna were with us. The week we spent in Chudovo was like hell: bombing day and night. Chudovo no longer exists. So many dead and injured! And little children among them. A bomb exploded near the house where we stopped. The window frames and glass were blown out. Ninochka was hit on the cheek by flying glass. The wound is not serious and her little cheek is getting better. Father remained in Chudovo to evacuate a signals unit. Refugees moved along the road to Budogosh. Several times, Fascist fighter aircraft attacked us. Many of those with whom we travelled were killed. How we survived I don't know. We saw an air battle. Two of our 'hawks', blunt-nosed Ilyushin 16s which you fly, fought with four of the enemy. When a Fascist was shot down, everyone was pleased with our brave pilots. I watched and imagined it was you who had killed the Fascist; that you had seen our suffering and come to bring him down. Now I want to believe this, though I well know that you are far away near Leningrad.

I registered at the army recruiting office. Here in Vologda, an aeroclub is being formed. I am getting work as a flying instructor. Igor, don't worry about us. Everything is fine with us again. Greetings to you from your parents and all of us. Give our greetings to your comrades in arms: to Volodya Dikov, the mechanic, to Mikhail Ivanovich Bagryantsev, to Misha Fyodorov and Hussein.

Kisses, your Valya.

Gritsayenko stood listening to the letter holding his service cap in his hand. I read as far as the last lines and he still stood for some time before me in silence. He found it difficult to say anything; then at last, 'Yes,' he said, 'Greetings to Bagryantsev, Fyodorov, Hussein. . . .' There was more silence. Once more, this time to myself, I read through the letter.

'But you know,' said Gritsayenko a little later, 'it's good that they live in other people's thoughts.'

I understood that he was talking about Bagryantsev, Fyodorov and Hussein.

'And let Valya believe it. The letter's affectionately written.' His face brightened. 'Somehow heartfelt. . . . Thank you, Commander.' He replaced his service cap, then stroked the fuselage of the aircraft. 'Our "hawk" pursuit plane is not blunt-nosed. You must write to her about that. Give her our greetings. She is good to you. She doesn't complain at difficulties and all's well with her.'

Sasha, out of habit, again busied himself about the aircraft, thinking over something to himself. On the eve of war, 21 June, with the permission of the Commanding Officer, he had taken his family to Leningrad. The next morning, still not knowing the war had begun, he saw off his wife, Anna Petrovna, and the children to his parents' home town of Novaya Karlovka in the Ukraine. There were four little ones: Vera – six years old, Tolik – four, Kolya – two, and Gena – only ten months. 'Have a good holiday,' thought Sasha as he waved goodbye from the platform when the train departed. 'They'll have plenty of milk and fruit, and they'll sunbathe, and there'll be room to run about as far as the eye can see on the steppe, and nearby is the River Konka.'

Sasha found out on his return that the war had begun. By that time, the squadrons were already flying on military operations. Probably, now he was thinking that the Fascists were somewhere near Zaporozhe. Could the front have moved towards Novaya Karlovka? Were enemy aircraft flying over them? It was a long time since he had received letters from them. How were they getting on there? What would Anna Petrovna do? Where would she go with such a brood? And there was no one to look after the old people. Thoughts, thoughts . . . .

He Could No Longer Survive Without The Sky

We gradually made ourselves at home in the new place. For the time being, Gritsayenko, Alferov and I organized ourselves in an aircraft shelter. Alferov dragged from somewhere a whole pile of hay and spread aircraft covers on it. It made a luxurious bed. For the first two nights, it was not very cold as we slept but the next day it was nearly freezing. Freezing, because my aircraft was not in the aircraft shelter. We wrapped ourselves from head to toe in the covers but the autumn wind whistled and seemed to say to me: 'You won't give your machine to others. You won't . . . you won't.' But how can that be? I asked myself. How can that be if someone has not the means to fly? We go on patrol and he remains on the ground. For a day he doesn't fly, then for two. What does he do if his machine is not repaired? His friends are fighting for Leningrad and he, this pilot, walks to and fro as if he is an outcast, as if he's of no use to anyone. He bustles about everywhere with nothing to do. Rolling up his sleeves, he tries to help the technicians in order to make his machine serviceable sooner. But will they permit him? They won't be sleeping all night, but they will preserve the pilot's strength: 'Take a rest, Lieutenant, you have to go into battle.'

Poking my head out from under the cover, I looked into the darkness of the shelter and I was distressed. The shelter was actually empty. For two nights, with the aircraft as my neighbour, I had become used to making out in the darkness its strong wings, its forward-thrusting sharp nose and the blades of its propeller, like the ears of a giant animal. It always seemed to me that the fighter was listening attentively, in the night time silence of the front-line aerodrome, like a sensitive young horse.

But my war horse was not there. No, and my No. 13 fighter would never be there. And what was even more difficult and bitter was the fact that our wonderful pilot, Vladimir Shirobokov, who had not returned that day from a military sortie, was not alive. And how he had asked me to let him, just once, fly in my machine! 'Just once, Igor. . . . My comrades have saved my life when flying. How can I now sit on the ground doing nothing when it's so hard for them?' he emphasized, persuading me to take a rest and publish another camp news-sheet. How I cursed myself for agreeing. It would have been better if I . . . .

And how had this come about? I was already sitting in the cockpit preparing to take off when he came up to me. He came up, as always smartly turned out, even in the worn raglan which had seen much service, placed his hands on the side of the cockpit and looked at me with such hope.

'Do you understand? I have just been to the CO. He said, "Ask Kaberov. If he agrees, I shan't object." So, Igor, I shall have to share with you. Before long, they will repair my undercarriage.'

How quiet, how shy was Volodya Shirobokov in a circle of friends on the ground, yet how audaciously he fought in aerial battles. I lay and thought, thought as the wind whistled. I never imagined that somewhere on the other shore of the gulf, in the Strelna region, the remains of an aircraft would lie and beneath it, beneath it . . . .

'Aren't you sleeping, Commander?' Alferov turned towards me. 'Oh, Volodya, Volodya. . . .'

'Yes, Boris, Shirobokov was a fine man, brave, honest, good. An excellent pilot, a wonderful comrade. . . .'

'That's true, quite true.' Alferov sighed deeply. 'But just the same, you must sleep. There's work again in the morning. We stay on the ground, but you're flying.'

'Flying in what?'

'In an aircraft, of course. They'll give you someone's.'

'But whose? There aren't any to spare.'

'Well, why not? Shirobokov's machine will probably be ours now. Tomorrow they'll repair it.'

Alferov fell silent and I left him to his thoughts. He was a peculiar man. Boris was sure that in aviation there was a deep-rooted and crying injustice. In his opinion, technicians at the front live 'in the bosom of Christ', but pilots carry an unjustifiably heavy responsibility.

'Even when a pilot flies in after battle, I am ashamed to look him in the eye,' admitted Alferov at times.

'Yes, you're a good chap, Boris, good, brave,' I thought to myself. 'But you aren't right in your opinions. Is military action as a pilot, its victory in aerial conflict even thinkable without your participation . . . ?'

Then once again I brought to mind the details of the fight in which Shirobokov was killed. Already Kostilyev had told us several times about this fight. It seemed to me now as if I could see with my own eyes how everything had happened. Messerschmitts dived out of the sun. Our pilots turned but failed to counter attack. Kostilyev was the leader of the group and the Fascists aimed the first attack at him. In order to save the Flight Commander, Shirobokov threw his aircraft in the space between the enemy and Kostilyev's fighter but the burst of fire intended for Kostilyev fell on Shirobokov's machine. . . .

I was lying covered by canvas, looking into the darkness of the night and, only at that moment it seemed, I really began to understand what kind of a man Shirobokov was, what noble heart beat in his breast. Volodya's feat of gallantry seemed to me in some ways like that of the fearless infantryman who, in the battle for Novgorod, when helping his comrades who had come under Fascist machine-gun fire, threw himself on the weapon and, at the price of his own life, saved the situation. A week before, when we were in Nizino, a political officer from Kronstadt had arrived at the squadron. It was he who told us about the glorious deed performed by the heroic infantryman. In the morning, I looked through all the newspapers we had, but mention of the Soviet soldier who had thrown himself at the enemy machine-gun was nowhere to be found. However, many years later, I found out the details of his action and the name of the hero. On 21 August 1941, in Novgorod, when storming the Kirillov monastery, which the Fascists had turned into their strong point, a detachment led by a political officer, Aleksandr Pankratov, came under the deadly fire of a machine-gun. Breaking away from the others and moving forward, Pankratov threw a grenade and wounded the enemy gunner. The shooting stopped but not for long. When a fresh burst of fire came, Pankratov made a last dash and threw himself on the machine-gun. The company took the fight inside the monastery walls. And moreover, I found out that Aleksandr Pankratov was a fellow townsman of mine. It was the very same Sasha Pankratov who had studied with me at school and worked at the Vologda steam locomotive and rolling stock repair factory. Now in Novgorod, on the bank of the River Maly Volkhovets, an obelisk stands. A golden inscription shines on it:

> Instant death
> Became eternal glory.
> PANKRATOV
> Aleksandr Konstantinovich
> covered the enemy machine-gun with his body.
> 24 August 1941 in the battle for Novgorod.

And every time when I stop in front of this obelisk, I remember not only Sasha but Volodya also. In life they did not know one another, but in their feats of heroism they were brothers.

CHAPTER SIX

Defending Kronstadt And The Baltic Fleet

A Difficult Hour For The Battleship Marat

Shirobokov's machine had been repaired and handed over to us. The technicians gathered beside the aircraft. It was as if everyone was waiting for something to happen. It seemed as if, presently, Volodya would come there; as if he would arrive, smiling shyly and take his seat in the cockpit. But the CO walked up, examined the aircraft, touched the patches covering the bullet holes, tapped them to test their strength, patted the fuselage with the palm of his hand and turned to me.

'Shirobokov was a good man. . . . Look after his machine, Comrade Kaberov. . . .'

I, having taken charge of the aircraft, decided to wait for the next sortie in the cockpit and curled up for a while. But pilot's dreams don't last for long. Soon, above dispersal, two green rockets went up.

'Take off!' shouted startled technicians, who had hardly managed to refuel the aircraft.

'Help our matelots! Aerial attack on the *Marat*!' they shouted at dispersal.

Raising clouds of dust, the six of us took off: two Yak 1s and four LaGG 3s, the pride of our squadron. Senior Lt Myasnikov led the group in his Yak. His second-in-command was a new pilot whom I knew slightly. We used to meet at gunnery competitions. Now he was in our squadron, and he was no helpless novice. On Lvov's tunic the Order of the Red Banner flashed, which he had received for bravery and skill in battle during the time of the Soviet–Finnish conflict of 1939–40.

The engines of the fighters roared threateningly as they took off. Yegor Kostilyev and I went last. Enveloped in bluish smoke, the battleship *Marat* was lying in the sea canal opposite Strelna and firing its gigantic guns at the advancing Fascist forces, which had already taken Nizino, Peterhoff, and were making for Leningrad. Strelna was burning, Uritsk was burning. The battleship's anti-aircraft guns were firing. The sky was peppered with the black shell bursts. I was impatient to strike the enemy dive-bombers as quickly as possible. But just at that moment, the left leg of the undercarriage had to break free from its lock and hang treacherously under the wing of my aircraft. There and then, over the radio came a command from the authorities: 'The pilot whose undercarriage leg has dropped – land immediately!'

Somehow, in response to the command, I automatically broke away from the formation, made a circuit of the aerodrome, reported what had happened and tried to retract the undercarriage. But it repeatedly fell down. What should I do? My five comrades flew on but many Fascist aircraft were getting close to the *Marat* and the anti-aircraft guns on the battleship increased their fire.

Damned undercarriage! Land when my comrades were about to clash with such a gang? No, that was impossible. Once more I pressed the red button to raise the undercarriage, holding it and firmly pushing it with my thumb. I reported that I had raised the leg and that everything was in order, then banked steeply and flew off at full speed towards the battleship. But the button was making my thumb numb. I hadn't the strength to hold it. What should I do? I had to resign myself to the fact that the leg was again hanging below the wing. Over the radio, orders to return to the aerodrome were still being broadcast, but I was already turning a deaf ear to them. Our fighters had forced their way into the middle of an attacking formation of Junkers and Messerschmitts. I accelerated and raced to the help of my friends. They were already fighting an aerial battle with an enemy who outnumbered them by ten to one.

I approached the ship alone, attacked by no one; then made for the nearest Junkers at speed. This 'lapotnik'[7] (this is what we called the Fascist Ju 87 because of its fixed undercarriage) had already started to dive. I followed him. My machine swung sideways, caused by the undercarriage leg which had fallen. It was awkward to take aim, but now there was nothing I could do to correct it. I chased the Junkers and aimed, allowing for the sideways drift. The burst reached the target! It was as if the dive-bomber were convulsed. The heavy bomb jettisoned and fell beyond the target, and the dive-bomber itself, enveloped in flames, quickly lost height.

'I've got one!' I shouted, switching on the intercom.

'I've got another!' responded Yegor Kostilyev.

Trailing a ribbon of black smoke behind it, yet another Junkers fell heavily. Meanwhile, the aircraft I had set on fire was still flying above the water – trying to reach the shore. It did reach it but crashed there. A tall column of flame and dense oily smoke rose into the sky. I flew over the fallen Fascist aircraft: 'That's for Shirobokov, you reptile.'

A battle, a very heavy battle, was going on, but just for a moment I noticed that one of the LaGGs was missing. Could it be that one of us had been hit? Who? There were five of us, but the Fascists seemed to have thousands. And over the radio I heard: 'Retract your undercarriage. Who has a wheel down? Retract it!'

But I wasn't able to, even though it attracted the attention both of my comrades and the enemy pilots. My comrades understood how difficult it was to do battle, but our opponents saw in me an easy prey. I no longer kept an eye on the battleship or the dive-bombers. Messerschmitts flashed before my eyes. How many were there? My head swam. Again they attacked me. The enemy fighters gave no rest to the aircraft with its wheel down. But a powerful engine, the good manoeuvrability of my machine, and also the protection my comrades gave me made all the Fascist attacks futile.

A Messerschmitt was behind me. I threw the aircraft into a deep side slip and switched off the engine. My Lagg seemed suddenly to stop. Almost colliding with it, the Messerschmitt passed by; moreover, it was on fire. Who did that? Who helped me at such a difficult moment? LaGG No. 63 sped past after the Fascist. It was Yefimov's. Thanks, Matvey, thank you, my friend! The Fascist pilots, having lost four Ju 87s and one fighter in the battle, flew away to their aerodrome. The *Marat*, though, was still firing its guns and it was, as before, pouring an avalanche of fire on the enemy.

Five of us regrouped. Who was missing? Then I saw it was Volodya Khaldeyev. Could he have been hit? Yet clearly none of us had fallen. Usually an aircraft damaged in aerial combat, whether it is burning or not, is distinctly noticeable. We crossed the Gulf and flew towards the aerodrome. I looked back. The dark silhouette of the *Marat* could easily be seen. What a hero was the master of this ship of the line to have withstood such an attack by the Junkers! Maybe not all the enemy bombs missed. In that case, there could have been casualties on the *Marat*.

After landing, we gathered together beside the CO's machine. We searched the sky for a long time, expecting the possible appearance of our comrade.

'Did no one really notice where Khaldeyev went?' asked Myasnikov, anxiously looking out to sea and shading his eyes.

'I'm here, Comrade Commander, here!' How astonished we were when we turned and saw the smiling Khaldeyev.

'You're alive!' The Commanding Officer embraced the pilot. 'Well, now we can put our minds at rest. How were things with you? Where have you been? What happened?'

It turned out that, in the first minutes of the battle, an enemy fighter damaged the lubrication system of Khaldeyev's aircraft. He successfully withdrew from the fight and made a landing on the headquarters aerodrome. From there, he returned home in a U 2 aircraft.

But now I would like to tell briefly the story of how fate brought a certain interesting person and me together after the war. Viktor Ivanovich Novikov, Captain, First Class, was living in retirement in Novgorod not far from me. He was already in his sixties. It was widely known that Viktor Ivanovich's health was not one hundred per cent, but he wasn't downcast and he continued to work at one of the businesses in the town. We knew him as an active person in public life. I was not only busy writing my book but also chairman of the sports flying club DOSAAF,[8] flying myself and engaged in public activities. Nevertheless, Viktor Ivanovich and I sometimes found an hour or two in order to meet as neighbours, sit down and have a chat. Anyhow, one evening he called on us. We dined, talked about this and that and reminisced about the war. I started to describe how we defended the battleship *Marat* from the air.

'So that was your task!' Viktor Ivanovich became animated. 'Well, of course! I remember that battle very well. I even remember the date: 16 September 1941. You see, I was serving on the *Marat* as the ship's party organizer.'

At that, I took out my front-line diary and, finding the right page, gave it to Viktor Ivanovich. Putting on his glasses, he read: '16 September 1941. Fierce aerial battle over the battleship *Marat*. Six of our fighters against forty Ju 87s and twenty Me 109s.' Novikov removed his glasses and looked at me with astonishment. 'So that was us, old chap. We've been friends for a long time and until now I didn't know that we were in the same battle!'

Viktor Ivanovich and I talked for a long time that evening; each living once more the events of those far-off times.

Bullet Hole In The Wing

Not having succeeded in breaking through to Leningrad quickly, the Fascists' large-scale aerial forces attacked the fleet's main base. For several days in a row, battles, unprecedented in their ferocity, took place above it. Groups of forty or fifty dive-bombers, protected by large numbers of fighters, made for Kronstadt one after another. Neither the anti-aircraft artillery nor the small number of our fighters were able to oppose such a force. But we gathered all that we had, and our MiGs, Yaks and LaGGs took to the air again and again. Umansky and I were in LaGGs, Myasnikov and 1/Lt Chepelkin, a pilot who had recently joined the squadron, in Yaks.

That day about forty Ju 87s in flights of three dived on the ships and targets on the base. Messerschmitts literally swarmed around the dive-bombers. They intercepted us at once while the anti-aircraft guns fired like mad. Shells burst, sometimes among the tightly woven trails of the aerial battle. Our attempts to impede the Junkers were in vain. Neither Myasnikov nor Chepelkin, neither Umansky nor I could tear ourselves from the tenacious claws of the Messerschmitts.

It was hot in the cockpit; no air to breathe. And there was also a double danger: enemy fighters and flak. But what could we do? Kronstadt was defending itself; it had to use its anti-aircraft guns. And high in the sky, in a regular square as if on parade, approximately sixty twin-engined Ju 88 bombers were flying. Black kites with swastikas on their wings – they eclipsed the sun. Almost five hundred bombs were released simultaneously from the planes in level flight on the town and ships. The aircraft flew a little higher than us and I saw how the bombs, at first horizontal then turning over, plunged earthwards. So I threw my machine aside. The whine of falling bombs muffled the roar of the engine. I froze inside. An explosion of frightful strength shook everything around. It was as if gigantic hands had grasped my fighter, thrown it upwards and turned it over. With difficulty, I kept my machine under control, but still I couldn't understand what had happened. Beneath me in the thick of the battle, a black cloud swirled. Fragments of an aircraft flew out of it to all sides. No doubt, one of the bombs had hit a fighter. But whose – ours or the enemy's?

The Messerschmitts, having recoiled from the explosion, flew away. The enemy dive-bombers also left. We looked for one another with some difficulty in the slowly cooling and clearing skies of Kronstadt. Three of us met: Umansky wasn't with us. Could it have been the explosion? I couldn't believe it. . . . We returned home in silence and landed. I leapt from the cockpit and ran to Myasnikov.

'Umansky?'

'Yes,' he uttered painfully, wiping sweat from his flushed face with his sleeve. Myasnikov slowly got out of his aircraft, picked up a splinter lying under the wing and drew the outline of Kotlin Island on the ground.

'Just here,' said Myasnikov, outlining with the splinter the eastern part of the island, 'he came down by parachute. He was below me. I think the ack-ack got him.'

'What parachute? What ack-ack? What are you saying, Aleksandr Fyodorovich? There was such an explosion. Only fragments were left.'

'Yes, fragments of a Messerschmitt,' said Chepelkin, removing his flying helmet. 'The bomb exploded in a Messerschmitt. I was chasing it, you understand, and at that moment. . . . And look,' he pointed at the torn wing tip of his aircraft, 'I was a little fortunate.'

'Well, where is the CO then?' I asked.

'He baled out. I saw him as well,' said Chepelkin. 'He jumped. I'm telling you the truth.'

That evening, the squadron heard that Capt Umansky, who had baled out, spent almost an hour in the water somewhere near Kronstadt and was then picked up by a rescue launch and sent off to hospital.

A day later, on 23 September, the Fascist air force again began fierce attacks on our main naval base. Thousands of bombs of different sizes fell on it. It seemed that no stone would remain on another. But at last the enemy aircraft flew away. Everything that could burn, burned, but Kronstadt survived. We could see this easily from the air. Perhaps, even if only by the end of the day, the town, and with it we too, would be granted respite. But it wasn't to be. The Junkers appeared again. True, this time there were only three. We were also three in number: Myasnikov, Babernov (he joined the squadron with Chepelkin) and myself.

My comrades chased two of the Junkers which were flying ahead. The third flew at a respectable distance from them, but like them, made course for the base. The crews of the Fascist aircraft, seeing our Yaks, clearly lost heart. The leading Junkers dived and, having dropped their bombs, made for Strelna.

I was interested in the third enemy aircraft. It had an unusual appearance. Like the Ju 88, it also had long engine nacelles but twin fins on its tail unit like an Me 110. However, looking at it more carefully, I realized it was a Ju 86. I could see from its behaviour that the crew were taking photographs. Our ack-ack opened fire on it and there was no way I could approach the bomber. Nevertheless, I chased it, got closer until I was only a short distance away and opened fire at almost point-blank range. However, at that moment my fighter received a jolt. It almost turned round. I heard a rumble and had the impression that somewhere far off there had been an explosion. I controlled the aircraft and saw a hole the size of a saucer had been torn in the root of the left wing. Ack-ack shell? Yes, by all appearances.

'Why are you devils shooting at your own aircraft?' I shouted as if my voice could reach the gunners.

And in fact the firing stopped. The Junkers I had hit went away. It had already turned towards Peterhoff and now side slipped, trying to extinguish the flames. I caught up with it and gave it another burst of fire. Dropping its nose and listing to the right, the Junkers flew towards the shore. It fell on the shore side of the Peterhoff Park not far from the fountains. A blazing fireball rose where it crashed. I circled above the shore. The ruins of Peterhoff passed under my wing. I saw the ruined building of the palace, the smashed railway station, the chimneys of burnt-out houses.

1/Lt Babernov was unlucky in this battle. He attacked a Junkers with his Flight Commander, but in doing so, he failed to reach shore and ditched in the Finnish Gulf. It is shallow by the shore near Lakhta and this saved the pilot. Myasnikov and I flew over him. The fin and propeller blade stuck out of the water. The cockpit light was visible. Babernov himself was standing in the water, waving his flying helmet at us and indicating his intention to make for the shore. We had hardly landed on our aerodrome when Gritsayenko immediately fixed his eye on the hole in the wing root of my aircraft.

'Someone has given you a treat . . . !'

'Sasha, it's a greeting to us from the Kronstadt anti-aircraft gunners.'

'They what? Have they gone mad there? Are they firing at their own aircraft?'

'They were a little off target and they touched me there,' I explained.

'It seems to me they were on target not off,' Gritsayenko remarked.

'They missed the Junkers.'

'I understand, but where's the Junkers then?'

'There, beside Peterhoff; it's burning on the shore.'

'So does that mean you shot it down?' Boris asked, and receiving an affirmative reply, shouted to everyone at dispersal: 'Hurrah! Another one! Well done!'

After about two hours, 1/Lt Babernov arrived at the aerodrome soaked to the skin.

A few days passed and again much changed in our squadron. Sergey Sukhov and Nikolay Sosyedin returned from hospital. But several days later,

Nikolay was killed during a military operation. In the region of Pushkin, his fighter was hit, caught fire and he jumped out of his plane. His comrades saw him fall and waited for him to open his parachute. But the figure of Sosyedin quickly became smaller in size. Finally, it started to merge with the ground beneath it and was lost from sight.

After some time, Khaldeyev and Kirov were sent on an official trip. They didn't return to the Baltic. Umansky, who was wounded in the head, was posted to the rear. Myasnikov became the squadron CO. Out of all the young pilots who started the war in our squadron, only Sergey Sukhov and I remained. But we were no longer considered young.

The squadron had two types of fighter: LaGG 3 and the Yak 1. Both aircraft had the same engine. The LaGG 3, a wooden machine, was heavier, but the Yak 1, a fighter of mixed construction, was lighter and more manoeuvrable. Myasnikov, Lvov, Babernov and Chepelkin preferred the Yak 1. Kostilyev, Yefimov, Sukhov and I were confirmed LaGG 3 flyers. At that time, we called ourselves, in jest, the Yak group and the LaGG group.

1/Lts Semyon Ivanovich Lvov, Vasiliy Ivanovich Babernov and Sergey Ivanovich Sukhov were sworn brothers. Lvov and Babernov each wore the Order of the Red Banner, Sukhov – the GTO[9] badge.

'It's to prevent a hole being drilled into the tunic,' joked Sergey.

Nobody Believes The Silence

There had been silence over the main base of the Baltic Fleet for three days. The weather was fine and not a single enemy aircraft was in the sky. It was as if there was no war. Since morning it had been the turn of Yefimov, Sukhov and me to be on duty. To begin with we sat in our cockpits; then the CO allowed us to leave them but ordered us not to move away from the fighters. The three of us gathered beside my aircraft. Being rather cold, we jumped up and down and exercised.

'What's this, are you frozen?' said the engineer, Sergeyev, coming towards us. 'Well, warm up, warm up.'

'If presently we were to fight, we would get warm at the same time,' replied Sukhov. 'Isn't that so?'

'That's right, Comrade Commander. If we are all on duty, why not fly?' asked Alferov, the fitter.

'We aren't flying because the Fascists aren't flying.'

'But why aren't they flying?'

The engineer placed a hand on the fitter's shoulder: 'Oh, Alferov, there's no need to go into details. I'll tell you this: in the last three days, the Fascists have been clearing away the kites we destroyed – that's one. They are burying their dead – that's two. They are doing repairs – that's three.'

We all smiled. We liked Sergeyev's optimistic mood. Alferov listened to the engineer, standing to attention. Then he went off to the hangar, where fitters always have much to do.

'We could have a week of calm,' Sergeyev pondered aloud. 'We could do with a little break or the technicians will be asleep on their feet. Well, all right,' he suddenly remembered, 'here I am chattering with you and I also have things to do.'

We sat down on aircraft covers, heaped in a pile. The conversation was about the time in the distant future when our army had driven the Fascists from Leningrad. 'The quicker the better,' said Sergey thoughtfully. 'I would like to bring down the last Fascist aircraft over Berlin. . . .'

Duty over, I ran to our clerk, Zhenya Duk. He had recently returned from hospital and was already on the next edition of the camp news-sheet.

'Zhenya, I've got an idea. Don't stop me. I'll start composing.'

Shortly before lunch, we hung up the latest number of the newspaper. In it was the poem which I had just written:

> We'll get even with our enemies
> Our reckoning with them is simple:
> Just let the bandits show themselves –
> And we'll send them to their graves.
> With the speed of eagles
> We'll take to the air –
> And over the city of Berlin
> Bring down their last aircraft.
> To strike and see how, enveloped
> In acrid smoke and flames,
> The thrice cursed Fascist falls
> In his own black lair . . .
> Although still we cannot set about this task
> However much we scan the skies,
> Yet the desire to do battle
> Makes our fingers itch!

Friend Or Foe

Far from Leningrad, in the rear of the enemy, the heroic Soviet garrison on the Hanko Peninsula was fighting right up to December 1941. But for our forces to hold out longer at Hanko was senseless and the staff at supreme headquarters took the decision to evacuate them to the beleaguered city of Leningrad. The evacuation would be conducted in several stages.

On 2 November 1941, the western part of the Finnish Gulf as far as Gotland was covered in an unbroken layer of fog. Taking advantage of this, a group of ships from the Red Bannered Baltic Fleet sailed from the Hanko Peninsular and, observing radio silence for secrecy, made for Kronstadt.

The Regimental Commander, Hero of the Soviet Union, Maj P.V. Kondratyev, showed us on the map the place where we were supposed to find the ships, and warned that radio communication in flight to the target was strictly forbidden. Our problem was to discover where the ships emerged from the fog and report in code over the air their number and location. On the basis of this information, an escort would be organized. So our fighters were airborne. There were three of us: Matvey Yefimov (Flight Commander), Yegor Kostilyev and me.

The weather was clear and calm as we passed Kronstadt. I watched the sky attentively. To the left of us on an approaching course was an aircraft. 'Evidently, one of us has been on reconnaissance and is now returning,' I thought, but just in case took the safety catch off the trigger. However, there was no cause for alarm. An SB bomber, having noticed us, rocked its wings and passed to one side. We replied to his greetings in like manner.

However, a professional interest compelled me to turn round. I followed and looked at the aircraft. What interested me was: why was his undercarriage lowered? After all, he was above the sea and was flying at a great height. The SB was already almost invisible but I had the feeling that we were mistaken. It was a pity that I couldn't utter a word to my leader. Radio contact was forbidden. The silhouette of the bomber finally dissolved in the blue sky, but I was still disturbed and thought: 'Alone and in such clear weather, without fighters. They could easily bring him down. No, there was something wrong here. Moreover, quite recently an order had been given to all units and formations equipped with SB bombers that, as a result of heavy losses of these aircraft due to enemy fighter action, they would be transferred to night operations. But he was flying by day . . .

Soon our flight approached the very edge of the fog, beneath which, somewhere, the ships were sailing. We had hardly managed to turn, when the first ship appeared out of the fog. Behind it, a second, a third. It turned out that the Commander's calculation was accurate. We descended to low-level flight and passed along the line of ships. The decks were full of people. The soldiers and sailors – the heroic defenders of Hanko – greeted us, shouted, waved their arms, threw their caps in the air. For them, we were good news, the first sign of their homeland from which they had been away so long.

After Yefimov had led the flight away from the convoy of ships and had informed headquarters of their position, I openly reported to him my doubts, which had been aroused by our meeting with the SB. 'What SB? Let's not hang about.' said Yefimov. He didn't want to listen to me and, maintaining top speed, hurried home.

But just the same, I attentively surveyed, now the smooth surface of the sea, now the sky above it. For a time, no one could be seen. But after a while, having lowered one wing, suddenly a twin-engined aircraft flying just above the water became visible.

'There he is!' I shouted to my friends over the radio and put my plane into a dive. Yes, it was the very same SB. Only now he was making for Vyborg. It seemed as if the pilot had noticed me. The bomber again signalled by rocking its wings. Oh no, my dear chap, we've already met; but let's have a really good look at one another. As I dived, I did not cease to be tormented by doubts. Could it be an enemy? How many times had we escorted just such aircraft! Our Russian lads had piloted them; but who was flying the plane which was before me? Why was this aircraft behaving so strangely? What was it doing here in broad daylight? Why was its undercarriage lowered? Maybe it was, nevertheless, one of our aircraft which was carrying out some kind of special operation. Maybe it was searching for Fascist submarines, in order to protect our ships travelling from Hanko to Kronstadt.

Suddenly, it was as if I had been scorched with a flame. I looked and could hardly believe my eyes. On the wings of the SB, the enemy's identification marks were clearly visible! I turned sharply and chased the bomber. It tried to move away from me. The cat knows whose meat she's been eating!

'No, don't go away, you vile creature. Your song is sung!'

But I didn't succeed in taking aim properly and, meanwhile, the bomber vanished in the white shroud of fog hanging over the area around the island of Somers. The upper edge of the fog was all of 100 metres above the water. As I entered it I thought: what if it begins at sea-level? Would I plunge into the Gulf?

But the shroud of fog turned out to be no thicker than 2 or 3 metres. I had hardly broken through it when the enemy air gunner gave me a burst of fire. Tracer bullets passed by and the SB was lost in the fog again. I followed him and the gunner poured a hail of bullets at me for a second time. The bomber again plunged into the fog, but I could see its wheels from below. They were like flies running across a white ceiling. I held them in my sights. A short burst decided the outcome of the duel. At this point, the fog was left behind. I could see clearly. The port engine of the SB was burning. The pilot threw his aircraft into a side slip, trying to put out the flames, but he hadn't the height. The last metres of the inglorious flight of the enemy reconnaissance aircraft remained. At that moment, Yefimov and Kostilyev flew over the burning aeroplane at great speed and set fire to its other engine. Enveloped in flames, the SB struck the stony sandbank beside Somers Island and broke into pieces, blazing on the stones near the shore.

At low altitude, we circled above the island. I saw clearly how three soldiers ran to the place where the aircraft crashed. One of them stopped and raised his arm. Completing the circuit, I noticed that he was threatening us with his fist. Probably, down there they thought that we had killed our own flyers. Never mind, later it would all be investigated.

Well, they did investigate, but not immediately. At first a telegram came from Somers Island in which it was said that an LaGG 3 had shot down an SB aircraft. We still hadn't returned before the authorities were demanding an explanation from the Commanding Officer of our regiment. After landing, we were in trouble because clearly we had shot down our own SB. Things took a serious turn. I was ordered to surrender my revolver. But the second telegram made matters clear. The SB, it turned out, was an enemy reconnaissance aircraft. When the aeroplane crashed on the rocks, the pilot and navigator were killed, but the air gunner was thrown from his turret into the water and lived.

I still didn't know about this telegram when the telephone rang in the dugout. Someone spoke so loudly that even I could hear him say: 'Give Kaberov back his weapon and apologize.' The Officer who received the instruction breathed a sigh of relief, rapped out 'Aye-aye' and hung up the receiver. In silence I took up my pistol from the table, saluted and left the dug-out.

All the same, how do we explain the appearance of the ill-fated SB over the Finnish Gulf? The enemy, for sure, knew nothing about the evacuation of the naval base from Hanko, but the lull in military activity around the peninsula must have disturbed him. In order to solve the mystery, the enemy decided to undertake a deep aerial reconnaissance over the waters of the Finnish Gulf. With this aim in mind, a damaged SB bomber was obtained and restored by the enemy. As to the undercarriage, evidently it remained faulty during the flight.

However, as the reader knows well, cunning cost the enemy dear.

Warm Yourself With A Song

The weather got worse. During the day it drizzled, towards evening it froze. A white shroud of fog covered the airfield. Sometimes it was so dense that nothing could be seen three paces away. It was the second day that we had not flown. On 6 November – the eve of the twenty-fourth anniversary of the October Revolution – they announced that the well-known singer, Klavdiya Shulzhenko, was coming and everyone hurried to the club for the concert. Duk and I had only just finished preparing the celebratory number of our news-sheet, 'For the Homeland'. Zhenya immediately hurried away to his friends. I had intended to go to the club with Chepelkin, but he seemed to have disappeared into thin air. I met engineer Sergeyev and asked whether he had seen Chepelkin.

'In an aircraft at dispersal,' Sergeyev whispered. When I ran to the aircraft shelter, Pyotr was sitting in the cockpit, a flying helmet on his head.

'What's this – night duty? And if not, why aren't you going to the club?'

'I'll go to the club later. Let's listen. There's a meeting to celebrate the occasion in Moscow.'

'But can our station receive Moscow?'

'Yes, when Leningrad relays it. I tuned in and found it. True, at times there's interference.'

Chepelkin twisted the left earpiece. I tried to listen with him, but it was uncomfortable. It was better to go across to my own aircraft. Gritsayenko and I got the spare accumulator going, switched on the radio and listened to Stalin's familiar voice. I listened to the report and was plunged in thought. A cruel battle was going on in which the fate of the Homeland would be decided. The enemy was at the gates of Moscow, and yet by tradition a solemn meeting, dedicated to the twenty-fourth anniversary of the October

Revolution, was taking place there. What did this bear witness to if not our strength! The Soviet government, the Central Committee of our party, firmly believed in the fact that the hated Fascist plunderers would be utterly defeated!

To use an aircraft radio on the ground was strictly forbidden. Therefore, as soon as the duty technician appeared (he had come to close the dispersal area and place it under guard) I hurriedly switched off the radio and leaped out of the cockpit. Chepelkin came up to me.

'Well, how was it?'

'I listened for a while. A pity that there was interference.'

'But did you hear about Goering? The bloodthirsty creature, the cannibal. "Kill, kill," he said. "I shall answer for everything." It appears that murderers are in power. Never mind, we'll show them what's what!'

Chepelkin looked at his watch. 'It's just time. Probably we're still not too late to get to the concert. Come on, hurry!'

'Go ahead, I'll catch you up!' shouted Gritsayenko to us from behind.

The path leading to the club wound between pine trees. You couldn't force your way through the crowd in the hall. Klavdiya Shulzhenko, accompanied by a jazz orchestra under the direction of Vladimir Koralli, was singing the lively song 'Retrousse'. It was cold in the club. The audience was dressed in winter clothes, but the artists appeared in lightweight garments, as if in a summer variety scene. Klavdiya Shulzhenko was wearing a light sleeveless dress. She needed a warm flying jacket!

She had hardly finished her song before thunderous applause broke out. One of the airmen climbed on to the stage and presented the singer with a branch of fir with cones. Everyone felt this was an appropriate gesture. Klavdiya Ivanovna appreciated his gift. She pronounced her words of gratitude with emotion and wished the soldiers glorious military victories over the Fascist plunderers.

The CO of the regiment, Maj Kondratyev, pushed past us on his way to the exit and asked me to follow him. 'When the concert ends, take my car,' he said in the foyer, 'and drive Klavdiya Ivanovna, her husband and son to Poklonnaya Gora. In the headquarters mess, give the artists refreshments. Is that understood? Well, off you go.'

'What about the rest?'

'The rest we'll try to feed here. We'll think of something. Go now!'

We arrived late at Poklonnaya Gora. I gave the cook the CO's instructions and he made an effort to please us. The artists had supper and warmed themselves with hot tea. At table, Klavdiya Ivanovna asked me how the war was going: was it not frightening to fight the Fascists in the air? She was interested to know where in the aircraft the machine-guns were mounted and what Hitler's forces looked like.

On the way back, she asked me about the pilot Kaberov.

'The CO said that he writes verse,' she said. 'So I'd like to know whether he has any lyrics. We could put the words to music and sing them on stage.'

It was just as well that it was dark in the car and my companion did not see my blushes. 'Klavdiya Ivanovna, I am Kaberov, but it would be a mistake to describe me as a poet. I write for the station news-sheet, that is all. You have been misinformed.'

However, when she bade farewell, once again she returned to her idea about verses. 'Comrade First Lieutenant, just the same, if you do compose a lyric, send it to me and I'll sing it.'

The next day, Chepelkin and I, at the instruction of Commissar Isakovich, conducted political meetings about Stalin's report. Pyotr chatted with the young aviation specialists, I with the technical staff. Then, while the airfield was shrouded in mist, we all took a bath using a birch switch. Our mood became even more healthy and happy. I wrote letters home, put my diary notes in order, explained to Sgt Haustov, our new party organizer, my notes for the news-sheet. Then I set off for the regimental headquarters. As I walked, I looked up and examined the green tops of the pines bathed in mist and I almost bumped into Capt Koreshkov.

'Good-day, Comrade Captain!'

'Hello, Kaberov! I was just hoping to see you.' He pulled a newspaper, giving the latest news, from under his raglan coat and offered it to me.

'Have you read it?'

'What's in here?'

'They've awarded you a decoration, Igor!' Koreshkov shouted at the top of his voice. 'The Order of the Red Banner, don't you know!' I raised my eyes to the Captain, looked at his pleasant, beaming face, which was spreading in a smile and I didn't know what to say.

'Congratulations!' he shook my hand. 'I congratulate you with all my heart. I have just come from Leningrad. Here,' he pointed at the paper, 'it's about you and Kostilyev and Sukhov and Yefimov. . . . You'll read it all here. . . .'

Koreshkov embraced me and slapped my back with his strong hand. 'You have a fine group of people in the squadron. Pilots, the CO, the party organizer. They're friendly and determined. A real front-line body of men. Well done! . . . And you know, it seems they've also given you the Order of Lenin.'

'But what are you saying, Captain! It can't be!'

'It's true, but for the time being keep it under your hat,' he warned. 'We must get details. However, the information comes from extremely reliable sources.'

Stunned by such news, I became completely lost for words.

Escape On Crutches

Yes, Koreshkov was right. I soon read in the newspaper, the Edict of the Supreme Soviet of the USSR concerning those airmen, myself included, who had been awarded decorations for outstanding service in battle. After some time, I received the two awards together. That was on 26 November 1941.

Recalling that day, I can see myself in the cockpit of my aircraft, ready for action. Winter had already set in. Snow whitened the roofs of the dug-out and the aircraft shelters, and lay in clumps on the spreading branches of the pine trees. It was cold in the cockpit. I moved the lamp and looked through the glass at everything around me. Sukhov's voice woke me from my meditation.

'Hey, guardsman!' Sergey knocked on the cockpit canopy. 'Get on parade!'

'But what's that? What's going on?'

'High ranking officers have arrived. No doubt they'll be giving us our orders.'

'I can't. It's not time yet. There's still twenty minutes.'

'Well, come on. It's freezing.'

The staff officers and all of us gathered close to the aircraft shelter in which Kostilyev's aircraft was standing. I saw a table covered in red material and beside it people unknown to me. The Regimental Commander, Kondratyev, the Commanding Officer of our squadron, Myasnikov, and Commissar Isakovich were also standing there. A technician told me that Rear Adm N.K. Smirnov, a member of the military Soviet from the Baltic Fleet, and representatives of the air force headquarters staff had arrived. A large group of our pilots and technicians would be handed war medals.

I observed the grand award ceremony with interest from the cockpit of my fighter. One after the other, my friends walked up to the table on which lay the boxes containing the war medals. I heard the emotional sounding words, 'I serve the Soviet Union!' and with everyone else, I applauded.

Then, unexpectedly, my surname was called out. Comrades beckoned to me: 'Come on, quickly!' Without removing my flying helmet, I climbed from the cockpit and ran to the table. The admiral himself undid my raglan coat, pierced a hole in my tunic with an awl and fastened to it the Order of Lenin and the Order of the Red Banner.

'I've heard you're from Vologda, like myself,' he said, shaking my hand.

'That's correct, Comrade Admiral.'

'I've had to hand out awards many times, but to do so like this – two at the same time and such medals! This I don't remember. Well done, fellow townsman!'

I replied with the regulation: 'I serve the Soviet Union,' and ran to my aircraft. My friends surrounded me and eagerly congratulated me. And I them. At this moment, Commissar Isakovich came up.

'Well then, show me the awards, and congratulations!' he said, grasping me in a powerful embrace.

Then something unexpected happened. In order not to fall, I had to take a step back. There was a snow-covered hole behind me and my foot slipped. I screamed with pain. Mikhail Zakharovich let me go but continued to shake my hand. I fell into the snow. I shook my leg but it still hurt. I tried to remove my boot but couldn't. Then Matvey Yefimov took his Finnish knife and cut it off. To my astonishment, I discovered that the leg was swollen from foot to knee. With the help of friends, somehow I managed to reach the dug-out.

That evening, I was transported to the divisional hospital and the next day I was transferred to the naval hospital in Leningrad. The hospital was overcrowded with wounded. The doctor examined my leg.

'Well then, it's clear to me . . . .'

Taking his time, he uttered the evil sounding word 'blockage' and made a dozen injections in the area of the injury. 'Now try to move about the ward without crutches.'

I was afraid to walk with the swollen leg but I tried and, to my great astonishment, felt no pain.

'Well, that's fine. When the swelling goes down, you can return to your unit,' said the surgeon.

Four days later, I persuaded the nurse to help me collect my clothing and rations for the journey and, taking my crutches just in case, stealthily left the hospital. I thought that everybody must be secretly laughing at me. Well, how about that! The man hurt his leg in such pleasant circumstances – accepting congratulations from his friends.

The tram stop was nearby but I had to wait about twenty minutes for the tram going to Poklonnaya Gora. At last it appeared. An elderly woman helped me to climb on. She offered me her seat. I assured her that I could stand but she insisted that I sit down.

'Are you a pilot? Have you been wounded?'

In reply, I muttered something inaudible, sensing that I was blushing.

'How brave you people are!' she continued. 'Recently, I watched a dogfight over the town. First, I saw how our "hawks" shot down a German; how he fell leaving a trail of smoke. Then one of ours started to fall. I covered my face with my hands. I couldn't watch. You know, we're prepared to work night and day, without leaving the factory, just in order to defeat the Fascists as quickly as possible.'

'We'll defeat them, never fear,' said the man standing near me. 'I thrashed these curs in the German and civil wars.' He raised his powerful fists. 'And, if necessary my son, I'll take up arms again.' Unexpectedly, he unbuttoned his old greatcoat and opened it. 'There you are, an old guard!'

Everyone standing nearby saw on the jacket of this man, now no longer young, the George Medal on a striped and faded ribbon, and the Medal of Honour.

'Thank you, sir!' I shook his hand.

Meanwhile, an old man, who had been sitting in silence, moved towards me. 'Tell me, young man,' he said, displaying interest, 'have you any medals?'

'He's only just begun his service,' the bemedalled man answered for me. 'He has yet everything to do. Is that not so, my son?'

I didn't know what to say. I must admit that I wanted to show these people my medals, but I feared that this might look like boastfulness.

'No, no, don't be shy,' said the old man, evidently understanding my reserve. 'You can only be proud of medals.'

I slightly opened my greatcoat. The old man's eyes opened wide. 'The Order of Lenin? The Order of the Red Banner? What's this for?'

'Well . . . show me, show me!' The old soldier turned to me and opened my greatcoat himself. 'Yes, so it is!'

He looked for a while and finally made me feel embarrassed by removing his cap from his already greying head. At this, I wished myself elsewhere. Fortunately, we had already reached Poklonnaya Gora. Hardly had the tram stopped before I clambered off and, overcome with pain in my leg, began walking on crutches. 'Foolish show-off!' I cursed myself. But somewhere within me there remained a warm feeling for my fellow travellers, simple working people who followed the successes and misfortunes of our army with all their hearts.

At combined headquarters, they informed me that our regiment had abandoned its former airfield and was now based in the Ladoga district, but that my aircraft remained in the old place. In the morning, I set off on my way and by midday somehow arrived on crutches at the airfield. No one was at dispersal. My aircraft stood alone under cover. But suddenly: 'Kirrill, hurrah! Our Commander's arrived.'

Alferov ran out from the dug-out and after him Yevseyev, the technician.

'What a surprise! How is it that you're here?' I was astonished.

'The engineer left me here as a supernumerary in order to see you off,' explained Yevseyev.

'And Gritsayenko?'

'Sasha's at the new airfield. Fly there and you'll start work with your technician straight away.'

'Yes, perhaps that makes good sense. Well then, come on in.'

We walked into the dug-out. Kirrill stretched his hands towards the red-hot little stove.

All night the tractor rolled the snow smooth. By morning, a take-off strip was ready. The lads brushed the snow from the aircraft and warmed up the engine. I clambered into the cockpit with some difficulty. My crutches lay in the fuselage wrapped in a cover.

'I don't know how you'll manage with only one leg,' said Alferov doubtfully.

'Never mind, somehow . . . .'

I couldn't press the pedal with my right leg. Bandaged in something soft, it lay above the pedal. In order that I could more easily use the good leg, Yevseyev fastened it with cord to the left pedal. Alferov looked at this contrivance and only shook his head.

'It would be interesting, Commander, to know what the medics would say about this.'

Finally, I raised a cloud of fine snow, taxied for take-off, waved to my friends from the cockpit and opened the throttle. Now I felt at home in the cockpit of the fighter as it moved forward. It was my secluded corner, my bright celestial chamber. Here it was warm, cosy, comfortable. I could relate to the aircraft as to a living creature. I would talk to it. We were friends. But before I flew away on course, I turned, dropped down and flew low over the heads and waving hands of Yevseyev and Alferov.

'See you soon, my friends!'

I gained height. How familiar everything was around me. Snow covered Kronstadt, and the Finnish Gulf, just gripped in a young frost. Through the smoke, the ominously quiet Peterhoff shore, occupied by the Fascists, could be seen. The painfully familiar contours of a Leningrad now blockaded by the enemy floated past beneath my wings.

CHAPTER SEVEN

At The Volkhov Front

A Third Front-Line Dug-Out

At the new airfield, I immediately found myself in the hands of the medics. I was ordered to rest in bed and keep the foot warm. I took long fur boots from behind the stove and pulled them on. The Squadron Commander, Capt Myasnikov, explained to me that our regiment was giving aerial cover to the ice roadway and showed me its position on the map. I also found out that only our squadron was based on this airfield. Low-flying attack aircraft were also based with us. Our task was to give them aerial cover. Commissar Isakovich brought me a bite to eat and the CO poured me something from stores into a mug.

'Well then, this will warm you up. . . .'

One after the other, the pilots came into the dug-out. Pyotr Chepelkin sat next to me. Yegorushka Kostilyev and Semyon Lvov lay on bunks.

'Our chaps have arrived,' said Myasnikov, looking out of the window. 'They've been flying over the road.'

Soon Yefimov and Sukhov appeared on the threshold. 'Look, Matvey, he's actually home!' Sukhov shouted from the door.

'Hi, hopalong! How are things? How's Peter's city?'

Everyone was interested in Leningrad. Unfortunately, I could not console them in any way about conditions in the town. Seeing the gloomy faces of his friends, Yefimov took our new bayan from under the table in its dust-covered case.

'One hundred days of war – one hundred camp news-sheets,' he said significantly.

The fact was that on the hundredth day of the war, 29 September 1941, the brigade newspaper *Victory* devoted all of its first page to the one hundredth number of our squadron news-sheet. Here then, an order was placed by the Brigade Commander to award the editor of the camp news-sheet a valuable gift. Following which, Hero of the Soviet Union Col Ivan Grigorevich Romanyenko, who had given this order, flew to our airfield.

'If you're an accordion player,' he said, chatting with me, 'here's a kopek for you; pop in to Leningrad and choose yourself an instrument that you like.'

Powerfully squeezing my hand in his enormous palm, he gave it a friendly shake.

'Play, make the squadron happy!'

That was how we came by our bayan, once I had exchanged my old instrument, which had seen better days. I gradually got used to it, and by the time of our transfer to the Ladoga district, had taught myself to play fairly well.

'Something of ours from Novgorod,' ordered Myasnikov. 'Even if it has to be "Katyusha".'

'Since when has "Katyusha" become a Novgorod song?'

The lads laughed. I played and watched my friends as they sang and listened to the voices and bass notes of the bayan. It must be said, it was a fine instrument! . . . At the sound of singing, Sergeyev looked in at the dug-out.

'Comrade Commander, all the aircraft are ready for take-off but the weather's bad.'

Myasnikov looked out of the window, then telephoned regimental headquarters. Moving from the phone, he explained to us that in ten minutes, according to headquarters, the snow storm would move away and the attack aircraft would set off on a military exercise in the area of Lyuban station. We would give them cover with our flight of six fighters.

'To your aircraft!'

The dug-out quickly emptied. (By the way, this was our third front-line dug-out.) I was left alone, but I didn't sit still. Though my leg was still very painful, I walked out in my fur-lined boots with the help of a stick to the river bank. The Volkhov! How wide it is there by Novaya Ladoga! Even when ice-bound, it does not lose its majesty. The powerful river ends its journey there and flows into Lake Ladoga. I returned to the dug-out and thought over a plan for the next number of the station news-sheet. I wanted to make it as striking and interesting as possible. While I was forbidden to fly, I would have sufficient time to do that.

Day followed day, each bringing with it some important event. The troops on the Southern Front had driven the Fascists from Rostov-on-Don. The forces on the Volkhov front had taken the town of Tikhvin. On 13 December, we were informed in a radio broadcast that our army outside Moscow had launched a mighty offensive.

It was good to see how happy Sergey Sukhov was. And why not! On 13 December, his native town, Kalinin, was liberated. Matvey Yefimov, when free from flying and other duties, literally never ceased to watch the map. He studiously moved the flags which marked the liberated towns and even the comparatively small populated places.

'Ah, we should have attacked Mozhaysk!' said Yefimov, thoughtfully looking at the map. 'Vyazma is not far from there. From Vyazma to our Yartsevo is only a stone's throw. And my native town of Beryozhok is nearby.'

'Why don't you write to headquarters,' advised Sukhov, jokingly. 'Say like this: We, people of Smolensk, beg . . . .'

Sergey had flown with Matvey since the start of the war. Great friends, they were inseparable on the ground and in the air. Sukhov valued this friendship; he valued Yefimov's experience of life highly. It was well known that Matvey had been a collective farm's young communist leader, then chairman of the village soviet.

'You should be a commissar, not a pilot,' Sergey would say at times. But he also knew of Matvey's enormous love for aviation. It was this love which had brought Yefimov to the Eysk aviation school after he had finished university.

Matvey marked the direction taken by our victorious army, and we all followed the movement of the red flags westward from the capital. For us it was a relief. How uplifting it was for the aircrews, patrolling the Ladoga ice highway, to know that our forces had driven the Germans from Voybokalo station and the town of Volkhov. Supplies were flowing again to the ice road along the railway between Tikhvin and Volkhov. The enemy had not succeeded and would not succeed to encircle Leningrad with a second blockade.

It was now unbearable for me to sit doing nothing. 'I'm well,' I said to our doctor. But the leg was still swollen and his order was short and to the point: 'Sit and don't hop about!'

I was reminded that sometimes in aerial combat a pilot had to use his parachute. To land on a bad leg wasn't easy; it could cause harm to a healthy person, but in winter moreover, when far from home it could mean death. Finally, what I did to prove that I had recovered produced some impression. I climbed a pine tree and jumped down from a fairly good height. The medics took note of this and gave in. So I began flying with Pyotr Chepelkin. We flew over the ice road. There were many lorries on it. The weather was bad and there were no Fascists about.

We celebrated the New Year quietly. Since dawn we had been thoroughly prepared for action. While on duty, we sat in our cockpits. A signal rocket bursting interrupted our conversation.

'Scramble!' shouted the technicians.

We taxied, took off and rose to a height of 50 metres. All around was brilliant white; only the forest and an occasional bush helped us to orientate from the air. Over the lake it was like swimming in milk. Soon we came upon the highway. I peered into a thick white haze and at last saw the transport. The road!

Pyotr flew close to me, not falling behind: a good airman who knew his job. Not a word over the intercom. Once we flew up above the road into weather where Fascist fighters would dart about. Meanwhile motor vehicles were moving along the road – but not all. One of them was standing at an angle to the direction of movement. Lying beside it on the snow were people, probably victims of an aerial attack.

Pyotr and I crossed to the right side of the road in order not to meet any Messerschmitts head on if they came at us; but the ice highway came to an end. Beneath us was Lake Ladoga station, the Karelian shore. Turning back, we saw a cluster of vehicles. Here something else had happened. People waved their arms in the direction of the lake. The Fascists, it seemed had only just gone.

Again we flew to the right of the road, but now in the direction of Kobona. We climbed to a position just below cloud level in order to be less noticeable. Something like two minutes passed before beneath us a pair of Fascist fighters dashed across the roadway on a northerly course. While we were turning, they vanished. I judged that the enemy pilots could hardly have seen us. Probably, they had only just arrived there to take the place of a previous pair. In such visibility, the Messerschmitts would certainly turn to the left. A fighter pilot holds the joystick in his right hand. To observe and turn left is always easier for him, the more so in difficult weather conditions at low altitude. That meant that the Fascists would emerge on the road near Lake Ladoga station, where there were many vehicles.

I accelerated. Chepelkin was beside me. They mustn't give us the slip! We mustn't let them go!

'There they are, Petro!' I shouted over the radio to Chepelkin. Meanwhile, the pair of Messerschmitts flew low above the lorries. First I took aim at the second Messerschmitt, but it unexpectedly banked to one side and disappeared from view. Then I chased the leader. He had already fired a burst at one of the vehicles. I opened fire. The enemy fighter, enveloped in black smoke, turned sharply aside, turned on its back and fell to the ice.

'That's the way to wish a Fascist a Happy New Year!'

Red flames and a plume of black smoke showed against the white snow. People were running across the lake's virgin snow to the place where the Messerschmitt had fallen. But where was the other aircraft? We couldn't see it. Probably, somewhere in this area, the enemy had a station for eavesdropping. The second Messerschmitt had not made off without a reason, for I had only shouted: 'There they are, Petro!' The leader had evidently hoped to strike the motor vehicle and slip away, but he wasn't so lucky.

Three times we flew along the road as far as Kobona and back, but didn't meet any enemy aircraft. At dispersal, Chepelkin ran up to me beaming.

'Beautifully done!' he said, having in mind the attack on the Messerschmitt. And a little later Pyotr boyishly proposed: 'So that the whole year may be victorious, let's swap raglans!'

'Well, it's a deal!'

We made the exchange and it turned out that my raglan fitted Chepelkin better, and his – me. To the sound of approving exclamations from technicians, who were there watching the exchange, we ran to the dug-out to report the result of the patrol to Myasnikov.

'That really makes a Happy New Year!' he said, shaking our hands.

'Congratulations on your new victory!' said Mikhail Zakharovich as he embraced us.

Our aircraft went on patrol over the road all that day, but did not meet the enemy again. Sqn Cdr Myasnikov took off in the evening, supported by Chepelkin. The two Yaks turned over the airfield and flew away into the gloomy haze of Ladoga. At this hour a heated fight developed. The Fascists attacked the squadron commander, but Pyotr was in time to help him and shot down an Me 109. A second enemy fighter preferred not to engage in the fight any longer.

This was now the fifth victory over Fascist pilots for Chepelkin. Not for nothing did the Order of the Red Banner shine on his chest. The commander thanked Chepelkin for his help during the battle but Pyotr didn't know where to look for embarrassment. But most of all I was pleased that our squadron had begun the New Year so well. Two enemy aircraft had been shot down! The air force Commander in Chief reported our victories to Zhdanov and by 2 January the regimental commander had received a telegram of congratulation from the Military Soviet on the Leningrad Front. Unfortunately, I don't remember it word for word but Chepelkin and I were mentioned in it.

On 2 January, Semyon Lvov and Pyotr Chepelkin shot down yet another Me 109 over the ice highway when enemy fighters were trying to strafe motor vehicles on the way to Leningrad.

'Yes, we gave them what for!' said Chepelkin to Lvov as they returned from their flight. 'But a second got away again.'

'Evidently that second one was young and inexperienced,' concluded Lvov. 'The attack came to nothing. The first one is no more; we took him down a peg for his arrogance.'

'Oh no, they're still not finished,' retorted Chepelkin. 'Yesterday, the CO and I ran into some dangerous opponents. They took us on without the advantages of visibility or altitude. Both the leader and the second pilot were experienced wolves. So we still haven't destroyed all these impudent Fascists.'

'Very well,' Lvov smiled, 'but we'll destroy them yet.'

Before long, Capt Myasnikov was summoned to the headquarters of the 57th Attack Aircraft Regiment, based on our aerodrome. When he returned, he informed us that from time to time we would be ordered to accompany attack aircraft to their target and back. Of course, the patrolling of the ice road remained for us the most important duty.

The CO walked up to the map and explained the situation on our front. Continuing to advance successfully, the land forces had reached the railway line between Mga and Budogoshch, had bypassed Kirishi, forced a crossing of the Volkhov and established a bridgehead on its western shore. The German command transferred part of its forces from other parts of the front in order to exert a more stubborn opposition to our forces, which now were particularly in need of aerial support. From that day, we all started to fly with attack aircraft more frequently, delivering blows with them to enemy positions close to Maluksa and Pogostye stations in the area of Shapki and Posadnikov Ostrov.

The names of the brave pilots of the 57th Attack Aircraft Regiment – Karasyev, Klimenko, Potapov, Stepanyan, Mazurenko – were always in newspaper reports at that time. These famous lads lived with us. In bad weather, when there was no flying, they loved to sing a favourite song with us to the sound of the bayan.

Nelson Stepanyan, a cheerful chap, full of *joie de vivre*, reminded me of Hussein Aliyev. I remember how Pyotr Chepelkin and I wandered into the dispersal area for attack aircraft. At that time, the armourers were hanging bombs under Stepanyan's aircraft and fixing 132 mm missiles on racks.

'Whom do I see? Igor, Petro!' exclaimed Nelson Georgyevich in a Caucasian accent.

'We've come to look at your dive-bomber,' I said.

'It's not only a bomber but also a fighter!' Stepanyan began to lavish praise on his aircraft.

'But it has bombs, Nelson, yet you call it a fighter.'

'It depends who's flying it,' Stepanyan proudly remarked, and started to tell us how, in October 1941 during a bomb attack on one of the enemy's airfields, he himself had shot down two Ju 88 bombers.

'It was like this, you understand. We had reached the target and already gone into the attack, but there were two Junkers over the airfield. Well, I fired on the aircraft at dispersal and then went after the 88s.'

'Nelson Georgyevich,' Pyotr asked then, 'so in one day, you sometimes made as many as four sorties, and every time came under a hurricane of fire from the ground. Tell me frankly, weren't you frightened?'

Astonished, Stepanyan took an enormous missile from a pile.

'Look, what a beauty! There's no need to be afraid with one of these.' He tenderly stroked the nose of the missile and, placing the tips of his fingers to his lips, kissed them with relish. 'It's not a missile, it's a peach! Understand?'

You Have No Right To Get Killed

We were now at the very end of January. Winter had been remarkably cold with heavy snowfalls and frost, but in our dug-out it was warm and cosy. That morning we received good news: the forces defending Moscow were continuing their advance. The Commissar and the party organizer were interpreting the signs of movement on the map. Red flags were placed on it at Kaluga, Sukhinichi, Kirov, Mozhaisk and Toropyets.

Heatedly, we discussed the pace of our troops' advance outside Moscow. Eyes turned involuntarily towards the map on which the limits of the Volkhov front were delineated. These limits were also marked by flags, but these were moving nowhere. Hopes that our forces would immediately break through the blockade around Leningrad remained, for the time being, simply hopes. Our flags on the map stood stock still on the line from

Gruzino to Kirishi, Pogostye, Voronovo and Lipki. From Lipki along the shore of the lake was all of 12 kilometres to Shlisselburg. Were the enemy forces so strong on the Sinyavinsky Uplands that they could not be overpowered?

'We should send our attack aircraft there,' said Sukhov. But for some reason, Sukhov's recommendations were not taken into account. Orders were given to send fighters, not attack aircraft, to the region between Voronovo and Lipki. When the CO received this unexpected order, he replaced the receiver and looked at me.

'Come on then, go there with our novices. Take off in ten minutes.'

Gromodvinnikov, Borisov, Kochur and I got dressed. At that moment, the CO gave me a letter. 'I almost forgot. From Vologda. Probably from your wife.'

As he said, it was from Vologda. I opened the envelope and, first of all, found a photo enclosed. Valya was holding our little daughter in her arms. On the back of the snapshot was written 'My daddy is killing vile Fascists.' In the letter, my wife explained that our Nina would say that when people asked her where her daddy was. Myasnikov examined the photo and smiled. 'Kills vile Fascists. . . . Well done! . . . My Yurka is a little older. He'll soon be six. He plays soldiers with his friends all the time. He wants to be a pilot like his dad.'

The new pilots in our squadron, Capt Gromodvinnikov and Borisov, and Senior Lt Kochur, came to us from civil aviation. We got into our aircraft and flew off on our mission. I put the letter in my pocket and fastened the photo into the frame of the deviation graph. Valya and Ninochka could watch me as I flew.

For fifty minutes we gave cover to a part of the front line. I must admit, I much preferred to fly like this over a forward area than to accompany attack aircraft. Here, as they say, the initiative was in our hands. Almost beneath us were the blackened stations of Mga and Shlisselburg, which had been taken by the enemy. We saw Kolpino and the smoking chimneys of the heroic Uzhorsky factory beside the front line. The ice-bound River Neva was lost in a white smoke hanging over Leningrad. The ice road could easily be seen with the black dots of vehicles moving along it. But there were enemy aircraft in the sky. We flew to a height of 300 metres, just below cloud level. I looked at my watch and heard over the radio: 'Cannon 46, return to base.'

'Message received. Shall return,' I responded, but not without regret, and led the group back to base. A whole hour and the flight had been in vain. But if we're ordered to return, home we go. Beneath us was Naziya station. Suddenly at this point, on a course towards us, two Me 109s tumbled out of the clouds. The leader, seeing four soviet fighters in front of him, gave a burst of machine-gun fire. This he did, probably without aiming, and went into a steep climb. Both enemy fighters made off. We chased after them but they vanished into the grey mass of clouds.

Igor Kaberov, Novgorod Flying Club Instructor, 1939.

This was taken on one of the first days of the war. Seeing the photographer at dispersal, Matvey Yefimov suggested: 'Why not take a snapshot of the lads as a souvenir?' We gathered beside the aircraft. From left to right: Volodya Tenyugin, Sergey Sukhov, myself, Yegor Kostilyev, political officer M.Z. Isakovich, Squadron Commander I.R. Novikov, Husein Aliyev, Misha Bagryantsev and Nikolay Sosyedin. Boris Godunov is standing wearing the white helmet. Further to the right – Matvey Yefimov and on the extreme right Volodya Khaldeyev.

There was no time to hold a meeting, so party organiser, Yefimov, without interrupting flying duties, conducted the business under the wing of his aircraft. From left to right: Major I.R. Novikov, political officer M.Z. Isakovich, Flight Commander Mikhail Alekseyev, mechanic Vladimir Linnik, party organiser Matvey Yefimov, mechanic Kirrill Yevseyev. (1941)

I look at this photo and remember you, my dear friend Misha Fyodorov, a remarkable pilot, a man full of *joie de vivre* and a master when it came to dancing or cheerful conversation. Our lads found you such good company. I treasure this photo, taken in March 1941 at the very moment when you marked on the map the route for my training flight.

To this day, Boris, Shura Verina hasn't forgotten you. We all remember how on one occasion in the mess you said to her, 'Shurochka, direct your eyes at us, the peasants have returned from work!'

'I could have kissed him in front of everyone, hearing these words,' said Shura. 'But not just me! All our girls were in love with him.'

A cheerful person and brave in aerial combat, you were the soul of our military group, party organiser Boris Godunov. (1941)

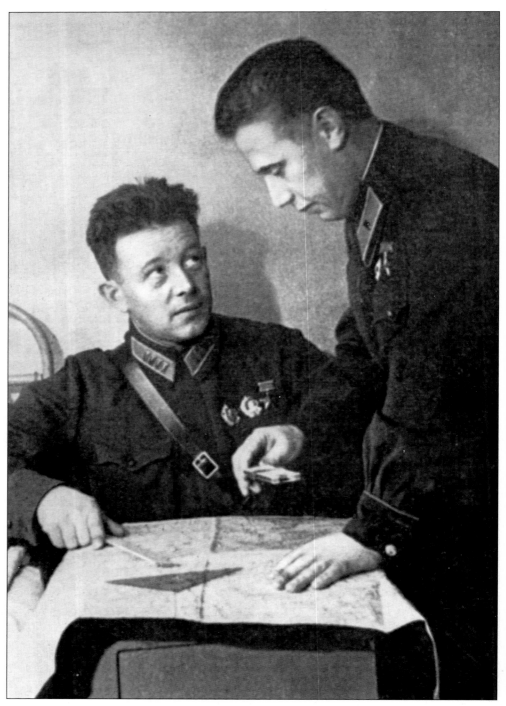

'The first Russian over Berlin!' – that's what they said about Colonel Yevgeny Nikoloyevich Preobrazhensky who led a group of Soviet bombers that struck a blow at military targets in the fascist capital on 8 August 1941. Next to Preobrazhensky is the navigator of the flagship, Pyotr Ilich Khokholov. (1941)

Pyotr Antonovich Brinko. He was already Hero of the Soviet Union on the twenty-third day of the war. By September 1941 Brinko had shot down fifteen enemy aircraft. Before our eyes he destroyed an enemy observation balloon. It took him only a few minutes to do it – take-off, a burst of machine-gun fire and landing. (1941)

Captain I.M. Umansky (in this photo he is a major) whose watch in the squadron was reckoned to be the most precise since it showed 'commander's time'. But watches are just watches and you for us dear Isaak Markovich, were the man from whom we learnt bravery, justice and kindness. (1942)

This was how Hero of the Soviet Union Pyotr Brinko dealt with a Heinkel bomber in September 1941.

During a short break the lads eagerly demanded music and I took up the bayan. I played, watched my friends as they sang and listened to their voices and the bass notes of the bayan. It must be said, it's a fine instrument. (1942)

'Whenever do you sleep?' the correspondent from a military newspaper once asked mechanic Sasha Gritsayenko. 'We'll catch up on sleep after the war,' he answered. My aircraft, serviced by technician Gritsayenko, never let me down in the war. Thank you, Sasha!

These witty cartoons were drawn by B.I. Prorokov in 1942. Depicted in them are Yegor Kostilyev (George and the Dragon), Engineer Sergeyev (the careful nurse), Matvey Yefimov, Sergey Sukhov and me (Hunters at rest) and me again (Moon Waltz). Bottom right the artist has drawn Pyotr Chepelkin shooting down an enemy aircraft.

The regimental commander, Major N.M. Nikitin, and the regimental commissar, I.P. Lukyanov, in a cheerful mood. Things were going well in our regiment. (1942)

He came to receive his party membership card but hearing the air-raid warning, ran from the dug-out and was soon in the air. Having shot down a Junkers, Kostilyev returned and apologised to the members of the party commission for his temporary absence due to official duties. In all, Yegor Dmitriyevich Kostilyev destroyed forty-six enemy aircraft. Here regimental commissar S.S. Bessonov (left) hands Yegor Kostilyev a third military medal. The printing on the wall reads: Defenders of Leningrad have one slogan: Death or Victory! (1942)

Matvey Andreyevich Yefimov beside his aircraft. Count the stars on the fuselage. Each one means an aerial victory over an enemy. Commissar Yefimov's aircraft was 'target number one' for Fascist fighters, as it later became clear. But not one of them had the strength to withstand his attacks. (1942)

Those twelve circuits and two zonal flights with aerobatics which Zhenya Duk and I made in a U 2 aircraft in 1943 determined his future. He became a first-class fighter pilot. (1950)

Our discovery – LaGG 3 fighter No. 59. Nobody knew whose it was. Pyotr Chepelkin spotted it returning from a sortie. The machine was lying in a swamp. Technicians dragged it out and renovated it. There was no time to test fly it after repair, so in February 1942 I immediately flew off in it on a military operation. If our technicians repaired it, that meant it wouldn't let you down.

In one of Sasha Potyemkin's first battles he had to bale out of a burning aircraft. The canopy of the parachute was torn. Potyemkin fell but landed on a slope on the northern shore of the River Neva and by a miracle remained alive. When Sasha resumed flying, he eagerly adopted the fighting experience of his comrades and soon became a threat to Fascist pilots. (1942)

Ivan is tired but he's in a good mood. The battle had been difficult but, as always, it ended with victory for Tsapov. This remarkable pilot shot down about thirty enemy aircraft in the Baltic Skies. Pictured here is Captain Ivan Ivanovich Tsapov after an aerial dog-fight. Another pilot, Captain Minayev helps him remove his parachute. (1943)

Semyon Grigorevich Bondarenko – squadron commander. He made 284 military sorties and shot down 17 enemy aircraft. When Semyon and I were sent to a rest home, after two days, Bondarenko phoned the regiment. 'The daily routine here,' said Semyon, 'is for me counter effective. That's my first point. Secondly, there's a war on now and we are stuck here. Thirdly, whatever happens I shall leave.' And leave he did. (1942)

A cheerful disposition, courage, strength of will and humanity characterised these two men. You see in this photo comrades in arms, Heroes of the Soviet Union commander of the aerial brigade I.G. Pomanenko and the commander of our regiment P.V. Kondratyev. (1941)

The aircraft have left on a military exercise. You may allow yourself a minute's break; but only a minute. A photographer takes a snapshot and each man then returns to his task, Zhenya Duk (on the left) will run to put the headquarters papers in order, Boris Alferov to help the lads to repair a damaged aircraft, armourer Avdeyenko to busy himself with weapons. (1943)

Squadron commissar Nikolay Kosorukov – calm, unruffled on the ground, he was like a meteor in the air. Observing from the ground how Kosorukov conducted the battle, his comrades would say, 'The handwriting of a commissar.' Wounded, he flew in a damaged fighter, and I conducted him away from the fight. Had he been on the ground, the doctors would have saved a man who had lost consciousness; but in the air. . . . What a terrible loss. (1942)

Never did I fly so confidently as a leader with anyone as I did with Sergeant Nilolay Shestopalov. He was only nineteen when he joined us from flying school. Kolya had only to take off and I was sure that next to me was a real fighter. He had something of his own, a Shestopalov quality – the ability to see everything about him. He was swift, courageous and disiplined. More than once Nikolay helped me at difficult moments. (1944)

Dawn has hardly broken before reconnaissance pilot, Vasiliy Chernyenko takes off into the sky. Returning, he reports that enemy ships have been discovered here and there on the Finnish Gulf. We sound the alarm and Stormoviks supported by fighters go to the target. Chernyenko, a skilful pilot, shot down twenty enemy aircraft. Here Vasiliy Chernyenko (right) and the squadron commander, Viktor Terekhin discuss the details of the aerial battle in which they had just taken part. (1943)

The author, Igor Aleksandrovich Kaberov, still at work during retirement at home in Novgorod.

Forty years on comrades in arms Igor Kaberov and Ronald Clutterbuck meet for the first time, Watford 1985.

Igor Aleksandrovich Kaberov, Distinguished Military Pilot and Hero of the Soviet Union, 1917–95.

Once again, I gave the command to make for home. Myself: I followed behind the group. It was at this moment that the engine of my aircraft for some reason suddenly cut out. Then it started to work, and then stopped again. From beneath the engine cowling, steam was streaming out. The water temperature was over 100 degrees. I reduced the engine speed in order to cool the motor, but the needle of the thermometer stayed at maximum. The oil temperature was also at maximum but the oil pressure, on the other hand, had fallen. The engine wouldn't stop! As if in reply to this thought, the engine gave a sharp thud. The three-bladed propeller stopped dead.

'What's happened? Could it be a stray bullet from the unaimed burst of fire?' I wanted to inform my comrades what had happened, but the radio didn't work either. The road to Ladoga stretched through the forest like a narrow ribbon. Probably I would have to land here in an open place close to a village. After all, it wasn't like the rye field covered in boulders where I had landed my plane in Bolshaya Vruda. Undercarriage up in snow – nothing to fear. The fighter would slide along about 50 metres as if on skis; everything would be fine. . . .

While I thought about this, the aircraft lost height. The altitude was already 200 metres. There was a village and the forest on the right. I slackened speed. At a height of 100 metres, the aircraft plunged into a mist as white as snow. For a moment or two, I broke through the shroud of mist. Beneath me was the dense forest with the tops of its sharply bristling spruce trees. I turned the aircraft to the left towards the edge of the wood, but I hadn't enough height. The wings were already brushing the tops of the trees. Twigs began to fly. I could see nothing in front of me, but felt a sudden jerk. It seemed as if someone had grabbed the aircraft by the tail. It immediately stopped in mid-flight and slid down. I managed to throw my hands forward to avoid hitting my head. Then came a slight thrust and I was thrown half out of the plane, suspended by my harness and hanging from the cockpit cover. A cloud of snowflakes settled. It became quiet. I felt myself. It seemed that I was in one piece. I unfastened my straps, looked round the cockpit, took the photograph from the instrument panel. My wife and daughter looked at me with a fond expression. 'Don't worry, my dears; the worst is over.'

I got out of the cockpit but then became stuck in deep snow. I tried to pull myself out but a stern command made me stand stock still.

'Stay where you are! Hands up!'

Above me on the edge of the gully, parting the branches of a bush, stood a soldier. His automatic was aimed at me. The determined look of the man promised nothing good for me if I made but a single careless movement.

'Are you a Fascist? Lay down your arms.'

'I'm one of yours. A Russian, a Soviet airman. But I can't give you my weapon; my arms are raised.'

'Throw your weapon here!'

I unbuttoned my belt and threw the pistol and all my equipment at the feet of the soldier.

'And now come out!' he shouted in a bellicose tone. 'Presently, we'll sort out who you are.'

'Calm down, Comrade soldier. As you can see' – I pointed at part of a red star still left on an undamaged part of the fuselage – 'it's a Soviet, not a Fascist aircraft. Moreover, I'm a captain. I beg you to behave more politely.'

'We know you,' he didn't give up, 'the other day, we also caught one here. He also spoke Russian. He said he flew a Yak and had been shot down by Germans. And he wore a raglan, like yours. But he was an ugly-faced enemy who had hidden his parachute somewhere in the bushes.'

I remembered my own parachute, clambered on to the wing and pulled it out of the cockpit.

'Mine's here, no need to hide it.'

Only now did I see that the aircraft had neither wings nor tail. The cockpit and fuselage were above ground. The rear half of the fuselage with its tail unit was swaying on high voltage cables. The stanchion for the tail wheel held it fast on them.

'The line has no power,' I said to the soldier, 'otherwise the current would have killed me. If it's not live, that means that starving Leningrad is still without electricity.' The soldier looked at the electric power cable, at the tail of my plane swaying above him and then, somewhat less angrily, ordered me to come out of the gully. Some time later, he brought me to the village, to a house beside which stood a sentry. In the house, a major in combined services uniform stood up to greet us.

'I've caught a German pilot, Comrade Major!' the soldier reported smartly.

They both looked at me, and then I realized the raglan, which I had obtained from Chepelkin, had no blue tabs and the collar of my shirt was not visible from under my woollen sweater. That was why the soldier was suspicious. However, the Major sorted this out at once. Once he had dismissed the soldier, the commander asked me to describe in detail everything that had happened.

'Yes, you were very lucky,' he said, having listened attentively. 'You can be sure that we shall touch nothing on the plane. I'll order sentries to stand guard beside it until your comrades arrive.'

The Battalion Commander gave orders to provide me with rations but regretted that he couldn't transport me to the airfield. However, he did give me a guide who knew how to reach the road.

'Be careful,' the Major advised me as we parted. 'Sometimes enemy patrols are about in the forest. Don't run into them. As for the soldier who brought you here' he smiled, 'we'll express our gratitude to him for his vigilance.'

At first with my escort, and then alone, I walked with my parachute on my shoulders along the forest road. Just in case, I carried a pistol at the ready. It was eight o'clock in the evening when I walked up to our base. A newcomer met me, a sailor on duty whom I'd never seen before.

'Where are the others?'

'Having supper.'

On the table lay a small note. My eyes involuntarily caught sight of my surname on the paper. 'What's this?' I started to read: 'Comrade Isakovich! Take your car and have a word with Myasnikov as to where you might look for Kaberov. Take a map and torch. Talk to the people who are living there. Take all measures to find Igor. Lukyanov.'

Everything was clear. I walked to the mess. For some reason, it was extremely quiet. Everyone was talking quietly.

'You understand, we were on our way home and approaching Voybokalo.' I heard the voice of Capt Gromodvinnikov as I opened the door of the mess. 'You remember how he gave the order to regroup? He gave the command and said that he himself would fly behind us and catch up. After that, he gave no reply to my enquiry. He disappeared somewhere. . . .'

I quietly closed the door behind me.

'Maybe, but what about those two Messerschmitts?' said Yefimov.

'No,' objected Sukhov, 'more likely he simply put down somewhere out of necessity. He'll arrive, you'll see, he'll arrive. . . .'

At this, I couldn't restrain myself. 'Quite right, Sergey! See, I have arrived.'

What happened after that I shan't begin to describe. I'll only say that it was more dangerous than landing on the edge of the forest. As with Sergey a week before, my friends almost smothered me with joy. It all finished by pouring 100 grammes into my glass and giving me food to eat. Then, once they had asked me about my adventures, brought me the bayan and begged me to play dance music. Of course, the first to step into the circle was Seryozha. A reckless dance began to a chorus of licentious verses.

'Play, play, Igor! You have no right to get killed. . . . Because you're the only bayanist in the squadron.'

The next day, technicians went to the place where I had come down and brought back the radiator which had been pierced by a bullet.

'Look, Comrade Commander.' Sergeyev showed Myasnikov the hole. 'Just one bullet and see what happened.'

Myasnikov carefully turned over the radiator to examine it. 'Nothing can be done. It's the water cooling. This is the main fault with this aircraft.'

'The battalion commander is a really understanding person,' said Sergeyev. 'Everything he's said to us has been helpful. He apologized for putting Kaberov under escort, but regulations demand it. There's nothing can be done about the aircraft. Of course we removed the tail unit from the high tension cable. Pity we didn't have a camera; we'd have obtained some unusual photos. I saw the wreck, and to crash the machine and receive not a single scratch. . . .' The engineer shook his head. 'No, Kaberov, you were born under a lucky star for sure!'

On Foot Round Leningrad

That day the Squadron Commander, meeting me on the airfield, spoke to me more strictly than usual:

'Why are you here, Comrade Kaberov?'

'Where should I be but here?'

'As far as I can remember, today is your day off.'

'How can that be, Comrade Captain? The other day, you gave me a day off after my "soft" landing. Is today another day off?'

'I don't know.' Myasnikov led me to the dug-out. 'Here's the list. Yesterday, Sukhov had a day off; today, it's your turn.'

'But what shall I do at home alone?'

'But you're going to "Peter".'

I couldn't make out if he was joking or serious. The CO took off his cap and stroked what was left of his hair. He had this way with him. He would look slowly at the person he was talking to in order to find out what impression the words had on him.

'To Leningrad?' I asked.

'And why not? You could take the ferry aircraft for repair at the same time.' Myasnikov smiled. 'Fly back in the repaired U 2. They're expecting you at headquarters.'

Well then, the task was to my liking. I travelled to the mess by car and drew two days' rations. The adjutant issued instructions for my trip. The CO again came up to me at the aircraft.

'Does your friend in Leningrad smoke?'

'Yes, he does.'

'Give him this little gift from us.' Myasnikov handed me a box of mild tobacco.

'Many thanks.'

I taxied, took off and, having circled above the airfield, set course for Leningrad.

A day off! Is it possible to talk about such a thing in wartime? It would seem not. Yet while the first battles were going on, Commissar Isakovich had proposed to introduce such a day with the aim of conserving the strength of the squadron's pilots. We each rested in turn. The man granted leave could stay with relatives or friends in Leningrad.

That day it was clear and frosty. In a fighter it was fifteen minutes to the city as the crow flies; but fighting was going on there. The ice highway was a lifeline to Leningrad. I flew a little to the north of it where it was usually quieter. On the horizon, Leningrad could be seen through the frozen mist. On its northern edge lay the headquarters aerodrome – a comparatively small airstrip among aviation workshops. I lowered my undercarriage and flaps and landed safely.

Having arranged for the repair of the aircraft, examined the U 2, which had already been repaired, and verified the time when I would fly it to my regiment, I hurried to the tram stop. There wasn't a soul about. I looked about me; the streets were empty. The few passers-by made their way with difficulty along narrow paths. Snow, which had not been cleared away, lay on the pavement. The tramways were buried in snow. It was a fair distance from the headquarters airfield to the town centre, but there was nothing I could do but to go there on foot. On my way, there was much that horrified me.

Somewhere near Leo Tolstoy Square, a man was lying face down on the pavement. I walked up to him and tried to lift him. 'Citizen . . . citizen. . . .' I turned his face upwards and was convinced that I was looking at a dead man. I spoke to a woman who was passing. I asked her where I should phone so that the corpse could be taken away. But the woman looked at me with weary expressionless eyes and slowly walked on.

By the Kirov Bridge I stopped another woman and found out from my conversation with her much that I had not known. For example, I discovered that special vehicles were going around the town. The corpses of people who had died on the streets and in the squares were being carted away in them to the cemetery.

'They will take this man away,' said the woman. 'So don't be upset.'

Walking along Sadovaya Street, I came out on to Nyevsky Prospekt and saw the half-burnt and blackened building of Gostiny Dvor with black gaps where once there were brightly lit shop windows.

Everywhere traces of bombing and the cruel shelling could be seen. Many shop windows were covered in sandbags. At the foot of buildings, on street corners, were blackened gun ports. One of the side streets had been turned into a store for anti-tank devices. At any rate, the town was prepared for street fighting.

Quite unexpectedly, an army patrol stopped me.

'Show us your papers!'

Once the senior man had carefully inspected my identity card and travel warrant, he advised me to cross to the opposite side of the road because an artillery bombardment was expected. I looked at the Anichkov Bridge from a building called the Pioneers' Palace and didn't recognize it. Where were Peter Klodt's famous horses? Passers-by explained to me that the sculptures had been removed in November 1941. Nyevsky Prospekt was unusually silent. Pedestrians went about their business quietly. They stood silently by a shop in a queue for bread. Only the engines of patrolling fighters gave full voice to their song, flying above the town in the frosty blue sky.

Not far from the Moscow station, a woman walked out of the archway of a corner house. With difficulty she pulled a sledge on which lay the bodies of dead people wrapped in a sheet. As it changed direction, the sledge tipped over and its load fell on to the snow. I ran to help the woman and asked her whom she was taking. In reply, a feeble half whisper reached me.

'My husband and two sons. My husband died the day before yesterday and my children – yesterday.'

'Where are you taking them?'

'To Okhta.'

There was neither a teardrop in her eyes, nor a note of complaint in the voice of this mother and wife who was enduring so much suffering. I estimated the distance to Okhta. No, she hadn't the strength to walk that distance. I picked up the rope from the roadway and pulled the sledge. I moved slowly; the woman couldn't walk quickly. We passed the Moscow station and came out on to Suvorov Prospekt.

'Thank you. Now I can manage on my own,' she said, fixing an eye on my badges. 'Are you a pilot? My eldest wanted . . . . He would have been sixteen. . . . How he wanted to be a pilot. . . .' She became silent, turned away and covered her face with her hands. I stood benumbed. I hadn't the strength to comfort her. Somewhere behind the station a shell exploded, and a second later, another.

The bombardment went on for almost an hour. Vosstanie Street was closed by a patrol. In order to get to my friends, the Sokolovs, I walked down Mayakovsky Street. There was Kovyensky Lane. The corner building standing next to the Polish church had been reduced to a pile of ruins, but the house where the Sokolovs lived was standing. I stopped, looking for its familiar windows. They were not so easy to recognize. One was plugged with a pillow, another covered in plywood. An old lady was standing in the porchway.

'Where are you going, young man?'

I shrugged my shoulders in astonishment. 'To my friends.'

'This is no time, son, to visit friends.'

'The Sokolovs live here, granny. I'm calling on them.'

'Who are you calling granny? I'm here to guard and protect the house and I'm not allowed to let strangers in.'

She blocked the entrance to the staircase like a sentry.

'Comrade guard,' I addressed the old lady, 'I'm a military man and recognize good order, of course, but the Sokolovs live here – do you understand? I must visit them without fail. Aunt Lida, Uncle Vanya and their daughter Nina live in a flat on the second floor.'

'Your Sokolovs have been evacuated for sure.'

'But that's not so, they're here,' I continued, trying to convince her.

'Well, all right. Show me your documents.'

The strict old woman took my travel documents. 'I can't see without my glasses. But it's all right. I'll believe you. Come in.'

I climbed to the second floor and knocked on the door.

'Are you alive here?'

'We're alive,' said Aunt Lida quietly as she opened the door. 'It's rather dark, that's true, but so far, we're alive.' How thin she had become! But somehow she was still cheerful. Nina came out of her room.

'Ah, Igor!'

I didn't have too much time. I pulled some dry rations from my suitcase (half a loaf and some sugar lumps) and suggested we arrange a tea party.

'Well, since you both smoke,' I said, 'my friends have sent you some tobacco. The CO himself asked me to give it to you.'

'Golden Fleece! Strong tobacco.'

Nina turned the box over in her hands. 'Thank your Commanding Officer.' Straight away, they both started to smoke and the aroma of tobacco spread through the flat.

The head of the family, Ivan Ilich Sokolov, was fighting somewhere outside Leningrad. He was a senior lieutenant in the signals corps. Sitting at table, we remembered him and all our relatives and friends. Aunt Lida brought boiling water, gave everyone a lump of sugar and a small slice of bread. Music was playing on the radio. Outside it was already dark.

'Tell us,' asked Nina, 'are we now in a position to break through this damned blockade?'

I shrugged my shoulders.

'As a pilot, you, with your bird's eye view, must be able to see everything,' she said, taking a drag on her tobacco and blowing blue smoke rings in my direction.

'You understand, Nina,' I said, 'the Fascists were in Tikhvin and 6 kilometres from Volkhovstroy. But now the front line passes 16 kilometres from Mga station and 12 from Shlisselburg. Our forces have driven back the enemy from Volkhovstroy almost 70 kilometres. And what a magnificent advance has been made outside Moscow! That means we'll break through the blockade. We must only consolidate our successes and conserve our strength.'

'But Leningrad is starving,' sighed Aunt Lida, pouring hot water into my glass.

The whine of the siren interrupted our conversation. An air raid warning. People went upstairs to the loft. Aunt Lida and Nina dressed hurriedly. They had to keep watch on the roof in order to render harmless any fire bombs. The Fascists were bombing Vasilyevsky Island, the region of the port. Flares were hanging in the sky. Searchlight beams were cutting through the darkness and, now and then, enemy aircraft were caught in them. Anti-aircraft guns were firing. Sometimes, silhouettes of our aircraft were drawn against the night sky. They cooperated with the anti-aircraft batteries in attacking the illuminated targets. Already, I had seen four enemy bombers fall to earth. Every time, the people standing next to me on the roof shouted out loud, 'Hurrah!'

When I left Leningrad, I carried with me the memories of these exciting moments. I carried away confirmation of the Leningraders' bravery, their yearning to deliver a fatal blow to the enemy and to achieve complete victory.

CHAPTER EIGHT

The Regiment Honoured

Landing Forbidden

5 February 1942: a clear cold day and a strong wind was blowing from Ladoga. My friends had left on patrol. Their machines, in fighting formation, quickly distanced themselves from the airfield in the direction of the ice highway. I remained on the ground for I had lost my wings. My old aircraft was undergoing repair and the new one was still in the forest near Voybokalo.

What should I do? I made for the dug-out. It's not easy for a pilot without his aircraft. At that time, they were repairing two of our fighters in Leningrad: a '35' and my '88'. I would be lucky to receive my machine by April. What had possessed me to give it even for a single flight to our new pilot, Borisov? My perfect plane had been damaged as it landed – my anger for this man knew no bounds.

Zhenya Duk was sitting at the table in the dug-out. He was putting some headquarters' papers in order. Borisov was lying on his bunk. He was smoking and telling Zhenya some funny story. You couldn't breathe easily for the smoke in the place which was as stuffy as a bath-house. I couldn't stand it.

'Why are you smoking in the dug-out, Comrade Borisov? You know very well the CO has forbidden it.'

'I'm sorry, I'll let some air in.' Borisov put out his cigar and opened a small window.

I walked to dispersal. There were neither aeroplanes nor technicians; only a piercing wind sweeping the snow low over the ground: depressing conditions. The lads were fighting and I was doing nothing. A few days before, Lvov and Kostilyev had shot down an Me 109 in the area of Lidov. Lvov and Yefimov also destroyed an enemy aircraft when they were covering the front line between Voronovo and Lipki. That day, Myasnikov and Chepelkin had shot down a Messerschmitt over the ice road in the region of Vistav, and Yefimov and Sukhov another over Kobona.

'You are not allowed to touch our motor vehicles,' Sergey Sukhov shouted when an Me 109 exploded following a burst of machine-gun fire. 'They are carrying bread to Leningrad, and you are . . . .'

In the dug-out, Yefimov told us about the battle so captivatingly, that I felt as if I had been in his intolerable position.

The roar of engines distracted me from my unhappy thoughts; our lads were returning. Craning my neck, I watched the aircraft as they swept over dispersal. One after the other, they quickly landed and taxied. The CO gathered the pilots together in the dug-out, de-briefed them and gave orders to prepare the machines speedily for the forthcoming take-off with the attack aircraft. I went up to Myasnikov.

'May I have a word with you, Comrade Commander?'

'I know, I know what you are going to say. But what can I say?'

'I have a proposal,' I said. 'Since there aren't enough aircraft, let's fly in turn.'

'It's not as easy as that. But in point of fact, it wouldn't do any harm if you were to learn to pilot a Yak. Incidentally, I did promise you that somehow . . . .'

'In which aircraft, Comrade Captain?'

'Go in mine. Let Makarov show you the cockpit. Do a circuit and in the evening when it's quieter, take off and pilot it within this zone.'

'Aye-aye, Captain!' I ran quickly to Makarov.

'Well, Sergey Sergeyevich, show me the aircraft. I shall be trying out the Yak. The CO sent me.'

Makarov was an experienced technician. He had serviced Maj Ivan Romanovich Novikov's aircraft when he fought the Japanese Samurai at Khalkhin Gol. Sergey Sergeyevich had also taken part in the battles on the Karelian Isthmus during the Soviet–Finnish conflict before the Second World War.

'Well, then, let's start from the left and take things in turn,' said Makarov. 'Here is the M 105 engine, the same as on the LaGG. The instruments are just the same. This is the lever to operate the undercarriage.' He pointed at a large lever. 'You use this handle when you need to lower the landing flaps. With the help of this control knob, you can change the pitch of the propeller. Everything here is simple,' smiled Sergey. 'Start the engine and fly. True, there are minor difficulties.' The noise of a rocket interrupted his explanation.

'Take off!' shouted the technicians and removed the covers from the engine. Capt Myasnikov ran up to the aircraft. I climbed out of the cockpit to make room for him.

'Well, how are things? Have you made yourself familiar with the controls?' he asked.

'Yes, there's little difference from the other aircraft.'

'That's true. Everything's very simple. And when landing it's quite miraculous – it lands itself,' joked Myasnikov and then continued seriously. 'Yefimov is leading a group in the region of Maluksa. I have been summoned urgently to regimental headquarters. There is no one else to fly. Maybe you can fly with Capt Lvov as a pair.'

'I understand, Comrade Captain.' Overjoyed, I returned to the cockpit. The attack aircraft took off and after them the fighters.

'Come on, Sergey, show me how the engine starts,' I hurried Makarov.

Nervously, he thrust his head into the cockpit. 'Wider, wider! Open up the starter. No, not that, this one. . . .'

Finally, the engine came to life and straight from dispersal, changing direction, I sped across the airfield. The machine ran softly over the smoothly rolled snow and, lifting away from it, speedily gained height. 'Oh, how easy you are!' I retracted the undercarriage, completed some circuits, caught up with the group and took up my position with Lvov.

Eight attack aircraft were flying far below and ahead of us. Behind them, on each side, four LaGG 3 fighters were following – a group providing first-hand cover, led by Yefimov. Passing to the west of Volkhovstroy, Semyon Lvov proposed by radio that I should gain height and view the airspace over Ladoga. We were already at a height of 3,000 metres. The sun was shining brightly. We looked round: nobody was there. I switched my weapons on and, turning the aircraft slightly away from Lvov, fired a short burst. Everything was working well.

'Let's go down,' said Lvov and rolled away. I intended to follow him, but on looking round noticed shadows in the blinding rays of the sun, turned sharply to the side and now saw more clearly four Me 109s diving on me.

Lvov had gone. He was already beside the group. I couldn't summon him for help. Of course, the enemy pilots would immediately discover the attack aircraft and pursue them. No, I must delay this group of Messerschmitts and meanwhile our aircraft would carry out the mission before them.

The sun prevented me from observing and aiming, and the enemy fighters were coming at me. There could be no doubt that they were about to open fire. It was impossible to get away; I couldn't dodge all four. Without thinking (when was there time to think?) I performed a barrel-roll. The Yak easily turned over. Surprised by the unexpected move, the Fascists swept over me.

Now this was what I had to do. With the sun behind me, I now occupied an advantageous position and could see clearly. The enemy fighters divided into two groups. One pair came straight at me, the other circled to the side in order to attack from behind. Knowing that our group, having hit the target, would return this way I tried to draw the Fascists away. This unequal battle lasted twenty minutes. We were already over Voybokalo station. At a suitable moment, I attacked. One Messerschmitt started to smoke and went away to one side. The three remaining were bedevilled by their lack of success. I had heard a little about the manoeuvrability of the Yak and I tried to conduct the fight flying vertically, as my friends had usually done. What a light machine was this Yak! The CO was right: it's not an aircraft – it's a dream!

From vertical flight (in which the Yak is an invincible machine), the Messerschmitts caught me on the turn. I pulled the stick towards me and the aircraft shuddered and shook all over as if in mortal fear of pulling out of the spin. Never fear, my friend, if that's the case, we'll die together! But there was a Fascist on my tail. Closer and closer he came. Crash! It felt as if a mallet had smashed into the rudder. The control column was torn from my hands. The aircraft turned over and went into a spin. From a height of 3,000 metres it was swept earthwards and turned at such a speed that it seemed that my head would be torn from my shoulders.

Having failed to bring the aircraft out of its spin, I unbuttoned my harness and tried to throw myself out of the cockpit, but some kind of devilish power pressed me to the armoured seat. I was half out of the cockpit but I hadn't the strength to tear myself free. It seemed that my end had come, but at this moment, quite unexpectedly, the aircraft stopped spinning and changed to a gentle spiral.

Once I had flopped back into my seat, I guided the aircraft out of its bank and pulled the stick towards me. The machine unwillingly lifted its nose and, at about 300 metres from the ground, swept over the forest. I controlled my nervous trembling only with difficulty. I looked about me – the Messerschmitts had gone. Evidently, having decided that I was finished, the Fascists had made off. I tried to hold the aircraft in level flight by pushing the stick as far forward as it would go, but it did not respond and continued to gain height. If it refused to be controlled, then the only hope lay in my parachute. Yet could I really abandon such a machine, especially the CO's? No, I must try to save it. I sharply pushed the stick right forward and waited. Slowly, and reluctantly, the fighter dropped its nose. This meant that the controls still worked, but with only slight effect: the machine obeyed only when the stick was moved sharply and to its full extent. I moved the stick forward as soon as the nose of the aircraft started to rise above the horizon; it only had to drop before I again jerked the stick towards me. I flew, alternately rising then plunging downwards. The altitude was now 1,200 metres. Both wings were holed with shell splinters. The rudder didn't respond to the movements of the pedals and the pedals themselves didn't return to their neutral positions.

I wanted to see what had happened to the rudder, but the high part of the fuselage hid my view of the tail unit. The engine was working well. The radio was silent. I gently banked the aircraft to the right and the ailerons caused the machine to swing slowly round. I flew along the railway line for five minutes – Volkhovstroy was already visible. Our aircraft were making their approach. I turned with the intention to join the formation. Every machine in the group was in its place. The attack aircraft and the fighters were all there. I immediately felt more light-hearted. It was good that I had succeeded in delaying the enemy fighters and had led them away from the Voybokalo area. A pity about the machine, of course, but, on the other hand, my friends had been able to carry out their mission calmly.

Strenuously working the control column, I approached them from the side. My aircraft found itself, now above the group, now below. Lvov came close and, using sign language, asked if I had seen what had happened to my machine. He clapped the palm of his hand to the earpiece of his flying helmet, meaning 'Can you hear?' Once he had received a negative reply to this and to other questions, he stretched his lips as if he were pronouncing the letter 'U', shook his head and moved away.

The attack aircraft and the fighters landed on the airfield. With the help of the ailerons, I described a large circle with some difficulty. At 1,000 metres, I lowered the undercarriage in order to check how the aircraft would behave. I added a few turning movements. The machine held on; it could still fly. I lowered the landing flaps. The speed immediately dropped and the fighter no longer responded to elevator movement. I lifted the flaps and accelerated. I could keep the aircraft in the air only with difficulty. Would I have to bale out after all? No, I had to try to land the machine. I had to make a longer approach and a gentle descent without flaps, keeping a straight course for the landing strip.

There was already a black cross made of two strips of cloth on the airfield. I had been forbidden to land. A crowd of people gathered by the cross. A vehicle of some kind was hurrying to the scene. I could see all this clearly, but my mind was made up. I lost height and prepared to land. The undercarriage was down and the flaps up. I was flying too fast, but what could I do? Bathed in sweat, I worked the control column like a pump. Three red rockets flew up from the end of the strip, signalling me not to land. Nevertheless, I made my approach. The aircraft still rocked as if in a storm. The engine now roared at maximum revs; now suddenly became quiet. At last, the machine struck the snow with its wheels, jumped, and seemed to hang in the air. The next moment, it again fell on its wheels. Leaping once more, the aircraft swept across the airfield without a sound and stopped at the very end.

After taxiing to dispersal and switching off the engine, I jumped from the cockpit, took off my flying helmet and wiped my sweat-soaked brow. I intended to report to the CO what had happened, but Myasnikov told me not to bother, embraced me and slapped me on the back.

'Thank you, thank you. . . .'

Then he walked round the machine in astonishment, shaking his head and looking at the broken tail unit.

'I don't understand how it stayed in the air. There's nothing to keep it flying. The rudder is broken clean off. . . . Half the port elevator has gone. Twenty per cent of the right is damaged. . . . To fly such a machine back to the airfield and land. . . . Well!'

Myasnikov counted the holes in the wings and fuselage, in what was left of the elevators. 'No, it's not anti-aircraft fire. This was a fight and, judging by all this, a fierce one.'

'Exactly so, Comrade Commander,' I confirmed, and reported all that had happened.

'Now do you see, Matvey Andreyevich,' Myasnikov turned to Yefimov, 'why we didn't meet the enemy?'

Looking at me, he gave a warm smile. 'And how did my aircraft fare in the fight? How did Yakushka behave?'

'A fine machine, Comrade Commander.'

There was a playful note in Myasnikov's voice when he asked: 'Well, how about the landing?'

'It landed as you saw – all on its own.'

Everyone laughed. We were all pleased that misfortune had passed us by.

About Flying Boots, Ailerons And Jupiter Lamps

A wartime dug-out: how many songs are sung about this simple creation made by human hands! Covered in snow, it stood on the very edge of a dense wood like a house in a fairy-tale. We had only just returned from a patrol, entered the dug-out and were singing 'The dug-out song'. The bass and treble notes of the bayan merged with the voices of my friends. Then unexpectedly the door swung open and several determined lads carrying a lamp on a tripod came into the dug-out and switched on this bright light. A man in a short white sheepskin coat switched on a camera.

'That's very good! Carry on, comrades. . . . A wonderful shot. We'll take that!' shouted the cameraman to someone and turned to us. 'Play, play on and sing please. . . . That's the way, many thanks!' The door closed; the lamp went out. 'You are making history,' concluded the cameraman somewhat loftily. 'Therefore, you must be patient. History will speak well of you.'

From time to time, not only photographers and cameramen looked in to our little airfield, lost in the woods, but also artists, actors and journalists. We were always pleased to see these visitors. Through them we were firmly tied to Leningrad and its people. When our unit became a guards' regiment, men of letters frequently came to visit us. This important event for us took place on the twenty-fourth anniversary of the formation of the Red Army. At the start of this festive occasion, the Commander of the Baltic Fleet, Adm V.F. Tributs, and a member of the Military Soviet, Adm N.K. Smirnov, handed us our regimental colours. From that time, our regiment changed its name to the 3rd Guards Aviation Fighter Regiment of the Baltic Fleet's Air Force. As before, we protected the ice road, accompanying attack aircraft and fighting to the death the enemy fighters who attacked them. True, such intense air battles as we had seen over Kronstadt did not take place, but three or four flights each short winter day was also no small duty. We had our work and the artists, journalists and cameramen had theirs.

In those grim times, Nikolay Chukovsky was well known as a war correspondent. The naval political authorities, heeding his wish to work in 'an interesting unit', sent Nikolay Korneyevich to our guards' aerial fighter regiment. One morning, I came to dispersal and saw Chukovsky beside my machine. Actually, he was sitting under the aircraft and examining something. What interested him was the way the undercarriage retracted. Then Chukovsky crawled from under the plane and turned to the technician with a new question.

'Excuse me, Aleksandr Nikolayevich, I only want to be quite clear. . . .
Oh, sorry, here is Comrade Kaberov. My point is . . . . Please understand,
it's the word aileron. . . .'

I walked up to the wing: 'These are ailerons.'

'Is that so?' The writer was not just astonished but became more
interested. 'Curious . . . but how do they flap?'

'Flap?' We just shrugged our shoulders. 'They give lateral steering. With
their help, the aircraft banks to the left or the right.'

'Ah, that's what they do!' Chukovsky suddenly burst out laughing so
heartily that tears came to his eyes. 'Well, they deceived me, the devils!' So
he told us that the evening before, he had accidentally heard a conversation
between Sukhov and Gromodvinnikov. One of them remembered that
during a fight a Messerschmitt had damaged his aircraft and the other
sharply remarked, 'You should flap your ailerons less. . . .'

At this, Gritsayenko and I laughed. We had to explain to Nikolay
Korneyevich that currently among pilots there was an expression 'to flap
your ailerons', which had the same meaning as the Russian phrase 'to flap
your ears' – meaning 'to listen without understanding'.

So on this occasion Chukovsky was able to define more precisely yet
another piece of aviation terminology. 'Do you see,' he said, 'a writer must
know about ten times more than he will use later when writing his book.'

'So you intend to write a book?'

'Yes, the material which I have collected here is so interesting that I would
like . . . .'

'That means we shall be reading it some time,' I said, and carelessly
glanced at my watch.

Chukovsky instantly closed his notebook. 'Are you in a hurry? I'll walk
with you as far as the dug-out. . . . Tell me, Comrade Kaberov, have any
fighters two cockpits? Understand, I would like to fly into battle with you, a
real battle with machine-gun fire.'

'Nikolay Korneyevich, it's very dangerous.'

'Never mind. Then I would see you in action.'

When we were near the dug-out, Nikolay Korneyevich asked me to stop
for just a minute. 'I have one small question to ask you,' he said. 'What are
'*untyata*'? You are wearing '*unti*' [high fur boots], but what are '*untya*' . . .?'

At this moment, I heard the voice of the guard. 'Captain Kaberov, the CO
would like to see you.'

I ran off, so I had no time to inform the writer that *untyata* are simply fur
stockings which you put on before you pull on your *unti*.

Chukovsky worked in the squadron without a break. He worked, not only
during the day but sometimes at night. One evening, I had some free time
and went up to him when he was writing. He moved his papers aside and
readily started a conversation with me. When talking to me about his work
on this occasion, Chukovsky threw open the lid of a small travelling suitcase.

'There, look.' In the case, his famous notebooks lay in piles. 'Do you see how many? And it will be necessary to write even more. These are detailed notes made after conversations with you, Kostilyev, Lvov, Yefimov, Sukhov and the technician, Gritsayenko. Now I must talk to Chepelkin and Myasnikov. . . .'

Once we had treated Nikolay Korneyevich badly, and even now I am ashamed about this. Chukovsky had agreed with Pyotr Chepelkin that he should come and have a chat after his flight. But Pyotr and I heard unexpectedly that the film *Fighter Aircraft* was being shown, so when we had finished our flying duties, we ran to the cinema. We ran like hares, taking a circuitous route through the woods so that Nikolay Korneyevich did not see us. He waited for Chepelkin and was offended. A day or two later, he disappeared from the squadron. We were all worried, but soon it became clear that Chukovsky was working with the squadrons of attack fighters. He filled up a whole notebook there, then tried to persuade the Commanding Officer to take him on a raid in an attack aircraft as an air gunner. The writer assured him that he could use a machine-gun and was prepared to use it in action. Fortunately, Chukovsky was not granted permission to do this.

He returned to our dug-out in a bad mood. In order to dispel this gloom, that evening we all talked to him about aerial battles, about all kinds of amusing incidents in the lives of pilots. Then his usual good nature, amiable disposition and cheerful spirit returned.

Alyosha Baranovsky Attacks

In the second half of May 1942, our regiment flew to a base in the rear in order to receive new aircraft. Meanwhile, Myasnikov, Yefimov, Lvov, Sukhov and I remained behind. We had four aircraft between the five of us. I was still flying in the Squadron Commander's Yak. Sergey Makarov fitted new controls in this machine; the technicians repaired the holes in the wings and fuselage.

As soon as the airfields had dried out a little, we said goodbye to Ladoga and flew to a base near Leningrad. But our fighters were so worn out that all four aircraft were rarely flying together. To relieve us, a regiment arrived already armed with new Yaks. But the pilots in this unit were young. They had no experience in giving cover to Il 2 aircraft. Our friends in the attack aircraft asked us to help the young fighter pilots. So we, who were carrying out sorties, took charge of groups of pilots from the new regiment. Together with them, we accompanied the aircraft which delivered attacks on enemy ships, airfields and other important military targets. Sometimes I had to conduct aerial reconnaissance. Twice I photographed the port of Kotka.

Once, returning from a flight, I met, face to face, Zhenya Susanin, a former student from our Novgorod aeroclub. Tall, mature, a pilot of experience with the Order of the Red Banner on his chest, Susanin was not happy on this occasion. He brought me sad news: Alyosha Baranovsky had been killed.

'Zhenya, what are you saying? When?'

'On 11 February.'

Aleksey Baranovsky. . . . My cheerful student to whom I gave a start in flying in 1939. It was he and his comrade who had looked for me in Nizino. It seemed as if only the day before we three had been chatting in the armourer's tent. Fascist aircraft had then appeared above the aerodrome and interrupted our conversation. I asked Zhenya how Alyosha had died.

'Unfortunately, I wasn't on that flight,' said Susasin, 'but it was like this: On 11 February, an intelligence report stated that troop trains had accumulated at Shapki station, and that petrol wagons were standing among them. A group of Il 15 fighters with bombs were sent to this target immediately. Baranovsky flew with the group, but rockets for attacking ground targets were attached to his aircraft, not bombs. What happened then? Many troop trains in Shapki station were overturned by the explosion of bombs. A blockage was caused but there was no fire. Lyoshka probably decided that he had to attack the petrol wagons. He set fire to one of these with two rockets. Enveloped in flames, it let out a ribbon of black smoke in the wind. Meanwhile, Baranovsky had four rockets left. He made a sharp turn, went into a dive and caused another explosion and fire with two rockets. Flames spread to other troop trains. Considering the mission accomplished, the CO led the group on a return course. There was no radio communication between the aircraft, and Aleksey could not ask the lads to wait for him. Nevertheless, he decided to make yet another attack. By this time, Messerschmitts had appeared over Shapki, but Baranovsky still made a third attack. The rockets he released spread over the target. When he came out of the attack and gained height, he had nothing left with which to fight a whole gang of Fascist fighters. As soon as his comrades saw this, they immediately rushed to Alyosha's aid, but the Fascists had already set fire to his aircraft, Aleksey climbed out of his cockpit and, evidently from fear that he was too low to bale out, immediately pulled the rip-cord. The parachute caught the tail unit of the fighter. That was how Alyosha died.'

Many years have passed since then. Yevgeny Ivanovich Susanin, that brave fighter pilot, made 620 sorties over the Baltic in defence of Leningrad, and shot down eight Fascist aircraft in aerial combat. Now he is a lieutenant colonel in the reserve. Four Orders of the Red Banner, the Order of the Red Star and other medals decorate his chest. Yevgeny Ivanovich lives and works in our town of Novgorod. We often meet, recall the grim days of war and our front-line comrades. We remember Alyosha Baranovsky, our good friend and fellow countryman.

On The Way I Visit My Native Village

Our small group, which had seen much action in battered and patched fighters, now stopped fighting. The time had come to receive new aircraft. Having taken the three last repaired machines into the air, Yefimov, Lvov and I circled over the airfield and took a course to the east. The rest of our comrades had to fly out the next day in a transport plane. Having completed our last flight as a team, we landed on our rear base airfield. It was the first day of summer, calm and sunny. Not far from the base, the waters of a picturesque rivulet meandered their way. As soon as we had climbed from our cockpits and removed our flying helmets, we made for the river. We undressed on the bank and immediately plunged into the river. So began a new time in our lives.

Squadron headquarters was accommodated in a small country house. Capt N.V. Darmogray, our new Adjutant, arrived. Capt Yefimov was appointed squadron commissar instead of Isakovich, who was posted on a training course. Snigiryev, an excellent flight technician, was unanimously elected party organizer by the communists. Maj Nikitin became the regimental commander and Lt Col Kondratyev, the brigade commander.

One evening it was announced that soon we would go to learn to master the new aircraft. Unexpectedly, the Regimental Commander proposed that I should pay a visit to my family. (Vologda from our base was several hours' flight.) I was due to fly in the U 2 but it turned out to be unserviceable. Never mind! Elated with joy, I set off on the long journey by road and rail (to Cherepovyets by car and from there on by train). Early the next morning, I was at the threshold of my family home.

I shall never forget those first minutes. Oh, what a commotion began in the house! Well I never, how unexpected! Mother broke into tears. ('Alive, healthy . . . my dear son!') Father began to bustle about, woke Valya and Ninushka.

'Get up, look who's arrived!' He hurriedly wiped his glasses and began examining my tabs. 'You've become a captain already!' He shook his head with an air of importance. 'Mother, listen, Igor's a captain!'

Mother bustled about the table and I went into the bedroom.

'Valyusha, Ninochka, my darlings!' I cannot convey in words what joy there was. 'Well then, show yourself to daddy.' I took my little daughter in my arms.

'Three years have gone by already,' said my wife a little absentmindedly as she straightened my daughter's hair, which had fallen into her eyes.

'There, Nina, this is your daddy.'

Ninushka looked at me attentively, slid down from my arms on to the floor and, without taking her eyes off me, grasped her mother's skirt.

In the next room, the table had already been laid. Sister Nadya woke up, and Aunt Liza, our neighbour in the flat, arrived. For a start, as usual, we drank a glass each to celebrate the occasion and then we talked and talked. The samovar came to the boil; father brought it from the kitchen and placed it on the table. Mother, as she always did, tossed a lump of sugar into the samovar chimney. The characteristic savour of tea-drinking, familiar since childhood, filled the flat. Mother busied herself at the table. She cut dried, salted cod into slices and tipped them into a dish of boiling water. The fish scales stood up, the slices curled and softened – my favourite food. Oh, if only there were scrumptious potatoes as well! But even potatoes had now appeared on the table! Meanwhile, father poured us out a second glass. He sat opposite me and looked fixedly at my medals.

'This one on the left is the Order of Lenin. But the next one?'

'Next is the Order of the Red Banner.'

Looking at my father, my mother, at Valya and Ninushka, at everyone sitting at the table, I still could not believe that I was at home. One thought struck me: 'How great it is, after all, when a man has his own home, a place with his family and people dear to his heart.' Meanwhile, father brought my old accordion from the bedroom and wiped the dust from it with his sleeve.

'Well then, play, I'm sure you haven't forgotten how.' And I had hardly managed to start playing when he sang:

> There on the road is my native village,
> The coachman is taking me back there.

Our new Adjutant, Capt Darmogray, had a wife and a little boy, who had also been evacuated to Vologda. He set off to see his family after me. We met while we were there and enjoyed a wonderful leave. But the happier the days, the shorter they seemed. Soon the U 2 air-ambulance arrived. We bade farewell to our nearest and dearest and in a short time were already with our regiment. Here, waiting for us, were the new English fighters, Hawker Hurricanes.

First of all, the size of the Hurricane struck us. Both in length and wing span, it was almost half as big again as our Yak. Humpbacked, on long 'legs', it seemed rather strange. All the measurements in the cockpit and various other inscriptions were made in English. However, that didn't prevent us from quickly mastering the new aircraft. We began flying in it and soon completed the programme of re-learning.

Altitude was in feet, the speed in miles per hour, the petrol, not in litres, but in gallons. It was necessary to get used to all this, and this we did. However, in no way could we resign ourselves to the armament of the Hurricane. It had twelve wing-mounted machine-guns of rifle calibre – six in each wing. After our Soviet cannons and heavy calibre machine-guns, we considered this insufficient. Nor did we like the armour behind the pilot's seat. It consisted of two vertically placed 4 mm plastic sheets, one above the other – and this at a time of high velocity cannons and armour-piercing rockets.

'Why, you could pierce it with a walking stick,' said Sukhov, and we all agreed with him. Headquarters got to know about our dissatisfaction. We were ordered to fly immediately to Moscow in order to replace the armour and weapons on the Hurricanes.

So there she was, our capital city, built of white stone. We landed at an aerodrome with a concrete landing strip and without delay handed over our machines to the factory.

'In ten days,' said the factory representative, 'your orders will be carried out. But now, take a holiday and get to know Moscow.'

Once I had a room in an hotel, I applied to Myasnikov for permission to visit my brother. He was studying near Moscow in a school for lieutenants. It goes without saying that permission was granted. I hurried to the Ryazan station. After forty minutes' journey on the electric train, I saw the large wooden barracks, part of a military camp, picturesque in its greenery. I asked if the gunnery school for lieutenants was located there. Yes it is, came the reply. The head of the school, a tall amiable man, greeted me affably and asked me who I was and what was the purpose of my visit. He spoke well of my brother.

'He's older than you, I would say.'

'Yes, eight years older.'

'He's one of the most modest and well-educated students,' said the Captain. 'Although he's not just a student. Aleksandr Kaberov conducts work in topography and gunnery. I'll tell you in confidence: when he graduates, he will receive the rank of first lieutenant and will remain with us. We need good instructors.'

I thanked the Captain for his kind words and went out on to the street. As I waited for my brother (they had already called him to meet me), I wandered about the coal-slack covered surface of the road. Then I saw him. Dressed in a soldier's shirt of an unusual leaden colour, breeches, boots and puttees, with a rifle and greatcoat roll on his shoulders, Shura was running towards the headquarters building. As he passed me, he changed to a ceremonial step and, according to regulations, saluted before resuming his running pace. He didn't recognize me. Well, that wasn't surprising; the last time we had seen one another was in 1934.

'Shurka!' He stopped still where he was, then straightened his forage cap and turned towards me and stood as if at his post. 'Shurka, it's me, Igor!'

We rushed towards one another. My brother's eyes became moist. He looked at me with joy and disbelief. 'Can it really be you, Igor?'

'As you see!'

He touched my medal. 'You've been shooting down Fascist aircraft, haven't you? While I haven't even seen an aerial battle. For sure, that's really awful. Not in this world. . . .'

The conversation turned first to Leningrad, then to Vologda. I told Shura about my trip home and asked him if he had received letters from his wife. Just before the war, she and their four children had gone on holiday to their parents in the Caucasus. The war had found them in Ordzhonikidze; to move out and return was then impossible.

Shura and I called on the school's commanding officer to apply formally for a leave pass, and then travelled to Moscow. The new khaki dress uniform looked well on Shurka. That evening, we spent our time with my aircrew friends in the hotel. I introduced my brother to Sqn Cdr Myasnikov and the Commissar, Yefimov, who had recently been made Hero of the Soviet

Union. My brother's wide knowledge of events, his grasp of technical matters and his familiarity with questions of foreign policy impressed them. Our conversations continued long into the night.

In the morning, we went to see Moscow and directed our steps along streets and across squares to the exhibition of war trophies in the Central Park of Culture and Rest. From the exhibition, we made for the circus and from there to the cinema. Late in the evening, I accompanied my brother to his military school.

'Shurka, what if, after your final examinations, they keep you in the school on the teaching staff? Could that be?' I asked.

My brother was silent, turning over something in his mind. 'No, Igor,' he answered at last. 'That wouldn't suit me. In Vologda, I wrote four reports, constantly trying to get them to send me to the front; but they posted me to this school. Now I intend to achieve my objective.'

'Think it over well,' I said cautiously. 'Here is where you are needed most, rather than there in the battlefield.'

'I've already thought it over.' Shurka started to get excited. 'You must understand. Our father went to war. Yurka fought and was killed on the Karelian Isthmus. Even Boris played his part in the Finnish campaign! Now, even you are fighting. But I, it seems, am some kind of select person. I have received a higher education and military training. Does it now follow that I am to sit it out in the rear?'

'I think it's not like that. The students in the school need your expert knowledge. Badly trained commanders die in the war – well-trained ones are victorious. That could be your victory.'

I could not make him change his mind. I returned to the Ryazan station by the last electric train and it was very late at night before I reached the hotel.

No, Shura did not heed my advice. Later, I learned that he did not want to remain at the school. In the battle for Oryol, commanding a company, my brother was severely wounded. When he recovered (he lay in one of the Tula hospitals) Shura went to the front again. In the battle for Ternopol, he was killed when the company he was leading was surrounded. Neither then in Moscow nor later did I have occasion to see my brother again.

The day when we left the capital remains clear in my memory. I switched on the aircraft engine and waited for it to warm up. At that moment, a motor vehicle drove up and a man dressed in a leather jacket with a zip-fastener got out.

'Whose aircraft is this?'

'Mine,' I replied and thought: 'There's something familiar about this man's face.'

'I am Kokkinaki,[10] the test pilot,' he said by way of introduction. 'Is it possible for me to take your fighter up so that I can see what English technology is like?'

'You may, of course,' I replied.

Kokkinaki asked me a few technical questions, climbed into the cockpit and took off. The flight took a little time, and when he had taken the Hurricane through a series of aerobatics, Vladimir Konstaninovich brought the machine in to land.

'Thank you,' he said, climbing out of the cockpit. 'Of course, it's not a Yak, but with types of cannon that have now been fitted into the Hurricane, I think it's possible to use it in aerial combat.' Kokkinaki said goodbye and drove away.

After an hour, our group of ten aircraft completed a farewell circuit above Moscow and took a course to our own airfield. Mountains of fantastic cumulus clouds floated majestically past the rocking Hurricanes.

'"Haritosha" flies straight, then bows and bows again,' said Kostilyev about the English fighter.

And actually, it was just like that. One characteristic of the construction was that in calm level flight the aircraft would first dip, then raise its nose. That's how it flew, bowing as it did.

Beneath the widely spread wings of the machine, the Volga and the town of Kazan could be seen. Did not these wings soar above the Thames and London? I thought. Moreover, I thought that the name 'Hurricane' hardly matched the technical qualities of the machine. The armament on it was now good – two 20 mm cannons and two heavy calibre machine-guns. One burst and pieces would fly off any aircraft. The armour plating (taken from our LaGG) was fine. Such protection was like a stone wall. The horizon indicator was also a wonderful instrument. It was easy to fly in the clouds with it. The radio worked magnificently, like a domestic telephone: neither noise nor crackle. But the speed, the speed. . . . No, this aircraft was far from being a hurricane. It was slow to gain height and was not good in a dive. As for vertical manoeuvrability – not good at all!

Yefimov, our Commissar, got it right: 'The aircraft is fine; it's metal, so it won't catch fire. You can shoot from it. But instead of manoeuvrability and speed – you'll have to use your Russian wits!'

CHAPTER NINE

Hurricanes Over Lake Ladoga

A 'Seagull' Flew Over The Gulf

One other pleasant surprise awaited me during our short stay at base camp in the rear. On 10 August, the morning had been spent preparing our machines for the flight and packing our things. I also placed my bayan in the aircraft. We were sitting and waiting for permission to take off; but permission was not given. Then after lunch, a car stopped under the windows of the headquarters building. I looked out of the window and saw that my wife was sitting in the back. I ran out.

'Valya!'

'Igor! How wonderful! I've found you after all!'

'But how did you get here?'

'Very simply. By train from Vologda. And from Pestovo your driver brought me here.' Happy, joyful, she jumped down on to the ground, brushed the dust from her dress and tossed away a lock of hair, which had fallen over her eyes. 'Hi! Aren't you going to say hallo to me?'

We went into the building. Valya greeted Yefimov, Kostilyev and Sukhov like old friends. Then she met Chepelkin and Lvov, whom she had known formerly.

The CO came out of his room. 'Is this your wife?' he asked me. 'I'm pleased to meet you.' He introduced himself courteously to Valya and kissed her hand.

'Why, everyone's got medals!' said my wife in astonishment. 'What fine fellows you are! But it's not very comfortable for you here. And not a single flower in the place.' There was a field nearby, so Valya and I went for flowers and picked a whole bouquet of daisies and forget-me-nots. My wife quickly brought order into the room. The flowers, which were placed on the table, gave a cosy atmosphere to the bachelor quarters.

We flew out the next day, my wife accompanying us to the airfield. She climbed on to the wing and I, sitting in the cockpit, showed her the aircraft's controls.

'Well, what a lot of instruments,' Valya was looking round the cockpit. 'It's not a U 2 for sure!'

Then I had a conversation over the radio with Chepelkin. 'Where's Valya?' he asked.

'Here with me.'

'Valyusha!' Petro shouted. I removed my flying helmet so that my wife could hear. 'Valyusha,' Chepelkin carried on. 'Regards to you from the whole regiment of guards. Give your little daughter a kiss. Wait for us until victory is ours.'

'I wish you all good luck!' Valya shouted into the headphones. I passed on her words to Chepelkin over the radio. The rocket went up and we started up our engines. 'Igorek!' shouted Valya in haste. 'Don't worry about us. Write, we'll be waiting impatiently for your letters.' She kissed me and jumped down from the wing.

We took off, circled the airfield and gathered together in formation. My wife was wearing a light coloured dress and for some time I could see her on the ground. Then she became a small white spot and finally completely vanished from view.

'Goodbye, dear. We'll meet again sometime.' Our formation passed over Tikhvin, Novaya Ladoga and Leningrad, crossed over the Finnish Gulf and landed at a small airstrip, surrounded on all sides by forest. This was our new airfield.

By the next day we had already started our military duties. We had been forewarned by headquarters staff that Finnish fighters, as never before, were becoming active. They were patrolling in large groups over the Finnish Gulf and frequently engaging in fights with our aircraft. There were times when the enemy pilots were flying in Chaykas (Seagulls) with our identification marks.

'Well, what disgraceful conduct!' said Kostilyev (that day he and I had been on patrol together). 'First in our SB bombers, and now in Chaykas.'

I was sitting in my cockpit and felt drowsiness stealing up on me. I closed my eyes for a moment and heard the alarmed voice of the technician. 'Comrade Commander, the rocket! Take off!'

I started the engine and was only just in time to follow Yegor. Orders had been received to follow a course to Kronstadt. Only after about ten minutes did some kind of aircraft appear from the Teriok region. It was moving at low level straight towards Kronstadt.

'Yegor,' I shouted at Kostilyev. 'Look, just above the water. I think it's a Chayka coming from the direction of Finland.' Kostilyev lost height with the speed of lightning. I followed him. Now we could already see the Chayka more clearly.

'It's disguising itself with star markings,' shouted Yegor and went in to attack.

The aircraft which was flying above the water turned towards the aerodrome where the 4th Guards Regiment in our brigade was based. We stayed with the Chayka and Kostilyev opened fire. It turned over. I also gave a burst. The machine fell just beside the airfield.

'It's good that we've succeeded,' shouted Yegor, 'or else it would have done its worst!'

We gained height and in ten minutes were patrolling over the Gulf until we received the command to land. When we landed, Yegor reported to Myasnikov.

'Comrade Commander, we've carried out our mission.'

Myasnikov stood with his back to us. Yegor took off his flying helmet and muttering wearily hung it on a nail.

'We discovered a Finnish Chayka,' he said, 'but . . . .'

'Say no more!' interrupted Myasnikov. 'I know what you shot down. But do you know whom you shot down?' We looked at one another in bewilderment. The CO stood as before facing the dull window in the dug-out.

'You can say you have opened the score.'

'Comrade Commander,' I spoke, 'we noticed the Chayka almost next to Teriok. It was making a course for Kronstadt. What mistake did we make?'

'What mistake? You shot down the commanding officer of the 4th Regiment, Lt Col Biskup.'

I started to tremble. Kostilyev seemed to turn to stone. We knew Biskup well. How could this have happened? The telephone rang. The Major lifted the receiver.

'So, that's clear. . . . Unharmed? I understand you. . . . But the aircraft? . . . In pieces. . . .'

Without replacing the receiver, Myasnikov looked at us. His expression brightened somewhat. He attempted a smile but there and then became serious again. 'So, I understand. . . . Was he flying around after the repair? But why did he go towards Teriok? Oh, he decided to make a trip. . . . So, that's clear. . . . Aye-aye, Comrade Colonel, thrash them both for vigilance!' The CO hung up the receiver.

Throughout that day, we all carried around the thought of what had happened. I must admit that even at night the thought of Biskup and his Chayka gave me no peace.

Next morning, the pilots gathered for a smoke on the green mound which served as a roof over the regimental command post. Maj Kutsov, the Headquarters Commander, came out of the dug-out.

'Trofim Petrovich, have you phoned the 4th Regiment?' Yefimov asked him. 'How is your colleague there feeling?'

'I rang,' answered Kutsov, unhurriedly, squinting in the sunshine. 'He's recovered a little. He asked that Kostilyev and Kaberov should not be punished. He said that he himself was at fault. He thinks that they acted correctly.' Well, Biskup we knew as a generous man. He could not have said other than that. But we also understood that we had acted hastily. But what's done is done!

Maj Kutsov threatened me with his finger. 'Look here, don't shoot down any more of ours!'

At that moment, the telephone rang in the command post and the Commander went down to answer. In a minute, it became known that Yefimov, Sukhov, Lvov and Chepelkin were about to take off. There were Stormoviks on our airfield. Their crew members were old friends of ours. Their machines, heavily loaded with bombs, flew away into the sky and with them Yefimov's group took off. Their aim was to deliver a blow to the enemy's shipping, but for some reason they were unable to find any ships. On the return journey, seven Finnish 'Capronis' tried to attack the Stormoviks. Yefimov's group engaged them in a fight. Our four, with Yegor Kostilyev leading them, flew to help them when the alarm was given. At first, when this happened, there was a misunderstanding. A pilot, Borisov, hurriedly climbed into my machine and took off. Like it or not, I had to fly in his fighter.

We met the Stormoviks over the gulf. There were no fighters with them. We received a command over the radio: 'Hurry to help Yefimov!' We quickly gained height but the enemy fighters had already flown away to their airfield. We could see only three aircraft in Yefimov's group. Where then was the fourth? We returned home and heard that Chepelkin had been killed. His fighter had been shot down.

It had been a difficult day. To crown it all, Borisov again damaged my aircraft. Coming in from patrol, for no reason he started to land in the direction of the landing mark. The aircraft rolled over the edge of the airfield's working area, unexpectedly flew into an anti-aircraft gun, nosed over and of course was damaged. The pilot, who had been lucky in similar accidents, climbed from the cockpit unharmed. It so happened that previously Borisov had crashed two of my aircraft; now he had crashed a third.

Incidentally, this man was no novice in our field. Before the war, he flew civil aircraft, then learnt to be a fighter pilot. But, as we were now convinced, he lacked the speed of reaction, so necessary for a pilot. What's more, he lacked training. Borisov was not particularly worried about improving his fighting skills and as a result, during his eight-month stay at the unit, he didn't shoot down a single enemy aircraft. It became obvious that he would never make a fighter pilot, and he was transferred from the regiment.

We continued to give cover to the Stormoviks. I remember one such flight. It was on 16 August 1942. Eleven Ilyushin 2s and eight Hurricanes attacked four enemy ships in the area near the islands of Seyskari and Lavansari. The Fascist naval transports were sailing across the gulf to Finland.

Hero of the Soviet Union Anton Andreyevich Karasyev, who until recently had been a metal worker in the Kirov factory, led the group of Stormoviks. Anton Karasyev was the first to release his bomb load on to the leading enemy ship. It exploded and the ship vanished beneath the waves in a flash. The next minute, a second transport burst into flames. It burned so fiercely that the crew could not extinguish the fire. The third transport sank by the stern and the port side, raising its bow high above the water. The crew of the fourth ship launched the lifeboats.

Our group of aircraft were approaching the island of Seyskari when, from the left, eight Capronis and two Me 109s appeared. We were put on our guard but they passed by on course for the sunken ships.

Messerschmitts And Junkers Burn

The next morning, we flew across to the area for refuelling, with the Stormoviks, and then took course for distant Lakhdenpokhya on the northern shore of Lake Ladoga. A lateral wind chased the waves across the lake: the shores could not be seen. The Stormoviks flew ahead and beneath us, skimming the water. According to intelligence reports, the enemy had built some kind of barge-like landing craft at Lakhdenpokhya. Valaam Island was already behind us. Approaching the shore, we could see the target. The Stormoviks gained height and went into the attack. I wanted to see more clearly what was beyond the barges, but we weren't able to do this. Above the four of us (Myasnikov, Lvov, Kostilyev and me) six Fokkers launched an attack. Terekhin and Ribin were somewhere below, guarding the Stormoviks. In the meantime, they had already set fire to something on the shore. The wind disturbed the smoke and things could be seen dimly in the background. The fire raged into the air. A Fokker fell, enveloped in flames; first one, then another. The enemy fighters fought stubbornly. They were close to their base, whereas we had to make our way home for almost 200 kilometres, about 170 of them over the water and along the shore captured by the enemy.

What was the score then? Having shot down two enemy fighters, we returned home without loss. Col Dzyuba, deputy commander of the air force, conducted an analysis of our combined operation with the Stormoviks. He looked once more at the photographs taken from over Lakhdenpokhya and informed us that the enemy were obviously building barges for a landing operation on Ladoga.

'Naval staff are worried about this,' said the Colonel. 'Tomorrow, at first light, you will have to make a second flight.' However, the circumstances changed and, as well as the Stormoviks, we changed stations.

As usual, our new airfield was not very level. We all landed safely. Only 1/Lt Yevgeny Teplov's fighter damaged a propeller blade when one wheel ran into a hole while taxiing. His annoyance increased when the pilots of the Stormoviks were informed that they were to prepare to deliver a blow against the enemy in the region of Nyevskaya Dubrovka. We were all heartened by this news, but Zhenya Teplov stood beside his aircraft in anguish and looked at the broken end of the propeller blade.

Engineer Sergeyev came up to him. 'Bring a saw,' he said to the technician.

'What kind?'

'An ordinary wood saw.'

He used the saw himself to trim the damaged blade and then cut off an equal amount from the two whole blades and ordered the technician to finish off the ends. In about forty minutes, the propeller was repaired. Sergeyev tested it by starting the engine.

'Not bad, it'll pull!' The engineer smiled. 'And you, Comrade Teplov,' he turned to the pilot, 'must remember that we have here foreign engineering. It likes delicate treatment, you understand. You aren't in our aircraft.'

When he had examined the propeller again, Sergeyev shook his head. 'A wooden propeller on a fighter! These old westerners have much to learn!'

But once again we were in the air. Zhenya Teplov was flying next to me. The blades of the propeller on his Hurricane had been shortened, but Zhenya did not lose speed. We approached the Neva and saw many of our aircraft. Stormoviks and bombers were there. So many bombs were dropped on enemy positions that it seemed that all the earth must have been turned over. During all this there had been no opposition. True, the anti-aircraft guns had been firing ceaselessly, but where were the Fascist aircraft? Hardly had this thought crossed my mind when out of the sun four Messerschmitts attacked us. Immediately a battle began, but we carried out the task which faced us and allowed no enemy fighters to reach our attack aircraft.

Another group of Hurricanes took off from a different airfield at this time. They escorted Pe 2 bombers which had to bomb enemy fortifications. There was a battle with Messerschmitts over these positions. In the battle, Capt E.P. Ribin, a brave and experienced airman, was tragically killed. The controls of the elevator on his aircraft were damaged and it fell out of the sky, leaving Ribin no alternative but to bale out. As he left the aircraft, he struck his head on the tail unit and lost consciousness. His parachute did not open. . . .

For two days the rain poured. When it stopped, a tiny little UT 1 aircraft landed on our airfield. Col Dzyuba climbed out of it. When he had gathered everyone together, both attack aircraft and fighter pilots, he showed us photographs obtained that morning by aerial reconnaissance. An hour later, eleven Il 2 attack aircraft and eight Hurricanes took off and again made course for Lakhdenpokhya. Capt Kostilyev led the group of fighters. I was his second in command. Kosorukov, Khamyetov, Yevgrafov, Chernyenko, Buryak and Terekhin flew with us. We flew over the lake again, for the time being trying not to attract the attention of the enemy.

The districts of Lakhdenpokhya and Keksgolm were defended by fighters, but we flew confidently towards the target. The island of Valaam was already behind us. We saw Lakhdenpokhya; on the shore were new barges and planed timbers. Attack aircraft turned and started to dive on the target. Bomb explosions shook the settlement. Fire broke out just as on the first attack. Clouds of smoke covered the shore.

Having delivered the attack, the bombers turned for home. Keeping close to the water, they flew further and further away; but over the island of

Konyevits an ambush awaited us. Hardly had we caught up with them than six Capronis dived on us from above. The enemy fighters confidently engaged in battle, but in only five minutes three enemy machines were enveloped in flames and crashed to the ground. In the confusion of battle, one Caproni broke through to our attack aircraft. However, Khanyafi Khamyetov, who was in the group of escorts, rushed to intercept but himself came under enemy fire. We didn't know what had taken place but heard Khamyetov's voice:

'Lads, help! I'm caught in an attack.'

'Kaberov!'

It was Yegor ordering me to support Khanyafi. I dropped like a stone to give help. I saw how the Hurricane was circling just above the water. The enemy fighter on his tail, not noticing me, was banging away at him. I caught up with the Caproni and found him in my sights. Fire! The enemy machine heeled over sharply, described a circle and, striking its port wing on the water, broke into pieces.

'That's it, Khanyafi!' I shouted. 'Make for home. He'll trouble you no more.'

The ailerons on Khamyetov's machine had jammed. It was turning to the left and Khanyafi could not control it. I helped him with some advice, protected him from enemy fighters and led him home. The Ilyushins flew away from us, further to the south; the Hurricanes accompanied them. Only Khamyetov and I flew quietly above the stormy lake.

Would Khamyetov reach the airfield? On my advice, he reduced speed and used both feet to hold the right pedal of the rudder. If only there were never engine failures! If only the pilot had the strength! Far ahead there were still almost 80 kilometres across the lake.

But Khamyetov held on. In the region of Morin Nos, we crossed the shore. After 15 kilometres' flight over land, Khanyafi's engine reduced speed sharply. Then it lost all power and finally Khamyetov successfully crash-landed in a small clearing. He leaped from his cockpit and waved to me. I circled above him and, having fixed his position, flew home. Soon, technicians brought Khamyetov's aircraft to the airfield.

To this day, I keep a photo of a poster on which is pictured one of the moments in an aerial battle between our fighters and the enemy Capronis. In the upper right-hand corner of the poster the artist has painted portraits of all our pilots who took part in this battle. Reproductions were given to us by the air force. Also I keep a photo of Khamyetov. On the back he has written: 'To my life saver and good friend, I. Kaberov. From Khanyafi.'

Next our home was the Oranienbaum bridgehead. The Germans were not far from there, but in that sector of the front it still remained quiet. On 30 August, Col Dzyuba's little UT 1 aircraft flew in. Five Stormoviks followed him and, a little later, seven Kittyhawks landed on the airfield. Cheerful young lads, with guards' badges on their uniforms, climbed from their cockpits.

'Where are you guards heading?' we enquired.

'We want to set somebody alight,' a tall blond sergeant answered cheerfully.

'Are you taking us, or will you fly by yourselves?'

'We've flown in to help you,' he said, neither in jest nor seriously.

We exchanged glances. So army pilots had arrived to help us. And Col Dzyuba was there. That meant there was to be some kind of interesting operation. Soon, all of us (the army pilots, too) were ordered to assemble in one place.

'Ahead of us,' Dzyuba waved a pointer at the map, then at a large photo, 'is Gorodyets airfield. It is situated 25 kilometres south of Luga. As you see, there are Ju 88s on the airfield. They are refuelling. The photo was taken two hours ago. Evidently, the bombers recently flew in from somewhere. Your task is to destroy them on the airfield. At its northern end, twenty-five Me 109 fighters can be counted. Follow my orders – then they won't take off. From our airfield, make for Samro Lake, then to Gorodyets. In the area shaded red,' Col Dzyuba again raised his pointer, 'are partisans. In the event of a forced landing, come down here. . . .'

Having defined the duties of the leading group, Dzyuba gave the command, 'Go to it!' Eight Il 2 Stormoviks, eighteen Hurricanes, seven Kittyhawk fighters and one Pe 2 aircraft taking photographs rose into the air. Fifteen of the Hurricanes were armed with rockets. Cameras had been fitted in two of the fighters (Maj Myasnikov's and mine), in order to take pictures.

We crossed the front line. The railway was beneath us. To the left was Volosovo. Beneath my wings lay Bolshaya Vruda where, on 10 August 1941, I had to land. I remembered that good Russian woman, Zinaida Mikhailovna Petrova, and said to myself, as if addressing her: 'Are you still with us, you who gave me shelter when I needed it? Dear Zinaida Mikhailovna, when Victory Day comes, put on the samovar. We'll meet again, sit down to tea and remember the past.'

While I was talking to myself with Zinaida Mikhailovna, we had passed over the Samro Lake and were approaching Gorodyets: there was the Fascist airfield. Everything as we had seen in the photograph; Junkers aircraft stood in three rows, and next to them petrol tankers. The Stormoviks immediately went into the attack, followed by the Hurricanes. Bombs and rockets exploded. The dispersal area was enveloped in flames. Again and again, our aircraft passed over it. One after another, the enemy machines burst into flames.

'Take that for Nizino! That for Bolshaya Vruda! That for Leningrad!' I shouted. Four Messerschmitts tried to taxi out for take-off. Two Hurricanes brought down a squall of fire on them. Pilots leaped from their cockpits, ran across the airfield, fell and lay motionless.

The sparse anti-aircraft fire did not trouble us. Once they had completed the task they had begun, the Stormoviks, Hurricanes, the Pe 2 aircraft (which had been taking photographs) and the Kittyhawks flew home.

Aleksandr Fyodorovich and I also photographed the burning airfield. As the cameras clicked, I heard Myasnikov's voice:

'Shall we give it to them?'

The CO questioningly glanced at me from his cockpit. I nodded. He turned his fighter and went into a dive. We passed over the northern perimeter of the airfield and fired at the fighters in dispersal with all our machine-guns and cannons. Another two enemy aircraft burst into flames. A large group of Germans, who had gathered together, fled in panic. Yet again we placed them under fire, then, at full speed, chased after our comrades.

Back home, we learned that, at the same time as the attack on Gorodyets airfield, there had been an attack on Siverskaya, where enemy fighters had been assembled. That was why we had not been intercepted. Without losing a single aircraft, we destroyed seventeen Ju 88 bombers and two Messerschmitts. That number includes only those that were burned or broken to pieces by bombs and rockets. But there were also damaged aircraft, possibly even rendered permanently unserviceable.

'Captain, Captain, Smile!'

Battles, battles! Our aircraft became fewer in number and the regimental commander formed combined groups from the pilots in various squadrons. On the morning of 2 September, eight of our Hurricanes were ordered to take off in order to give protection to our troops in the region of Krasniy Bor: Commissar Yefimov led this eight, and a second group of eight led by Lvov (I was one of the group) was ordered to be ready for action.

On the way to his aircraft, Semyon Lvov stopped for a moment beside mine. I could see that something disturbed him.

'They've called out eight on alert,' said Semyon, looking at the sky. 'What do you think? Why should they do this?'

'Difficult to say. Maybe the Fascists are sending their Junkers against our infantry.'

'But in my opinion, the enemy has decided to give battle in the air beyond Gorodyets,' Semyon thought aloud to himself. 'If we take off, let's climb to 3,000 metres. And it's most important that nobody breaks away from the group.'

I agreed with Lvov, but one question still bothered me. 'Tell me, Semyon, how do you understand what Yefimov said at the party meeting? He reckons that the landing craft at Lakhdenpokhya and the build-up of bombers outside Leningrad are part of the same plan.'

'I don't know,' Semyon shrugged his shoulders, 'but generally speaking it is difficult to refute the Commissar's logic. In fact, there is some kind of connection. True, Yegor thinks that they are fishing barges.'

'Yegor's not right. I was talking about it with him yesterday. Fishermen don't need such enormous barges. Moreover, their shape is wrong. And then tell me, Semyon: where have you seen a fisherman building a boat beneath the protection of anti-aircraft guns? As you know, ack-ack shells burst over Lakhdenpokhya.'

'Well, this is what I think,' said Lvov. 'The Germans are in Kirishi and the Finns are on the River Svir. Between them are some 120 kilometres. Are they not thinking of surrounding Leningrad again with a second encircling blockade? Are they not preparing for a combined offensive?'

Semyon went away to his aircraft and I sat in mine. I sat and thought: can a Hurricane stand up to a fight against an Me 109? The Hurricane is not an LaGG 3 and of course not a Yak 1 as Kokkinaki said. With Fiats, Fokkers and Capronis it was easy. But the Messerschmitt . . . . True, we were old hands, and had mastered the skill of flying Hurricanes quite well. But we still had not had real fights in Hurricanes with Messerschmitts.

Duk was standing next to the dug-out when from behind the forest, three Hurricanes appeared flying at low level. They immediately came in to land. Zhenya looked at them anxiously, then at me:

'But where are the rest?'

Yefimov jumped out of his machine and ran to mine. Meanwhile, a rocket shot through the air. It was the signal to take off. We switched on our engines.

'What news, Andreyich?' I asked the Commissar, who had climbed on to the wing of my Hurricane.

'Igor, evidently things will be difficult. Keep your head screwed on.' He wanted to say something else, but I had already increased engine speed. I had to hurry after Lvov. Yefimov jumped from the wing and waved to me. Lvov led us over the territory held by the Fascists towards Krasniy Bor.

A melancholy feeling swept over me. Could this be fear? No, no, I must dismiss it. Next to me, flying his fighter, was the young pilot Chernyenko. It was particularly difficult for him but he gave no sign of it. I saw how Vasiliy Ivanovich (we had already come to like this cheerful lad who was fearless in battle and, for some reason, sometimes called him by his forename and patronymic) turned his head and attentively looked from side to side. I started to feel uncomfortable beside him. 'Now then, Capt Kaberov,' I said to myself. 'Attack this feeling! If that's how it is, I mustn't hang my head. Well then, sing!' And at the top of my voice, I tried to shout above the noise of the engine:

> Captain, captain, smile!
> A smile, like a flag, is worth while.
> Captain, captain, smarten up,
> Only the brave . . . .

'Prepare for battle!' Lvov's powerful command interrupted this inappropriate concert. 'Junkers from the right!'

'Messerschmitts on our tails!' someone added.

I counted fifteen Ju 87s and ten Me 109s. We didn't approach the Junkers. The Messerschmitts repeatedly attacked. Usichenko and Teplov (he was still flying the fighter with shortened propeller blades) needed to leave the fight: their machines were damaged. There were still six of us. Just the same, Rudyenko managed to break through to the Junkers and destroy one of them. The bombers flew away and we fought with the Messerschmitts. Lvov, Chernyenko and I each shot down one enemy fighter. The battle went on for fifty minutes. The number of Messerschmitts did not decrease but increased. In the end, a group of army fighters came to our aid. We had run out of fuel. Looking at our fuel gauges, we took course for our airfield. Now it became clear that Lvov's and Chernyenko's aircraft were damaged.

We had caused losses to the enemy and lost no one from our own group. Of course, that was fine and we felt much better. But in my heart, I still felt some resentment at my momentary weakness at the start of the flight. It seems that man is so made that sometimes he experiences fear. It is so important that he should find the strength within himself to suppress this feeling.

Only when we returned home after the battle did we find out that the pilots in Yefimov's group of eight machines had been fighting twenty-six Me 109s for a whole hour. Yefimov's group shot down four Me 109s. In all we destroyed eight enemy machines.

The next day, the weather sharply deteriorated. The technicians carried out repairs on the aircraft and we, under the leadership of Lt Col Nikitin, discussed how we performed in battle, analysed our mistakes and successes and the qualities of the Hurricane. In the end, everyone agreed that this machine was certainly no 'hurricane', in spite of its name. However, it was possible to fight Me 109s in it. And with Junkers, even more so. The cannons made a lot of difference! In a fight with a Messerschmitt, I scored with them – it decided the outcome of the battle.

After lunch, we heard that M.R. Golod, an instructor from the political department, had arrived. Chatting with us, he talked for the most part about Leningrad, about the fact that the townsfolk were stoically enduring the difficulties of the blockade; that every one of them was heroically working at his task. There was competition to improve production for the front. Theatres were preparing new plays. The composer Shostakovich had dedicated his Seventh Symphony to the defence of the stronghold on the Neva. Our naval men of letters, Vishnyevsky, Azarov and Kron had written a play, *The Sea Stretched Far and Wide*. It will be staged in the Theatre of Musical Comedy.

Vsyevolod Azarov was with our unit many times and wrote poetry and articles about us. It was he who, after the war in 1963, made me take up my pen when he said, as Vishnyevsky once did: 'You see, things will go well for you. . . .'

But, once again it seems, I have digressed. Returning to our front-line working life, to the chat with instructor Mikhail Romanovich Golod from the political department, I remember, after his mention of the play by

Vishnyevsky, Azarov and Kron, Yegor Kostilyev, who loved a joke, said: 'What then are we to do? We cannot write a play, nor a symphony. So, on the side of our aircraft, let's scribble something that will make the Fascists' flesh creep. That we'll do!'

On that very day, Kostilyev inscribed the words 'For Rus'!' on the port side of his aircraft. At the suggestion of technician Tarakanov, we wrote 'For Leningrad!' on our Hurricane. At that moment, Sergey Sukhov came up to us.

'Not bad, but not very good either,' he said. 'It's too ordinary and expresses little. That won't make the Fascists' flesh creep. It must be simpler and more expressive.'

In the morning, when Sergey returned from a flight, I heard the technicians laughing at dispersal.

'Look what Sukhov's done!'

'Well, well . . . !'

Only then did we all see the bold inscription on the fuselage of Sergey's machine: 'Shoot the —— bourgeoisie!'

Of course, I do not present this inscription verbatim. Sergey included a word, describing the bourgeoisie, so caustic that it would have been hard to find one stronger. The laughter at dispersal took long to subside. Meanwhile Sukhov climbed out of his cockpit to meet Yefimov who was approaching.

'What's up with them, Commissar? They've found something to laugh at! Yet the Fascist reacted to the notice rather differently. As I saw it – straight into a spin. True, the cannons did help. . . .'

Yefimov himself, laughing till tears ran down his cheeks, wiped his eyes with a handkerchief and ordered the technician, Kudryavtsev, to paint over the strong word on the fuselage of Sukhov's Hurricane.

Soon we learnt that troops on the Volkhov front had started to advance. Aerial battles shifted to the Shlisselburg area, and we had to move our base again to the Karelian Isthmus. These were the heaviest battles. I shall never forget the first flight.

Our group of six had hardly reached the front line when sixteen Me 109 fighters attacked us. Meanwhile, above the positions of our land forces, Junkers appeared. Myasnikov and I broke through to them and I, at first burst of gunfire, destroyed a Ju 88. Without the close support of the CO, this could have cost me my life. Myasnikov succeeded in turning about to bring down an enemy fighter which dived at me. The Fascists were enraged. They succeeded in dividing us into two groups and set fire to Yevgeny Teplov's machine. Enveloped in flames, the Hurricane started to fall.

'Zhenka, jump!' shouted someone over the radio. But Zhenya evidently didn't have the strength to use his parachute.

Eventually, we succeeded in uniting in a single group. Before long, the Fascist vultures hit Commissar Kosorukov's aircraft from No. 1 Squadron. The CO ordered me to give him cover until he landed. I succeeded in breaking loose from the battle and caught up with Kosorukov.

'Lower the undercarriage! The undercarriage, the undercarriage – lower it!'

To this command, Nikolay Mikhailovich did not respond. Then I told him to switch off the engine and glide because the landing strip was nearby. But Kosorukov's machine reared, turned over, went into a spin and struck the ground. So died Nikolay Mikhailovich Kosorukov, a remarkable pilot, commissar and a most understanding person.

We returned to our airfield, depressed by the death of our friends and completely exhausted. I remember that I could hardly climb out of the cockpit. Every cell in my body ached. It seemed impossible to move my neck. But I was not allowed to rest. The engine fitters refuelled the aircraft, a signal rocket was fired and once again we took off into a smoke-filled sky where a no less dangerous battle awaited us.

The Fascist command threw against our forces in the region of Sinyavin more new regiments and divisions, taking them from other sections of the front in order to hold their position near Leningrad at any cost. Since the time that our regiment had taken delivery of the Hurricanes, we had destroyed in aerial battle twenty-nine Fascist aircraft, losing during that time five of our own.

The Fascist fighter Me 109 (F) was faster than the Hurricane by almost 100 kilometres per hour; and whoever had the speed could command height. Altitude guaranteed everything: both freedom to choose the target and the camouflage afforded by attacking out of the sun; also suddenness and speed of attack. But neither these advantages nor numerical superiority could save the enemy's aviators from loss. Soviet pilots and Soviet cannons could certainly strike down an opponent.

A Word About The CO

In 1936, a group of Soviet aviators arrived in Spain in order to defend the young republic. Among them were two extremely young pilots – Nikitin and Bagrov. One day at lunch time, Fascist fighters – a Messerschmitt and a Fiat – appeared over the airfield where their aircraft were standing. In a matter of minutes, Nikitin and Bagrov had taken off. The fight did not take long. Nikitin set fire to the Messerschmitt with a well-aimed burst of fire. Bagrov shot down the Fiat.

For heroism and bravery displayed in battle at that time, Nikolay Mikhailovich Nikitin was awarded the Order of the Red Banner. He received another such order after the Soviet–Finnish military conflict. Nikitin entered the Second World War a battle-hardened pilot. His country recognized his heroic deeds in those years by awarding him the Order of Lenin, a third Order of the Red Banner and the Order of the Red Star.

At the height of the tense fighting on the southern shore of the Neva, Lt Col Nikolay Mikhailovitch suddenly gave the order for a meeting of all pilots. We were puzzled. But the CO knew what he was doing. He conducted a strict and instructive analysis of the mistakes we admitted to have made in battle.

'Yes, we are in some ways at a disadvantage, but we don't count numbers when we fight,' said Nikitin. 'The manoeuvrability of our machine is weak but our cannons are powerful. And we have no right to make mistakes. Pilots, like mine-laying sappers, make only one mistake. But now for take-off. I shall lead the group. My second in command,' the CO turned to me, 'will be Capt Kaberov.'

Our group of eight in that battle came into conflict with twenty of the enemy's fighters. They were flying in a two-tier formation: Messerschmitts below, Focke-Wulfs above them. Attacks followed one after another. The enemy used his advantage of altitude and numerical superiority, but Nikitin knew how to conduct the battle and soon set fire to the first Messerschmitt. A second followed the first to the ground. However, the Fascist fighters managed to separate our leading pair from the other six aircraft. The CO and I were in a difficult position. He placed Capt Yefimov in charge of the six Hurricanes and said to me over the radio: 'Hold tight, come what may, we won't perish!'

So we held on. The CO's damaged engine was smoking and Nikolay Mikhailovich, like it or not, had to leave the fight. I repulsed several further sudden attacks by Messerschmitts and conducted the CO out of the danger zone. Only with difficulty did he reach the perimeter of the airfield and land successfully.

Soon all of our group returned to the airfield. We were pleased with the score, having shot down three enemy fighters while losing only one of our own. After this, I often flew paired with Nikolay Mikhailovich Nikitin.

'Now we'll have a go at them, come what may!' he would say, getting himself into a fighting mood as he prepared for another fight with enemy fighters.

The lads jokingly used to call him 'Come what may'. The CO took no offence. At work, he was strict, but when he relaxed he was a wonderfully understanding person.

I would also like to mention here one of Nikitin's personal characteristics – his astonishing resourcefulness, his smartness in battle. The following incident illustrates it: Nikolay Mikhailovich was leading six Hurricanes. We were giving cover to our land forces in the front line. When something like ten minutes remained before our spell of duty was due to finish, an announcement came over the radio: 'From the direction of Gatchina on course for Kolpino – enemy fighters.' We had hardly turned in their direction when a command followed: 'Stop the enemy aircraft, don't let them get to Kolpino!' It was easy enough to say – stop about forty Ju 87 bombers accompanied by fighters, but Nikitin answered 'Aye-aye, Stop them!' and rushed to meet the Fascist armada, taking us with him. We cut into the enemy's formation of aircraft at full speed. Fearing a collision with us, they dashed aside. Two Junkers collided and fell to earth in a ball of flame. The Ju 87 and the Hurricane were single-engine aircraft. The hump-backed English fighter was like the Junkers in shape and size; but the Junkers had a fixed undercarriage. Nikitin had a cunning idea.

Having slipped through the formation of Junkers, he immediately turned our six through 180 degrees and ordered us to form up in two flights of three, like Fascist bombers do, and to lower our undercarriages. Looking at my friends flying beside me, at our humpbacked Hurricanes with undercarriages lowered, only then did I understand the leader's idea. Truly, had we not become like Junkers? What a good idea of the CO's! We were flying in the same formation as Fascist bombers! And above us, the enemy fighters who had lost us were rushing about like madmen.

A Ju 87 loomed in front of me. It was already in my sights. The gunner on the Junkers (I could see him clearly) was twisting round in his cockpit, now aiming his machine-gun up, now to either side. He was looking for us, but in fear of the knowledge that Soviet fighters were near, he did not see the red noses of our machines, nor the bright stars on our wings.

Nikitin was already shouting over the radio: 'Everyone choose yourself a target! Attention! Fire!' We pressed our triggers.

I could no longer see the gunner. His machine, enveloped in flames, heeled over, put its nose down and plunged to earth, leaving behind it a belching trail of smoke. Burning and breaking up in mid-air, five more enemy aircraft fell to the point-blank fire of our pilots.

The Fascist bombers jettisoned their bombs without reaching their target, turned and fled in all directions. We retracted our undercarriages and also flew away. Only then, once they had located us, did the enemy fighters pursue us. Capt Yefimov's group, coming out to meet us, gave us assistance.

The concentrated aerial attack on Kolpino was broken up thanks to the bravery and resourcefulness of our CO.

CHAPTER TEN

Battles Over Sinyavin

On The Wrong Wavelength

'Where am I?' I asked myself suddenly, having just woken. I looked at the round faces of instruments. It appeared as if I were still in the cockpit of my fighter. There they were, control levers, dials, push buttons. As I sat there, I tried to come to my senses. The blood was throbbing in my forehead, my mouth was parched. I tried to get up, but I hadn't the strength.

What, then, had happened? My aircraft was standing at the very edge of the airfield. The engine wasn't running. Why, yes, it had stopped in the air at the last moment. My comrades ran up to me and asked if I was wounded. They asked why I had been so long, why I was alone and where Maj Myasnikov was.

'Myasnikov? . . .' I made an effort to remember what had happened to Myasnikov. But everything was mixed up in my mind. I walked to the dispersal area like a drunk. There it was, our tent, tattered by the wind. There was Capt Darmogray. He wanted information about the flight. Both of us, Myasnikov and I, had been counted dead. I was alive, but how about Myasnikov? Ah, yes, we had escorted the Pe 2 bombers from the 73rd Regiment. One of the pilots in a Pe 2 was a friend of Aleksandr Fyodorovich, and Myasnikov lost no time in joining the operation. Once airborne, they talked with youthful enthusiasm over the radio.

In the morning, before take-off, Aleksandr Fyodorovich was with our squadron where his aircraft was parked. He had become the deputy Regimental Commander, but flew with us as before. Earlier, he had succeeded in beating someone at chess and was in a good mood – joking a lot, laughing and talking happily. Then he wrote a letter to his Matrena Makarovna and his little six-year-old son, Yuri. But there was a telephone call from headquarters and soon we were in the air.

The Pe 2 bombers, with their bomb load, turned out to be faster than our Hurricanes. As we gained height, we fell behind them and met with Messerschmitts. We battled with the enemy fighters for about an hour. The bombers had departed and the enemy ack-ack had long since fallen silent, but still we could not break away from the Messerschmitts. There were twelve of them, only eight of us. They used the cover which the sun gave them. Nevertheless, we were able to shoot down two of them.

Without warning, another six enemy fighters appeared. They forced

Myasnikov and me away from the rest of the group. The two of us had to fight these six. The commander of our brigade, Hero of the Soviet Union Col P.V. Kondratyev, observed this aerial mêlée from his command post attached to the land forces headquarters. Following the dogfight, he helped us at difficult moments, gave advice over the radio, forewarned us of danger. He informed us that a group of Yaks were coming from the direction of 'Bolshoy' (i.e., Leningrad).

'Do you see the group?' he asked.

'We do!' I shouted, beating Myasnikov to it.

'They've been given their instructions; they'll help you presently.' Indeed, six Yak 1 fighters were approaching us. The Fascist pilots immediately left us in peace and took themselves off home.

'Thanks for the help, brothers!' we shouted over the radio to our rescuers and signalled our thanks by rocking our wings, before taking a course to the airfield. I must add that our fuel was running out. Evidently, the radio receivers on the Yaks were tuned to another wavelength. Meanwhile, our unknown friends mistook the Hurricanes for enemy fighters. Two Yaks suddenly broke away and started to attack us.

'They're attacking,' I warned Myasnikov.

'They're only Yaks,' calmly replied Aleksandr Fyodorovich. 'Our Yaks. They're joking.' But the leading Yak was not joking. The pilot fired a burst at Maj Myasnikov's aircraft. The machine caught fire and started to fall.

'What are you doing, you bandits!' I shouted over the radio on seeing how the Commander's aircraft, enveloped in flames, was falling. But my voice was drowned in the ether. The army pilots did not hear me. Only Col Kondratyev heard me. And he saw all that was going on in the air. The Brigade Commander informed me that they would now contact the Yaks. But already they had turned and were coming at me from two directions.

What could I do? I couldn't fire at my own comrades. I started to avoid action by turning away from the Yaks; but there were six of them. Moreover, they came fresh to their task. I had neither fuel nor strength. The engine could stop at any second. There was only one thing I could do: act as if my machine had been hit. But how? Put the aircraft into a spin? A notice fastened to the instrument panel of the Hurricane warned (and this I knew by heart) 'If the machine does not come out of a spin when you reach a height of 2,000 metres, abandon the aircraft and use your parachute.' Not for nothing had that warning been given: the English fighter, once it had gone into a spin, could not come out of it.

But there was no choice. Seizing the right moment, I put the machine into a spin. It turned, then again and a third time. The ground and Leningrad was transformed into a carousel which gathered speed. A fourth, fifth, seventh, ninth twist. 'Come out!' I shouted to myself for some reason, seeing the revolving earth rushing towards me. Defying expectations, the Hurricane responded to the controls. It came out of the spin and, lowering its nose, gathered speed. I was now in horizontal flight. The forest was beneath me. Altitude – 400 metres. Nobody was on my tail. I accelerated and took course for the airfield. What the engine was running on, I didn't know. The fuel gauge showed empty. 'Well, Hurricane, hold on, my dear, it's not far.'

I put the undercarriage down and glided towards the airfield. At that moment, there was a loud bang – the engine stopped. The blades of the propeller posed before my eyes, like a cockroach's whiskers. And so I landed.

Having written down everything I could tell him, Darmogray made haste to report to the authorities. I made my way with difficulty to my bed and fell into a deep sleep; but I didn't rest for long. The aircraft refuelled, Darmogray roused me. I jumped out of bed but Myasnikov was in my thoughts.

'I understand,' said the Adjutant, 'but what's to be done? You won't bring back Aleksandr Fyodorovich. They'll investigate and punish whom they ought. So sit down now and write an explanatory note. That's the Regimental Commander's order.' I wrote a short explanatory note and gave it to the Adjutant.

Soon they had us in the air, where again we were engaged in a fierce battle. We shot down three Messerschmitts and lost one of our own aircraft. And what an aircraft! Sergey Sukhov was killed. His Hurricane fell into a flat spin and, revolving like a lime seedpod, sped to earth. His comrades shouted to Sukhov to jump, but Sergey made no response at all. The plane fell on our territory, north of Nevskaya Dubrovka.

Returning to the airfield again and again, I recalled what a cheerful person Seryozha Sukhov had been, and what a happy mood Aleksandr Fyodorovich Myasnikov had been in that morning. Now they had gone, gone never to return. Their bunks were empty, their children orphans. In all this, the war was to blame.

Dear Matrena Makarovna, Dear Lenochka! In a few days, they would receive news of the death of their husbands. We didn't have the strength to console them, but we did have the strength to kill the Fascist scum. We swore to destroy them like mad dogs, for they were the source of all our troubles.

Bombs, A Storm And Music

The second autumn of the blockade came into its own when a powerful cold wind blew from Ladoga and maliciously tore the last leaves from the trees, covering the ground with a bright carpet.

Our steamer slowly cut through the waters of the Staro–Ladoga canal. We stood on the deck and watched Novaya Ladoga recede. It was strange to be returning to the regiment by such an uncomfortable mode of transport. My travelling companions – sergeant pilots, who had only just finished training at the Eysk aviation school – were bound for our regiment, commanded by the Chief of Staff, Maj Kutsov. The lads were joking, laughing, attracting the attention of those around them. They had still not smelt powder and their notion of battle was somewhat romantic. Trofim Petrovich happily clowned with them. However, gloomy thoughts again returned to me. I couldn't grasp the idea: first war and suddenly ordered to rest. True, to begin with, it had been difficult to resign myself even to a day off. But a rest home. . . .

All my friends had flown away to the Karelian Isthmus. Real work awaited them there. But Capt Bondarenko, Commander of the first squadron, and I had been ordered to take a rest. What's more: 'Don't think of moving!' Not just anyone's parting words, but those of the Regimental Commander himself.

What could we do? We raised and waved our service caps to the lads and started to wade through the mud on the road leading to the rest home. It wasn't too far – 8 kilometres – before we saw ahead a village surrounded by woodland. On the outskirts stood a small comfortable house, and nearby a rivulet. The food was excellent and there was nothing to do. A day passed, a second, a third. Finally, Bondarenko and I could bear it no longer and set off for Novaya Ladoga. We telephoned the regiment, tearfully begged to be taken away, but the angry voice of the commander denied us any hope of so doing.

But the next day they suddenly called me to the garrison. I ran, sweat pouring off me. Victor Nedyelin met me. We had been friends since Eysk aviation school days. He informed me that a fierce aerial battle had started again over Sinyavin; that Aleksey Rudyenko had been killed and that he, Nedyelin, had been ordered to fly to the front in my Hurricane.

'Rudyenko killed? Aleksya, Aleksya! . . . Such a pilot! No. Vitya, better that I fly it myself and you take a rest here in my place.'

'But the Regimental Commander has ordered me to fly,' said Nedyelin. 'I'll leave you the U 2. You'll take a rest and make your way to the regiment in it.'

What was I to do? They were taking my aircraft yet again. It was bad to fly into battle in a strange aircraft. It wasn't superstition. This was something different. Was it possible to forget how Shirobokov had been shot down in my aircraft? Just the same had happened with Sosyedin. Yes, and the Brigade Commander was shot down when, in the same way, he hurriedly took off in my fighter. I haven't even mentioned Borisov. . . .

'Don't worry!' Nedyelin reassured me when he noticed how upset I was. 'I shan't fly that much and I'll return your aircraft safe and sound.'

He quickly climbed into the cockpit of my aircraft, took off, circled above the airfield and vanished above the forest. I walked up to the U 2, which had been left at dispersal, drummed with my fingers on the fabric covering on the wing, only just holding back a roar of resentment.

The next morning, bad news reached us. In an unequal fight, Capt Nikolay Tkachev and Dmitry Buryak had been killed. Dmitry, Commissar of the 3rd Squadron, had completed 170 sorties and destroyed ten of the enemy's aircraft. Victor Nedyelin was also killed. He was killed that evening, soon after we had parted. It was his first flight in my Hurricane.

I returned to the regiment from the rest home, not in the U 2 (somebody from the headquarters staff had taken it), but by steamer. It was already dark when we came to Kobona. Here we were accommodated in an enormous metal box, fastened by a hawser to a small tug-boat. Even then we weren't able to cast off from the shore when, over Kobona and the convoy of ships stretching across the lake, enemy aircraft appeared. Flares burst in the sky.

Ladoga erupted. The Fascists thundered overhead. Now blue, now gold, the searchlight beams restlessly swept the skies. The joyful laughter of the young airmen ceased. They looked up intently to where shadows appeared for a moment, searchlight beams pierced the gloom and anti-aircraft shells burst.

'They've hit one! They've shot him down! Hurrah!'

A Fascist bomber traced its last fiery arc across the sky.

The old iron tub in which we had been placed thumped against its moorings. We saw how feverishly the dockers worked. Many had rifles slung across their backs. Here a strict rhythm of work was sustained. Despite the danger, orders were given for departure.

'Well then, you must get used to this situation at the front,' said Maj Kutsov to the airmen in his charge. 'This happens every night on Ladoga.'

The shore moved away from us. Rocking in our tin can, beneath star shells and candle bombs, we felt, to say the least, somewhat lacking in confidence. 'Ah, well, then, Kaberov, take up your bayan,' said Kutsov.

'That's right, play Comrade Captain. Am I lugging this bandura around in its box for nothing?' echoed his armourer, Shutov, in support. 'They say that bombs fear music.'

I don't know that bombs do fear music, but we felt better immediately. Singing, we reached Morye by morning, but it was still some way to the regiment. Only the next day at lunch time did we arrive at the airfield.

I counted nine aircraft at dispersal – all that we had now. These planes were standing a large distance from one another. It was as if the ground staff had left a special empty space for those fighters that had been shot down in aerial combat.

In my mind, I counted the number of enemy aircraft we had shot down after we had received Hurricanes, armed with Soviet cannons and machine-guns. It turned out that during that time sixty-eight fighters and bombers had been destroyed by us. At the same time, we had lost eleven of our comrades and fourteen machines. No doubt the regiment would receive equipment. New people would replace airmen who had died, but the severe pain of loss would stay in our hearts forever.

Dear Comrade Aircraft

New arrangements were always taking place. Organizational measures or, as they were sometimes called, 'orgs' occurred constantly. In October 1942, Semyon Lvov became the CO of the squadron; I was appointed his deputy. Ivan Petrovich Lukyanov was posted away on a course of study. His duties as regimental deputy to the Commanding Officer responsible for political matters passed to Matvey Yefimov.

Yegorushka Kostilyev, who had destroyed more than twenty enemy aircraft in battle and who had been given the title of Hero of the Soviet Union, was to lead a squadron in another unit. I deeply regretted that he was to leave us. We so often flew as a pair, and many times had rescued one another in battle. The Gold Stars of Heroes glittered on the uniforms of our wonderful friends in the attack aircraft – Nelson Stepanyan, Mikhail Klimenko and Aleksey Mazurenko. The only thing that grieved me was that I had not been flying for two weeks. But that day I was carrying out official duties at the Oranienbaum bridgehead. I was sitting in the dug-out with its only other occupant, Yevgeny Duk. An oil lamp made from a cartridge case was burning.

'Would you train me as a pilot?' asked Duk. He said this, not as a joke, for to become a knight of the air had always been his daydream. 'Would you take me?' he asked.

'Oh, Zhenya! If only it were that simple. You know yourself that it takes time to master the skills.'

'But I would quickly learn to fly a fighter,' he promised. 'Already, I have learnt all the commands, completed a course of flying training and know by heart the instruction manual for the LaGG 3 aircraft.' Zhenka looked at me, his eyes full of hope. 'Yes, yes, I'm quite serious. . . .'

A telephone call interrupted our conversation. There were orders from headquarters. I was ordered to join the regiment immediately and not wait until morning. The aircraft that was to deliver me had already taken off. So our meeting was short lived and Zhenya and I left the dug-out. In the evening sky, the familiar roar of the ubiquitous U 2 could already be heard. The Regimental Chief of Staff's deputy, 1/Lt M.S. Gozhev, and the Senior Political Officer, M.R. Golod, would come to collect me.

The aircraft landed and taxied towards us, guided by torchlight. With the engine still running, Viktor Terekhin leaped out of the cockpit. 'Igor, hi!' He shook me by the hand. 'I've come for you.'

'Hallo, hallo. But why have they suddenly sent a personal aircraft for me and, moreover, with a fighter pilot?'

'I'll explain presently,' said Terekhin. 'You and Yefimov are the only two who have flown in LaGG 3 fighters.'

'Does that mean that they've given us LaGGs? Hurrah, Vitka! What about that! We'll be flying in our own aircraft again! And you, Zhenya, must have been looking into a crystal ball. You did not study the instruction manual for operating the LaGG 3 in vain.'

In the mist, visibility was bad and not a light could be seen. The enemy were to the left and right. We couldn't permit the slightest deviation to either side. Yet Capt Terekhin confidently piloted our plane. At an altitude of 70 metres, we passed over the outskirts of Leningrad and the Commandant's airfield, but the fog had settled still lower and it was impossible to fly through to our airfield. We turned back. Judging by the time, we should have been approaching Kronstadt.

'Let off a flare!' ordered Terekhin.

An answering flare came from the ground and they switched on a search-light before we landed. All we could do now was to spend the night there.

Only by the evening of the next day did we succeed in reaching the aerodrome near the regimental headquarters. In fact, a matter of great urgency did await me. I had to take delivery of two LaGG 3 fighters in one of our units and ferry them to our base in the rear. Until our regiment had mastered the new technology, we were faced with completing training flights in these fighters.

I remember how a young pilot, Aleksey Parkhomyenko, and I took charge of the aircraft which had been made ready for us. The number 59 was marked on the first of them. It was our old regimental LaGG, which originally we had discovered in a swamp near Novaya Ladoga. Partly broken, it had been renovated by technicians and, as was now clear, had continued to fly until that moment. But next to it (at first I could hardly believe my eyes), stood my LaGG No. 88.

Its history was also remarkable. On one of those days when I was without an aircraft, Yegor Kostilyev had travelled to Leningrad, applied to the authorities and, having obtained for me with some difficulty the recently repaired machine, brought it to our airfield. And that was LaGG No. 88. Countless times had I taken off in it to meet the enemy. The fighter had been repaired yet again after Borisov, the pilot, had failed to land it properly. Now, once again, my warhorse stood before me in fine fettle.

'Hallo, my dear!' I said with emotion, and respectfully removed my cap.

Sgt Parkhomyenko became interested. 'What are you on about, Comrade Captain?'

'Well, how shall I put it? He was my dear old comrade!' I replied and joyfully embraced the aircraft, as far as I could, as a rider embraces his faithful steed. 'Many times together, we looked death in the eye. . . . Let me introduce him to you.'

Parkhomyenko walked up to the fighter. 'A trustworthy mount then?'

'Yes.' I sat down in the cockpit. My own aircraft! I was lost in admiration for it. What an unexpected and pleasant meeting!

We took off, passed over dispersal and flew away into the sky. Just look! I thought. This is a real fighter! It doesn't matter that it's made of wood; what matters is its speed and manoeuvrability! Moreover, it has the means to strike the enemy.

We landed beyond the River Volkhov at an intermediate airfield for refuelling and then continued on route for our base in the rear. Having delivered my fighter to the base, the next day I returned. Unexpectedly, somebody shouted: 'There's an aircraft on fire overhead!'

From the direction of the lake, an Il 2 attack aircraft, enveloped in flames, was approaching the airfield. 'Will he make it or not?'

Someone called the doctor and ordered stretchers. But the plane was already hitting bushes at the approach to the airfield and, without reaching it, dropped on its fuselage and raised a cloud of dust. The pilot and gunner, who had received serious burns, were hurriedly taken to hospital. The aircraft burnt itself out.

Meanwhile, yet another Il 2 was approaching the airfield from the same direction. It had a broken wing; a tail of smoke stretched behind it. The machine dropped on to the airfield without lowering its undercarriage. The medical staff gave help to the aircrew. We found out that 36 kilometres to the north of Novaya Ladoga, a battle was raging for the island of Sukho. The enemy had approached the island in landing-craft and barges and made a landing.

Someone told us the history of this tiny piece of dry land with the significant name of Sukho.[11] It seems that during the reign of Peter the Great, it was a shoal. Ships frequently ran aground on it. So Peter gave orders to transform the shoal into an island, and since it remained dry there, the new-born island became known as Sukho. In the last century, a lighthouse was built on Sukho. In the war years, when the enemy started to threaten Leningrad, a small garrison was established on the island. Now a battle was going on there. 'They were the barges we saw in Lakhdenpokhye,' I recalled. Col Dzyuba had been right. They were landing-craft, and evidently we had not destroyed them all.

Later, it became known that, seeking to intercept our lines of communication, the Fascist command had launched on to Lake Ladoga a large number of landing-craft, built in Germany, Italy and Finland. These craft were brought together into the so-called 'Detachment of Eastern Ferries'. Part of its mission was to destroy communications between Leningrad and the greater part of Russia. With this purpose, thirty-eight enemy landing-craft and self-propelled barges, under the cover of aerial and artillery fire, approached Sukho and started to make a landing. The island's defenders put up a fierce resistance to the enemy. They repulsed the onslaught with artillery and machine-gun fire and bayonet charges. Soon the ships of the Ladoga flotilla joined in and our aircraft delivered a heavy blow to the enemy, who retreated, having lost fifteen aircraft and nineteen ships. Our fighters and attack aircraft pursued them.

CHAPTER ELEVEN

January 1943: Squadrons On The Offensive

My Fellow-Countrymen: The People Of Vologda

There was much work involved in helping the pilots to master the skills needed to fly an LaGG 3 fighter. Day after day training went on relentlessly. When it was finished, I unexpectedly received orders from headquarters to fly to Vologda in the U 2 aircraft to collect a mixture of spirit and glycerine for use on undercarriages. I was in high spirits, for now I was to go home by plane. I collected my papers, prepared my route, thrust the map into its case and hurried to the airfield! What a fine machine this U 2 was. It sped forward for 50 metres and took off.

'Tell me, old friend, how many pilots have you taught in your time? And now you are going to war!'

I found out that it was being used on military operations. At the time when I was on official duties in the front-line area, it was intended to launch an attack, and a large group of U 2 aircraft had arrived. Bomb racks were fastened under the wings of every one of them. The pilots heaped praise on their machines. 'We have been working six months without loss,' said one of them. I was astonished.

'Yes, but as you know, your U 2 is only wood and cambric. What about the bullets and shrapnel from the anti-aircraft shells?'

At this, the pilot took a frying pan out of his aircraft; an ordinary frying pan on which you might cook potatoes. 'Here it is, our armour plating. I sit on it and keep on flying.'

We laughed at his resourcefulness. 'Intrepid lads,' I thought as I looked at this pilot and his comrades.

'And somewhere to the south, a women's regiment is fighting, equipped with U 2s,' he added. 'The aircraft have made the Fascists suffer great losses.'

I listened to the roar of the engine, recalled the conversation at the front and admired the broad expanse of my homeland over which I was flying. I made for Cherepovyets and passed over Ustyuzhina. I was already in the Vologda region, the land of my forebears. I was in such a mood that it was only possible to express it in verse:

> A wonderful picture glides below,
> Earth covered in a soft haze.
> The vast Vologda plain
> Beneath the U 2's blue wings.

I passed Cherepovyets. The station was visible ahead. I flew low, passing just to the right of the railway and read the name: Kipelovo. You could say I was already home. Once I had travelled there to pick mushrooms. Lumba, Dikaya, Molochnaya stations passed by, and ahead gleamed the golden dome of Vologda cathedral. And there was the factory where once I had worked. I turned and looked over our steam locomotive workshop, the brick superstructure crowned with a finial and the smoke-stained glass roof. I flew down low over the entrance and climbed away steeply. Nor could I deny myself the pleasure of flying over the house where my family were living. There it was, with its red iron roof. Next to it rose the fire observation tower. I had to avoid that. I circled once, twice, three times and then flew away to land. Once I had given the aircraft into the strict care of the aeroclub's official at dispersal, I hurried home. Valya and Ninochka met me on the porch.

There are no words to express the feelings which took hold of us. It seems that not only grief, but joy, can so affect the throat that you temporarily lose the gift of speech. Only Ninochka said something. She spoke so quickly and confusedly that I couldn't understand her. I took my daughter in my arms and we went upstairs. Now Valya helped Ninochka tell me how they had seen the aeroplane circling over the house and who was the first to guess that I had arrived. She tried to imitate the noise of the engine, to show with her little arms how the aeroplane circled, and her blue eyes shone with happiness.

So, the two days spent at home passed quickly, but I coped with all the duties entrusted to me and succeeded in visiting my old friend, Nikolay Nikolayevich Gulyayev, the former secretary of the works' young communist organization, but at the time of my visit, secretary of the town's young communist committee, and during the war, the chief of the local anti-aircraft defences. I remember we were sitting together at table and talking, while Valya and the mistress of the house were thinking over something in the kitchen, when suddenly Nikolay told me the stunning news: the people of Vologda had been collecting money towards an aircraft for their town hero.

'For which hero?' I asked.

'Well, who else? For you!' replied Nikolay.

'That can't be. What kind of a hero am I?'

'Very well then.' He put his hand on my shoulder. 'But you mustn't spoil our fun. They've already collected 25 million roubles.'

'How much?'

'25 million! And the collection is still going on.'

'Look here, that's enough for a whole regiment of heroes.'

'Well, what of it? We're not against it,' said Nikolay. 'But as far as you're concerned, say no more. With such medals! Nina!' he called his wife. 'Did you hear what our former railway engineer said?'

'I heard. I heard!' Smiling, she came into the room with Valya.

'On such an occasion, we must drink a toast. To the cooperation between those at the front and those at the rear!'

In the morning, I was again at the aerodrome. I bade farewell to my nearest and dearest and took off. The plane carried me further and further away from my birthplace. The cathedral's golden cupola was already lost from sight, the town melted in haze; but in my thoughts, I was still there inside my father's house. I could see my wife, hear her shy modest voice:

'Igor, my dear, in the spring, we shall have a little boy . . . bright-eyed, snub-nosed with dimples on his cheeks.' I kissed her and meanwhile she became thoughtful. 'But supposing it's a little girl?'

'That's fine!' I said. 'Pigtails and bows again – nice!'

'No,' she raised a happy face, 'it will be a boy. For some reason, I think so.'

Roads, streams, villages, copses floated past under the wings. The tireless engine sang its even song. It seemed to echo my thoughts: 'We shall have a son and we'll call him, like Chkalov – Valeriy! Maybe he will also become a pilot. . . .'

He Remained A Commissar

A large twin-engined Il 4 aircraft rose above us and then fell in the middle of the airfield. It struck the earth with a thud, broke into pieces and burst into flames. We switched off the engines of our fighters, jumped from our cockpits and found the strength to run towards the tragic accident. Someone shouted: 'Don't go near, it will explode!' And in fact at that moment there was a muffled explosion and we fell on to the snow, our heads down. Bullets from exploding ammunition flew whistling in all directions.

There, in that gigantic inferno, our comrades died: Matvey Yefimov, Trofim Kutsov, Khanyafi Khamyetov, Viktor Sigolayev and Boris Borisov, an aircrew led by its captain, 1/Lt Grigoriy Chervonooky. There wasn't the slightest chance to help them. Only twenty minutes later did we succeed in approaching what recently had been an aircraft. We walked towards it and removed our flying helmets.

The last tongues of flame died down and among the burnt-out pieces of the machine, we searched for the charred bodies of our friends. We recognized Kutsov by his giant figure, Yefimov by the Gold Star of a Hero which had melted on his chest. The rest were impossible to identify.

Why then did all this happen? The Il 4 bomber had as escort eight fighters as far as Novaya Ladoga. 1/Lt Chernyenko's flight took off immediately. My four escorts switched on their engines. The Il 4 prepared to take off. At this moment, Maj Kutsov appeared. He ran up to the aircraft carrying a small suitcase and begged the pilot to take him on board.

'Take me please, Comrade First Lieutenant!' implored Kutsov. 'Look, I've received a telegram. My wife has died. Only my little daughter is left. Do you understand? I only want to go across Ladoga. I shall manage to make my way to Tashkent from there. Take me. . . .' The machine was fully loaded and it seemed impossible to find a place for Kutsov. But Chervonooky, the kind person that he was, after some hesitation, gave orders to lower the ladder.

Possibly the disturbing conversation with Kutsov unsettled the pilot. Possibly fatigue played a part. Whichever it was, the pilot forgot after landing to put the elevator trimmer into the take-off position and began his take-off run. The machine reared as it rose into the sky. At an altitude of 100 metres, it lost speed, dipped its nose and making the half turn of a spin, struck the ground.

I looked at the smoking fire and recalled the previous day's conversation between the regiment's Commanding Officer and his political deputy. It was evening: pilots were reading newspapers and playing chess. I was writing a letter to my wife and Lt Col Nikitin was compiling a list of those who had to fly with him to the base to receive fighter aircraft. Matvey Andreyevich came up to the table and looked over Nikitin's shoulder. He said that it would be better if he, Yefimov, were to lead this group of pilots. The Commanding Officer had many duties there in the unit. The regiment had received new aircraft and it was necessary to keep a constant eye on young and inexperienced pilots.

'I'll try to return quickly,' Yefimov said with his good-natured smile.

Nikitin thought for a moment. 'Very well, you've convinced me, Andreyevich. So be it. You fly.' The CO crossed out his surname and wrote above it 'Yefimov'.

Oh, what a magnificent man Matvey Andreyevich Yefimov was. It was he who, at the start of the war, having found out that a group of fighter pilots were being selected to escort bombers intended to strike a blow at Berlin, first submitted a report with a request to include him in the group. Throughout the war, not one of Yefimov's wing men died. He, like no one else, vigilantly followed the course of the battle and at times, when a critical situation arose, immediately flew to his comrade's aid. Twice, Matvey Andreyevich personally got me out of trouble.

Matvey Andreyevich's rare capacity for work caused astonishment and admiration. He flew not less but more than all of us, and despite that, he managed to organize meetings, give lectures or reports, showed an interest in new literary trends, talked with the pilots and technicians and visited the sailors' quarters. He was the Commanding Officer's political deputy (that was his official title), but we, from habit, called him the Commissar. He was always the Commissar to us. The word had a particular meaning for us. People in the regiment saw in Matvey Andreyevich a man of the party with Leninist ideology who lived according to the glorious laws of the old Bolshevik guard.

'Matvey, you're another Furmanov!'[12] Sukhov said to him once.

Yefimov taught us: 'Victory does not come by accident but from know-how!' And it was he, our Andreyevich, who started – and not without success – to apply the teaching skills of an instructor and educator in battle. When it began to seem to a young pilot, Mikhail Alekseyev, that he 'simply wasn't having any luck', Matvey took the young man with him on the next flight. When they met enemy aircraft, he made the correct manoeuvre, boldly attacked them, hit one of them slightly, moved away and shouted over the radio to his wing man: 'Finish him off, then! Be brave, I'll give you cover.'

Mikhail delivered an attack. The enemy machine plunged to earth, smoking.

'Well, there you are!' shouted Yefimov enthusiastically. 'And you said you had no luck!'

In one and a half war-years, our Commissar made 352 military sorties, took part in 91 aerial battles and shot down 25 enemy aircraft.

Not one bullet, not one piece of shrapnel touched Yefimov during the war. He didn't lose a single aircraft in battle. Enemy fighters did not have the strength to shoot him down, although they constantly made him their target. As later it became well known, Hitler's pilots even made it their business to get him. They had a photo of him and he was known as 'Target No. 1'. The tragic accident removed him from our ranks, together with several other pilots in our regiment. But as a fighter pilot, he remained invincible. His image will always remain in the hearts and minds of everyone who knew him.

Blockade Breakthrough

Once again, as on many other occasions, the regiment was put on alert. A little time passed and we were moved and settled into a new aerodrome. It felt as if intensified preparations were going on for some big operation, but no one knew what to expect. However, we did not remain in ignorance for long. One evening at the regimental command post, it was explained to us that forces on the Leningrad and Volkhov fronts would assume the offensive with the aim of breaking through the Leningrad blockade on 12 January 1943. The Commanding Officer looked round at those who had gathered there with a significant glance.

'By morning, the second and third squadrons must be at full strength and ready to carry out the task of giving cover to ground forces over the battlefield.' A shout of 'Hurrah' shook the command dug-out.

A powerful rumbling like thunder reached the airfield at 9 30 a.m. It was the sound of artillery from the Leningrad and Volkhov fronts as well as the guns of the Baltic Fleet which had opened fire on enemy positions with an avalanche of fire and steel. From our dispersal area to Shlisselburg it was 20 kilometres, but even there we could feel the ground shaking beneath our feet. The artillery bombardment on the Leningrad front lasted two hours and twenty minutes; on the Volkhov front, one hour and forty-five minutes.

Despite low cloud, the first group of fighters left on their sortie and returned victorious. Shilkov, a young pilot, fought and shot down an Me 109 at a height of 200 metres. Meanwhile, the weather cleared up and we engaged some Focke-Wulf aircraft in a dogfight. It was the first time I had met the Focke-Wulf 190s in battle. However, at low altitude, it was impossible to judge what this machine was capable of doing. Colonel Kondratyev supervised the battle. I could hear his voice over the radio and it seemed as if I could see this cheerful, energetic, agile man. We said of him: 'The CO's not tall, but he's the big shot.'

The next morning, the weather again remained poor but we continued our fighting duties. We were ordered to cover land forces fighting the enemy on the left bank of the Neva. Our altitude was between 150 and 200 metres. We were flying along the Neva from Nevskaya Dubrovka to Shlisselburg and back again. In the region of Marin, infantry were crossing the river. They hurriedly emerged on to the left shore which had been torn up by shell fire. Our Stormoviks were attacking the centres of resistance. We returned home without meeting any Fascist aircraft. But Capt Tatarenko's group who flew out after us were already on the look out for Messerschmitts. Tatarenko shot down one of the enemy's fighters in a short battle.

On 14 January at midday, I again led a group of six over the front line and patrolled over Shlisselburg. Beneath us, the Stormoviks were working over the enemy positions. I saw how, as they were moving away from their target, a pair of Me 109s chased after them. I left four of the group with Shilkov leading them, and with Shestopalov, attacked the Messerschmitts. I fired a burst at the leading aircraft which was preparing to open fire on our Stormoviks. It turned over on its back, then slowly tumbled on to its nose and struck the ground in the vicinity of Chernaya Rechka. The second enemy fighter went into a climb and made off. In the evening, I flew out in the direction of Shlisselburg, leading five fighters. Suddenly, over the radio came a short clear command. This coded message meant that we must return. Very well – we went in to land. Aleksandr Shilkov and Nikolay Shestopalov succeeded in landing, but they sent us back. It turned out that no additional command had been given. This meant that the Fascists were confusing our pilots over the radio.

Three of us went to Shlisselburg together: our new flight commander, Capt Tsapov, Sgt Sasha Potyemkin and I. Two Me 109s were patrolling over the front line. We engaged them in a fight. Meanwhile, another pair of Messerschmitts came to us from above. They flew on past as if they had missed us, but immediately they attacked and set fire to Potyemkin's aircraft. Sasha climbed out of his cockpit and opened his parachute at a height of 2,000 metres, right above the Neva. A north-westerly wind carried him towards the enemy's positions. Enemy aircraft pounced on Potyemkin, trying to shoot him. We repulsed the attack.

How could we help Potyemkin? I gave Tsapov the order to follow and seizing the right moment, guided my machine under Sasha's legs. Caught in a current of air, his parachute drifted towards our shore. While I drove off the attacking Messerschmitts, Ivan Tsapov passed under Potyemkin's legs. By turns, we carried out this manoeuvre about fifteen times. Sasha was now already over the edge of the shore. But we couldn't protect his parachute from gunfire. The Messerschmitts made holes in it and only by a miracle did the air support it. When it was only a few dozen metres from the ground, the parachute cloth ripped and he disappeared from view like a white snake. Fascist mortars opened fire, from the opposite shore at the place where Sasha had fallen. Seeing that they couldn't take us and that the parachute was already on the ground, the enemy aircraft departed. Tsapov and I flew over the shell-scarred shore where our comrade must have landed, but did not discover him. We returned to the airfield with the bitter news: evidently, Potyemkin was dead.

But fortunately we were mistaken. Late that evening, information reached us of Sasha's miraculous rescue. And the next day he returned to us. He returned in bandages, but as always, cheerful and undismayed.

'This time, I have been lucky,' said Sasha. 'The parachute finally tore apart 70 metres from the ground. I more or less tumbled into a deep slope by the Neva and made a deep hole in the snow. I lay at the bottom feeling my limbs. It seemed that I was alive. I could hear mortar shells exploding on the shore. Then everything became quiet. Suddenly above my head, I heard a voice. I looked and there stood a soldier, carrying an automatic rifle. He was standing, shaking the lines of the parachute shroud and shouting: 'Now climb out, you stinker!' I corrected him: 'I'm no stinker but a comrade, rank of sergeant.' Finally, the lads of the artillery dragged me up out of the hole and gave me first aid.'

Sasha stopped talking and adjusted one of his bandages. Then, without a note of surprise, said: 'You know, that was my first parachute jump.'

'How can that be? why did they pass you out of flying school?'

'It was like this: when my friends jumped, I was ill in the sick bay for a few days. It was decided that at the first opportunity I should jump. But they shortened the training programme and before long we were discharged. I never managed to do my jump. Once I was here at the front, whenever I was flying, the thought of baling out was frightening. Today, however, it all happened. I saw that the aircraft was on fire. The flames were burning my face and hands. I don't remember how I got out of the cockpit. I felt myself falling and my first thought was: 'The ring!' But where was it? I grabbed but couldn't feel it. Then I looked. There it was. I pulled immediately. There was a jerk, of course, and my legs swung beneath me. Above my head, taut like a sail, the canopy. I almost sang for joy! But a second later I realized that my song could be my last. A Messerschmitt turned in my direction. Shots rang out. At that moment, one of you intercepted the Messerschmitt and the Fascist's bullets missed me. Only one line was cut.'

'And did you see that you were being carried towards the Germans?'

'How could I when I was watching the fight? But when you swept beneath me and the parachute really swung, I understood that the wind was dragging me towards the enemy. I understood and, of course, was relieved.'

Potyemkin looked at his bandaged hands. Beneath the bandages, the skin had been torn from his palms and his fingers.

'I pulled on the lines to slow my descent.'

Tsapov looked at me meaningfully and shook his head. He seemed to be saying: 'What dangers a man faces in the four minutes he takes to descend by parachute!'

On 18 January 1943, to mark the anniversary of our promotion to the status of a guards regiment, musicians arrived from Leningrad. There was a concert, during which the master of ceremonies, when announcing the next item on the programme, puzzled us by saying:

'Now here is the celebrated operator. . . .'

Someone cheerfully corrected him: 'You mean opera singer.'

But it turned out that the compère was not mistaken. 'Here is that celebrated – and presently you will know that I was right – radio operator from your regiment.' With a gesture he beckoned him on to the stage and added: 'In the last hour!'

We all sat stock still in expectation. The operator coughed and straight away, with the intonations of a singer, delivered these words: 'The armies on the Leningrad and Volkhov fronts have joined forces, comrades! The blockade is broken!' It is impossible to describe what happened next.

'Hurrah!' Both audience and musicians joined in the ovation which filled the hall. Our lads rushed on to the stage. They wanted to lift the operator shoulder high, but just in time he vanished in the wings, preferring to remain in one piece.

The blockade was broken but the bitter fighting continued. The Fascist high command hurriedly transferred to Leningrad all the new air force units. Severe aerial battles were waged in the region of Sinyavin from morning till night.

The next day, there was another difficult battle. There were five of us. With me were Tsapov, Shilkov, Prasolov and Shestopalov. Ivan Tsapov and Nikolay Shestopalov repulsed fighter attacks and the other three of us delivered blows on the enemy. At one moment, an Me 110 came into my sights. I opened fire. The starboard engine of the enemy machine was smoking. Recalling how Matvey Yefimov had taught young pilots, I shouted to Prasolov: 'Hit him, Petya. Finish him off!' He fired and the engine cowlings flew off the Messerschmitt. Enveloped in flames, it went into its last dive. 'Well done!' I said to Prasolov. 'Get into formation. Don't get left behind.'

But then, after the first group of Fascist aircraft, a second appeared. We drove a wedge into it and, using efficient teamwork, set fire to yet another Me 110. It flew on for some time, dipping first one wing, then the other. But the fire took control and the machine fell to earth.

Pyotr Prasolov, a small lad, who looked like a young boy, shot down the first Fascist bomber. He was twenty years old, but already a formidable fighter pilot. Pyotr was embarrassed by his comrades' praises, but at the same time proud of his victory.

All our lads fought with great enthusiasm. In the air, a group led by the Squadron Commander, Semyon Ivanovich Lvov, usually relieved my group. In one of the battles, he destroyed an Me 109; in another, when attacking the enemy with his partner, Pyotr Prasolov, he set fire to an Me 110. Also, the next day, Lvov and Shilkov shot down another two Messerschmitts. The pilots of No. 3 Squadron, led by that brave pilot from the Baltic Fleet, Dmitry Tatarenko, fought bravely. Coming on a group of Junkers, they repulsed attacks by enemy fighters and destroyed, in one dogfight, four Ju 88 bombers before returning home without loss. It wasn't the first enemy bomber that Ivan Tsapov, a flight commander in our squadron, had shot down. Ivan, who like Commissar Yefimov was from Smolensk, bore a strong resemblance to Matvey Andreyevich in battle. Intelligent, prudent, extremely brave, he helped his comrades who found themselves in trouble. Once he helped me. It was during a fierce aerial battle over the front line. I had to fight four enemy fighters for almost fifteen minutes on my own. It's difficult to say how all this would have ended had not Ivan Tsapov come to my aid. Together with Sasha Shilkov, he gained height and attacked the Focke-Wulf aircraft from out of the sun. Within a minute, they had lost one of their leading planes and the remaining three made for home.

In the days of the Leningrad blockade break-out, it was particularly hard for the young pilots in our regiment. I remember how one of them, Yuriy Shorin, had to make a belly landing because of an error. Owing to inexperience, he struck himself on the gunsight as the fuselage hit the ground. The next day, his face was so swollen that his eyes couldn't be seen.

On that day, our four were standing by on 'Red Alert'. It was cold and I asked the technician to place a cover over the cockpit. After a while, somebody knocked on the window. It turned out to be Lt Col Nikitin. He had brought some young pilots to dispersal in order that I should explain to them how to perform a belly landing, and to share my experience with them.

Sitting in my cockpit, I told them everything that had happened on each occasion. I recalled how I myself had landed on the fuselage several times and how I'd had to do this in different ways: with and without an undercarriage, on a partially lowered undercarriage, and on one wheel.

'Well then, do you understand?' I asked the lads, in conclusion.

'Yes,' they replied in chorus.

'And does Comrade Shorin?'

Shorin pulled apart the swollen lids of his right eye with two fingers and looked at me with one eye.

'Indeed I do, Comrade Captain!'

The young pilots laughed wholeheartedly at their luckless classmate. At that moment precisely, the signal for take-off was given. The technicians removed the covers from my fighter. The lads crowding close by ran to one side and I took off into the air. Shestopalov, Shilkov and Prasolov flew with me. As we were gaining height, a one word message over the radio was transmitted to us: 'Kolpino!'. Now we understood that evidently the Fascist aircraft were threatening the Izhorsk factory. I turned round and saw them approaching Kolpino. White puffs of anti-aircraft fire exploded in the sky above the town's approaches. I counted eight Ju 88 bombers and as many again of Me 109 fighters. There were four of us and those with me were novice pilots. But while the Fascists were thinking what was happening, we attacked the Junkers with the speed of lightning and three enemy bombers were gone: two on fire, and a third turned slowly and plunged vertically to earth.

However, the gunner in the Junkers which I attacked managed to make a burst of fire at the last moment and a high calibre bullet tore the cowling from my fighter. The oil pressure gauge in my machine registered zero. The cockpit was filled with smoke.

Whether I liked it or not, I had to retire from the fight. I asked Shestopalov to give me cover. My engine was already misfiring and my partner was repulsing the enemy attacks time and again. My bodyguard, Kolya Shestopalov, was still not twenty years old and he had few fighting skills, but he compensated for this shortcoming with courage. Unhurried in what he did on the ground, in the air Nikolay sped like a meteor to meet the enemy.

I was still about 10 kilometres from the airfield when my engine stopped. It became quiet in the cockpit. Shestopalov, who was flying alongside, knew very well that in our new LaGG 3 fighters there was no emergency system for lowering the undercarriage. So if the engine stopped, that meant making a belly landing. Nikolay asked how I felt.

'Excellent! We'll land now,' I shouted to him.

There was the airfield, but I needed to lose a little height. In order to correct this, I put the machine into a side slip. I came in to land close to where the bombers were dispersed, leaving room for the other fighters to land. The aircraft touched the earth, bending two of the propeller blades, and at the last moment slid on to its belly. A cloud of snow rose behind it.

A motor vehicle sped to the place where we landed. I climbed out of the cockpit and saw engineer Sergeyev, technician Tarakanov, the regimental doctor, Petrov, and several sergeant pilots headed by Shorin. The pilots looked with astonishment, first at me, then at the aircraft which lay helpless on the ground.

'Never mind, lads, we'll repair the machine,' said Sergeyev. He gave some orders to the technician and whispered in my ear:

'Well then, was the game worth the candle?'

I indicated with two fingers that we had bagged a couple.

'Oh, congratulations!' The engineer shook my hand. 'Did you hear that, Tarakanov? The Captain shot down two.'

'Here's the one you must congratulate.' I turned towards Shestopalov, who was running towards us. 'He managed to shoot down a Junkers and gave me cover. Without him . . . .'

Everyone turned towards him. He stopped, reported that his mission had been carried out, but could not take his eyes off the fighter lying in the snow with its bent propeller blades.

'How do you feel, Comrade Captain?'

'Quite normal.'

Shestopalov looked knowingly at me: 'You didn't strike your nose against the gunsight like some people do.' The remark was clearly aimed at Shorin, who understood and, taking no offence, allowed a smile to cross his swollen face.

It was only several kilometres from the Izhorsk factory in Kolpino to the first line of defence. Its chimneys were belching smoke under the very noses of the enemy and gave the Fascists no peace of mind. Evidently they knew that the factory was manufacturing weapons for the front and therefore tried to bomb it every day.

One day, I was yet again sitting in the cockpit of my fighter aircraft waiting for the signal to take off. As always in such a situation, I was feeling sleepy. I had hardly closed my eyes when someone knocked on the cockpit cover. This time it was Darmogray. I opened up.

'What's up?'

'They're bombing Kolpino.'

'Then why haven't they fired a rocket?'

'I don't know,' said the Adjutant, shrugging his shoulders. 'I telephoned headquarters, but they say that no orders have been given. Over the telephone I could hear such swearing and noise. Why were there no fighters, they asked.'

'Start up!' I shouted and at that the technician pulled the cover from the engine.

'Take off!' came the order to dispersal.

In a minute we were already above the airfield. I was leading a group of six fighters. I reported to the Brigade Commander, Col Kondratyev, over the radio: 'I'm on my way to the target.'

'Make haste!' shouted Pyotr Vasilyevich. 'I can see you. Lose height! On course ahead of you the last four Junkers are going in!'

We quickly intercepted these four. I sent Ivan Tsapov's pair above in order to give cover to our attack. The Junkers went into a dive but they still hadn't released their bombs. No enemy fighters could be seen. I caught up with the leading Junkers as it was making its dive. I could see the enemy machine growing in my gunsight and the rear gunner in his cockpit taking aim. The high tail prevented him from using his machine-guns. He feared damaging the tail unit of his machine and shot past me. Something like 50 metres separated my fighter from the Junkers. I pressed the trigger and, convinced that the bomber had caught fire, turned away and gained height. The enemy machine with its load of bombs plunged to earth.

My friends shared the remaining three Junkers and followed me. Now we were alone in the sky. Meanwhile, at our airfield (we learned about this after we had landed), a strange situation developed. Four minutes after we had left, a telephone message reached regimental headquarters: 'Duty flight of six – take off!' Lt Col Nikitin fired the rocket gun and flares rose from the dug-out. But no one reacted to the signal he had given. There was no roar of engines starting up. No aircraft taxied or took off.

They told us later that the CO came down to the dug-out and telephoned the squadron.

'Where are the aircraft? Why hasn't Kaberov taken off?'

The flight of six have already gone,' replied Darmogray, anxiously.

'Why have they gone? Where? Why without orders?'

'Six minutes ago. The flight left for Kolpino and is already fighting.'

The CO wiped the sweat from his brow. 'Yes, but who sent Kaberov, and are you sure that Kaberov has led the fighters to Kolpino?'

Capt Darmogray explained everything as it had happened and Nikitin no longer questioned him. He switched on the receiver, heard our voices and calmed down a little. When we landed, the CO met us at dispersal. I climbed out of my cockpit and, as instructed, was about to report the successful completion of our mission, but he took my hand and shook it firmly.

'Well, you know. . . . However, thank you, well done! In a situation of such tension and responsibility, to take off without orders. . . . Only why didn't they inform us about this matter in time?'

At the command post, frantic telephone conversations were taking place. Those in charge explained why the fighters had taken off late and who was at fault for the delay. It was decided that the telephone operators were at fault. Air force headquarters expressed gratitude for our decisive action. So the blockade was broken. The first train made its way via Vologda and Shlisselburg from Moscow to Leningrad.

We again returned to the Oranienbaum bridgehead from the Karelian Isthmus. Semyon Lvov handed over his duties to me and prepared to fly to Moscow. He was to work in the main naval aviation inspectorate. Young airmen held Semyon Ivanovich in respect. The Order of Lenin and three Orders of the Red Banner decorated his chest. In battles for Leningrad, he had shot down about thirty aircraft. On the day of his departure, we sat in the command post surrounded by young pilots and recalled past days. When the time came for leaving, Semyon got ready for the journey and bade us farewell. At the same time, the Regimental Commander came up to me:

'Get a group of eight together. In ten minutes you are going to give cover to forces in the region of Sinyavin.'

'But I have only seven pilots,' I replied.

'Do you mind if I make up the eighth?' Lvov responded unhesitatingly. 'I shall fly for the last time, make some cutting remarks to the Fascists as I ought and, having unburdened my soul, make for Moscow.'

'Don't do that,' I objected. 'You have your documents in your pocket. Just think, you're already in Moscow. While here there's still war.'

'What nonsense you talk!'

'Let him go,' agreed the Regimental Commander. 'He wants to help you.'

'I'll partner someone in the attacking group,' Lvov whispered to me, 'while you take command of the whole parade.'

He opened his case, took out his flying helmet, which was inside, and put it on. We walked to our aircraft, took off and were soon patrolling near Sinyavin. At first, the enemy didn't appear. Then we noticed a twin-engined Dornier making for Leningrad. It was flying above us.

'Semyon!' I shouted over the radio to Lvov. 'Do you see?'

'I do!'

'Attack!'

'Aye-aye!'

Semyon gained height. A few minutes passed and the enemy reconnaissance aircraft, which had been attacked by him, was falling, broken in two, into the Ivanov rapids on the northern bank of the Neva. Calmly, as if nothing had happened, Lvov reported to me that his task had been carried out and took his place in the formation of aircraft.

After landing, we gave Semyon Ivanovich yet another warm farewell. The whole squadron escorted him as he left. He waved to us from the cockpit of his U 2. The machine took a course to Ladoga, from where it would fly to our base in the rear, in order to refuel and then to Moscow.

There are two other characteristic episodes which remain in my memory from that time. On 13 January 1943, one of the Fascist pilots in a Focke-Wulf 190 fighter had to pass over the Ladoga ice highway. A little earlier, he had ordered his mechanic to adjust the interruptor mechanism on the cannons which fire through the propeller. Over Ladoga, the pilot, seeing vehicles moving across the ice, caught them in his sights and pressed the trigger. At that moment, the shells from the incorrectly adjusted cannons cut off all the propeller blades. The engine howled, the machine shook and the pilot could do nothing except make a belly landing right beside the road. Of course, the Fascist was taken prisoner. His aircraft was delivered to the Leningrad commander's aerodrome. In the evening of 4 February, fighter pilots were brought to the aerodrome to acquaint themselves with the enemy's technical novelties. The prisoner, speaking through an interpreter, gave an explanation. He was of average height, young, energetic and brown haired. He readily answered our questions concerning the characteristics of the machine and told us how the mechanic had let him down.

'He was probably a communist,' said the pilot.

We each in turn sat in the cockpit of the Focke-Wulf and examined the equipment. It must be said – the machine was not bad. A high undercarriage, electrically controlled radial engine. Armour-plated glass in front of the gunsight and thick armour behind the back and the head protected the pilot extremely well. But when the hood was closed the field of vision from the cockpit was rather limited.

'It's a high-speed machine,' insisted its former master. 'It's not possible to shoot down this aircraft.'

'We'll see about that!' laughed the lads. As time passed, in aerial battles against Fascist aviators, the Soviet pilots demonstrated the vulnerability of the Focke-Wulf 190.

In conclusion, there was an event of a completely different character. Soon after we had seen the new German aircraft, we were invited to the premiere of the musical *The Sea Spread Far and Wide*.

Without changing, in full summer uniform and flying boots, we took our seats in the Pushkin Theatre in Leningrad. As the second act of the musical comedy was being performed by an excellent company of actors, their voices were drowned by the noise of exploding bombs and shells. The enemy had launched a simultaneous aerial and artillery bombardment. The curtains closed. The leading actor came to the front of the stage.

'What shall we do, comrades? Take shelter or continue the performance?'

There was thunderous applause in the auditorium. The audience stood up. 'Continue!'

I shall never forget this. Having seen much during the war, yet we were astonished by the heroism of the actors and the half-starved people who filled the hall – the physically exhausted citizens of our besieged city on the Neva.

'Continue the performance!' What greater appreciation of a show or a play is possible? Produced in incredibly difficult conditions by Vsevolod Vishnyevsky, Aleksandr Kron and Vsyevolod Azarov, it found worthy performers and a noble audience.

CHAPTER TWELVE

Defending The 'Victory Railroad'

But We Live In Tsarist Mansions

It was already March in 1943 and the sun was shining as if it were spring. How quiet it was around us; a silence broken only by the pleasant metronome-like sound of falling drops of water. The little houses in the settlement where we were living were buried in snow. And that snow – how pure it was! Every snowflake reflected broken rays of light into space. We had been at the aerodrome since morning. Usually at this time I would have gone to my aircraft first of all and spoken to my technician and the engine mechanic.

Ever since I had become squadron commander, I had had other work, other concerns. Snigiryev, our Senior Technical Lieutenant and party organizer, came into the dug-out. Smiling good-naturedly, he removed his hat and sat down on the bed.

'Two questions, Comrade Commander.'

'I'm listening.'

'How do you feel about awards? Should we not make lists of those on the technical staff who should receive them?. We have been at war for two years. Technician Linnik has serviced more than 300 operational flights. Hero of the Soviet Union Yegor Kostilyev's faithful assistant, Technician Sitnikov – also about 300 flights. Commissar Yefimov, Hero of the Soviet Union, had flown in his aircraft since the first day of the war. And your technician, Gritsayenko? And Korovin, Shvets, Petrov, Kudryavtsev? And our engine fitter and armourer? And Engineer Sergeyev?'

Snigiryev waited for my reply: 'Well, how then?'

I looked at him and thought: yes, Yefimov knew who to give the job of party organizer to. There was no matter which this man would not have addressed. Everything concerned him.

'Well, what's to be decided concerning the list of awards, Comrade Commander?'

'You're right, Aleksey Alekseyevich,' I replied in support. 'It should have been done long ago.'

My deputy in political matters, Capt Gromodvinnikov, came into the dug-out. He also supported the party organizer. We invited the Adjutant and the Engineering Officer to consider who among the technical staff deserved to receive the highest awards.

Meanwhile, Snigiryev was solemnly turning over the pages of the newspaper *Red Baltic Fleet*. My portrait and an article under the headline 'Strike the enemy, son, in our aircraft' had been printed in it. Beneath the title in smaller print was: 'Fellow townsfolk of the distinguished fleet pilot, Igor Kaberov, have collected 25 million roubles to build aeroplanes!' I hurried to read through the letter, written to the newspaper by my father.

> Our dear Igor, hallo! (he addressed me), You write to say that you have learned about the collection made by our Vologda townspeople to build an aircraft for you. It was announced here over the radio. Everyone here was keen to make his contribution to build a Red Star fighter. The sum collected has now reached 25 million roubles. With our money, an aircraft will be built, not only for you, my son, but also, aircraft for your friends. Shoot down even more of the Fascist vultures with these planes. Give the predators a good Russian beating.
>
> I embrace and kiss you and your comrades in arms. I wish you success in the destruction of the Fascist vultures. . . . Cordial greetings,
>
> Your loving father, A. Kaberov.

For me it was so unexpected – the sudden information given by the newspaper in a letter from my father. I looked at my friends with some embarrassment.

'Really, 25 million!' said Gromodvinnikov.

'The people of Vologda have not done badly to collect such a large sum of money!' replied Sergeyev.

'You have good people in your part of the country,' said Snigiryev admiringly, 'but we must cut out this article and place it in the station news-sheet.'

After a while, Zhenya Duk brought the post to the dug-out. 'There are twelve letters today and I think they're all from Leningrad. No, one from someone called Markov. Probably from the north – the letter's taken twenty days to come.'

I unfolded the letter and quickly ran my eyes over the short text. 'Zhenya, it's my friend Volodya Markov, who's also fighting somewhere. This is the second letter I've received from him, but I don't know where he is. It's quite possible he's in the north.'

'Is he also a fighter pilot?' Duk asked.

'Before the war, he was Chief of Staff of our flying club in Novgorod. But now I think he's not in a flying unit. See, he writes: "We are fighting and at the moment defending our positions." So he's probably in the infantry or artillery.'

'I see,' said Duk and, smiling mischievously, handed me a bundle of letters. 'And these are all from girls. If your wife finds out, you'll get it in the neck, Comrade Commander!'

He was only joking, but our post, after the blockade, became much heavier. The people of Leningrad were reading about the fighting exploits of pilots from our guards unit in the papers, and hearing more on the radio. In the letters addressed to us, the citizens of the city on the Neva congratulated us on the victory we had won against the enemy. They told us about their own lives and shared their feelings, expectations and hopes with us.

But what kind of a message was this? What a strange address! Not even a field postal number, just 'To Kaberov'. How had it reached us? In the envelope, I found another envelope. On it, written in my wife's handwriting was: Field Post Office 1101, Postbox 704. It was a letter written long ago, which had been lost somewhere.

So finally, the last, the twelfth letter. Who was it from? From Nikolay Nikolayevich Gulyayev, my friend from Vologda, head of the Local Defence Volunteers in the town: 'I am pleased to inform you,' he wrote, 'that the sum of money, collected to build aircraft for our local heroes, has reached 35 million roubles. Dear Igor, I'm waiting for the happy day when I hand you the gift from the local people. May we soon meet in Vologda. I embrace you. Nikolay.'

Zhenya and I read the letter through together. Both for him and for me, 35 million roubles was an incomprehensible figure. I thought of my local fellow countrymen with pride – a great, good-hearted people. How dear they were to me! How pleasant to hear their dialect! More than one division did they, the people of Vologda, recruit and send to the Volkhov and Leningrad fronts. And now they wanted to send aeroplanes. Among the letters which Duk brought lay a folded note, addressed to Yegor Kostilyev (he was serving with us again – now as the deputy commander of the regiment). On the note, the sender's address was not written in any detail, simply 'Oranienbaum, to the Kostilyevs'. I guessed it was from Yegor's mother and hurried to despatch his letter.

Yegor lived locally. He was born and brought up in Oranienbaum. He told me all about his family and about his mother with great affection. I knew that she was called Agrippina Fyodorovna. Before the war, Kostilyev lived in one of the flats in a two-storey house on Sverdlov Street. The head of the family had been killed in an accident on the railway. Yegor's mother, his godfather, Dmitry Ivanovich Kostilyev, and sister Zoya remained in Oranienbaum even during the most difficult days when the enemy were 4 kilometres from the town.

The house suffered from the bombardment and the city authorities moved the family of Kostilyevs into Peter's Palace. Recently, Yegor had come to us in the Oranienbaum bridgehead and did not even have time to go into town and visit his nearest and dearest. When he took the letter from me, Kostilyev began to glow with joy.

'Ah, at last!' he said.

Having run his eyes once or twice over the letter, Yegor placed it before him on the table, carefully stroking it with his palm and became thoughtful. I detected a look of alarm in his eyes.

'Has something happened?'

'No, they're all alive.'

He took a deep breath and handed me the letter: 'There, read it.'

Our dear Yegorushka! (Kostilyev's mother had written). We are still living in Peter the Third's study and have already grown accustomed to these royal mansions. The palace has been severely damaged, but our part is still whole. We still have coal and there's a little more bread now. We're alive. Your godfather has taken to his bed. Zoya and I are not well but we can still move about. What joy all of us felt when the blockade of Leningrad was broken! We live with one thought: that now things will be easier for us. The day will come and the siege will be lifted. We believe so. We heard on the radio and read in the paper about your victory in the air. We are proud of you. We have cut out the portrait of you with your hero's medal from the newspaper and hung it on the wall. But how we would like to see you my son!

Kisses, Mama, Godfather, Zoya.

When Lt Col Nikitin heard about this letter, he gave Kostilyev his pass, and Yegor set off to Oranienbaum. Fortunately, in those days food parcels were arriving from various places at the regiment for pilots who were defending Leningrad from the air. (This was how local people were expressing their gratitude.) We gave some of these parcels to Kostilyev for his family.

How Stars Shine

A temporary lull in the bombardment came to Leningrad. The Fascists brought up powerful forces to the front line, hoping once again to close the gap in the blockade. Our forces strengthened the positions they had won. In less than three weeks, despite the frosts and snowstorms, the artillery bombardment and bombs, a railway was built from Polyana station to Shlisselburg. Its overall length was 33 kilometres. A temporary pile-supported railway bridge was built across the ice-covered River Neva. On 2 February 1943, the first train passed over it. On 6 February, the completed rail track was put into operation. The people of Leningrad called it the 'Victory Railroad'. On 9 February at 1 p.m., Fascist aeroplanes tried to bomb the bridge. Six of our fighters engaged them in a fierce aerial battle. The bridge was left undamaged.

Then, once again, we defended the Izhorsk factory, the chimneys of which belched forth smoke into the enemy's eyes and gave them no peace. There were five of us: Nikolay Shestopalov, Aleksandr Shilkov, Ivan Tsapov, Pyotr Prasolov and I. The Fascist fighters met us over Kolpino – six Me 109s and two Focke-Wulf 190s. I sent Tsapov and Prasolov aloft, while Shestopalov, Shilkov and I attacked our opponents. It was not easy for three to take on eight of them, but we had good reserves – Tsapov and Prasolov. They gained height and were ready to pounce on the Fascists from above. At one moment, Sasha Shilkov found himself in a dangerous position. A pair of Messerschmitts attacked him. They came at him from behind and attacked him from below.

'Sashka!' I shouted to Shilkov over the radio, and rushed to intercept the enemy aircraft. They climbed steeply but fell under the fire from Tsapov. Ivan Ivanovich's hand was steady and one Me 109 plummeted in smoke to earth. A pair of Focke-Wulf 190s came after me. In a fight, the best defence is attack. In a flash, I turned and now our aircraft were speeding to meet one another. 'A head-on attack', the thought flashed through my mind. The Fascist did not deviate from his path. And yet, usually, they don't like head-on attacks. As a rule, you only have to succeed in turning on an opponent and he climbs away from you; what's more into the sun, so that you lose sight of him. But this one went into the attack.

I could expect help from no one. My comrades were engaged in a fight with the Messerschmitts. 'Well then, "Focke", let's get to grips! If it has to be head-on then head-on it is!' I muttered through clenched teeth. Only . . .

> No Aryan can stand this – you're not up to it!
> You'll fear to lose your skin.
> I won't turn aside, for I'm a Baltic pilot,
> And I'm in a battle for my homeland.

Not long before, I had been sitting in the cockpit of a captured Focke-Wulf 190. 'So then, "Focke" I know your aircraft well. The air-cooled radial engine and bullet-proof glass in front of the gunsight would reliably protect you from such an attack. And four 20 mm cannons, malevolently squinting at me, of course make you confident of victory. Therefore you make your head-on attack with such enthusiasm.'

The Fascist fighter grew in size every second, and I lost count of time. I saw only the lines on the gunsight and in the centre of it the Focke-Wulf rushing towards me at full speed. One thought I had: 'As long as I'm not too late to open fire first. . . .'

> Still closer the enemy, louder the roar of the motor.
> Another second it seemed and then . . .
> But, unable to bear the Russian pressure,
> He tried to make a turn.
> Clumsily he made his cowardly move.
> Fire! And the Focke fell bullet riddled.
> They didn't help you, Fascist Focke,
> Neither the armour behind, nor the shield of glass.

The burning fighter still climbed for some time, but then turned over, dropped its nose and fell to earth like a torch.

The Messerschmitts ceased their attacks and quit the battle. Evidently, the Fascist who had been killed was no ordinary pilot, but the group's commander. I gathered my group, attentively observed the opponents' moves and, in general, did all that a flight commander should do, but no way could I control the nervous tremor which struck me like a fever. There had been such a concentrated nervous strain for a few seconds. How was it that I had not collided with the Focke-Wulf as I skimmed right beneath his tail?

The thought of the duel which had taken place would not leave me. No matter where I looked, before my eyes this yellow-nosed Focke-Wulf appeared, aiming at me. Now it was clear what a head-on attack was like. It is a fearful attack. You mustn't turn aside and you mustn't open fire before time. Otherwise, you die. It's a duel, not an attack.

In one fight, in just such a situation, the Regimental Commander, N.M. Nikitin, didn't manage to take aim before the Fascist pilot pressed his trigger. Nikolay Mikhailovich stayed alive only by a miracle. He was saved by the 37 mm bullet-proof glass which had been fitted in front of the gunsight in his Hurricane fighter. We were then convinced by this evidence and valued the armoured glass, regretting that similar glass was not fitted in our own fighters.

I sat in my cockpit for a long time at dispersal. I had never been so tired before, but now it was as if I had borne a heavy burden. The Focke-Wulf was still before my eyes. I recalled how the Fascist prisoner of war had affirmed that it was impossible to shoot down a Focke-Wulf 190. Wrong, it's quite possible! I removed my flying helmet and placed it on the gunsight. The winter wind passed its cold fingers through my hair. I pulled my cap down over my face and climbed out of the cockpit. Technician Gritsayenko, who was already arming the aircraft, suddenly stopped his work and looked at me.

'So does that mean, Commander, that another star may be drawn on the fuselage?'

'Yes, Sasha.'

'Boris!' shouted Gritsayenko to Alferov. 'Stencil, paint!' A new star shone on the side of my plane.

I went into the dug-out and almost collided with Duk and Darmogray, hurrying to meet me. 'Here's a gift for you to mark your twenty-eighth aerial victory, Comrade Captain. It's time to dance!'

'But where's the gift then?'

'Here's the telegram.'

'No, I must know; why am I to dance?'

'Well, if that's the case, play!'

Zhenya took the bayan, stretched the instrument's bellows and artlessly fingered the keyboard. Then I created such steps that the dust rose in the dug-out to the ceiling.

'Well, what about that? Is that enough for you?'

I read the telegram. So that's it! What news! I reread it: 'Son Valeriy has been born. Kisses, Valya.'

'Brothers! . . . No, just think! This is a reward for the Focke. . . . Yes, and what a reward! A son, Valerka! Hurrah!'

Both Duk and Darmogray gave me their friendly support: 'Hu-rra-ah!'

At The Oranienbaum Bridgehead

April 1943. Since morning, it had been rather cold but towards midday it was noticeably warmer. Although a fresh breeze was blowing from the Gulf, the spring sunshine was already giving plenty of warmth to winter's frozen earth. It was hard to believe that quite recently, there in the Oranienbaum bridgehead, intense battles had been fought. At that time it was quiet, as if there had been no war.

Zhenya Duk and I stood by our dug-out and, breathing the scented air of the pine forest, hearkened to that silence. Then, suddenly . . .

'Good-morning, comrades!'

'Hallo.' We turned and answered as we scrutinized a man, unknown to us, who was approaching. Judging from his shoulder straps, here before us was a senior lieutenant in the medical branch of the service.

'Doctor, who are you?' I asked, 'And where are you from?'

'Lt Bobilkin. I've been to Izhora, taken the wounded away and here,' he showed his bag, 'I've plenty of medical supplies.' His tired face brightened into a good-natured smile. 'I have been instructed to find a certain pilot as I travelled on my way.'

'Which pilot?' We began to take some interest.

The Lieutenant shrugged his shoulders. 'I don't know his surname. He shot down a Fascist reconnaissance aircraft over our farm. We call him "Spike".'

We viewed this Lieutenant with suspicion. A military man must come from a military unit, but he was from some kind of farm. We felt awkward about asking for his documents, so I proposed to Zhenya Duk that we conduct him to our regimental headquarters. However, soon the doctor reappeared in our dug-out.

'Comrade Captain,' he began as he appeared on the threshold, 'why are you so modest? It's you I'm looking for, and you took me to headquarters. But this doesn't matter. Now I know all about you. Your Regimental Commander said that he will give you a vehicle for the trip to our place. You must know that our sailors are expecting you as their guest! Until we meet at the Markov Farmstead.' We walked out of the dug-out. He waved to us and hurried to the car that was waiting for him.

The bad war-torn road slowly crawled beneath the wheels of our vehicle, which had seen much service. When we drove over cobblestones, although the car shook, it was able to move. Yet the driver, a young sailor, drove confidently. Finally the road went uphill, the mud was left behind and we felt calmer.

'Comrade Captain, what sort of a place is this Markov estate where we're going with a bayan?'

'The Regimental Commander advised me to take the bayan. "The infantry," he said, "you will entertain there if the situation demands." Ah, here's the place, evidently a military establishment and, I dare say, large. Well, Markov's a general for sure.'

'That's interesting,' smiled the driver, 'I've never seen a general.' The road wound through the forest.

'Is it true, Comrade Captain, that it was you who shot down the aircraft of which the medical officer was speaking?' asked the driver and, without waiting for a reply, continued. 'I was at headquarters when the doctor came to the commander. He spoke about an aerial battle, which everybody in their place observed.'

'In fact, there was no battle there,' I explained. 'At that time, we were returning from a military exercise. As leader of the group giving cover, I and my second-in-command, Nikolay Shestopalov, were the last to land, but an order came over the radio: "Do not land. You must go to the Lubensk lake district. At a height of 600 metres there is a Henschel 126 spotter plane. Destroy it!" We flew below cloud edge but did not see the Henschel. But shells were exploding on the ground. That meant that the spotter plane was somewhere about. "Target on the left!" shouted Shestopalov. "I see it," I replied and sped to attack. As the Henschel emerged from the clouds, he saw us, was about to go back into cloud cover, but failed to do so. I had already opened fire.'

'Well, what happened next?' asked the driver.

'The burst of gunfire hit the strut supporting the wing and the Henschel's left wing folded. The aircraft went into a sudden spin and fell into the bog. That was the only action there was.'

'You have dangerous work, Comrade Captain.'

'It's dangerous everywhere now. There's a war. You and I are driving up to the front line. It's dangerous there too.'

I had hardly pronounced these words, when the driver slammed on the brakes and our car stopped still. The roadway ended. In front of us was a gigantic crater.

'Look what we've come to!' I said. 'It looks as if we are not far from the first line of defence. Let's go back!'

The driver reversed and turned the car round; but then a junior nurse appeared from somewhere. 'Where are they taking you? Well, drive away from here before the Fascists open fire on you!'

'Nurse!' I opened the door and shouted. 'We're going to Gen Markov's place.'

'Go back a kilometre and turn right!' She waved her arm. 'You'll see a sign there. Get away from here quickly!'

There was the side road. We turned off and were lost in tall bushes bordering the road on both sides. Sensing that he was out of danger, the driver stopped the car and regained his breath.

'Indeed, Comrade Captain, lost in our conversation, we almost drove into the enemy's lines.'

The way across a small bog was paved with logs. We had hardly rumbled some 100 metres when, skidding on the damp planks, our vehicle's right-hand rear wheel jumped from the roadway and stopped. We were 200 metres from our destination. I walked up and showed my documents to the man on duty, informed him of the purpose of our visit and asked where we could find the Commanding Officer, Gen Markov. The guard moved his automatic rifle aside, looked at the documents and smiled.

'We're expecting you, Comrade Captain, but there is no Gen Markov. It's Maj Markov. He commands the 3rd Battalion of the 5th Marine Brigade of the Baltic Fleet. So, Comrade Captain of Guards, we are also sailors,' he explained, not without pride, and straightening his sailor's cap, which did not match his army uniform and had slipped to the back of his head, started to ring headquarters.

'Interesting,' I thought, 'among these forests and swamps are marines. . . .' As I was waiting, I moved aside and it so happened that between me and the sentry box was a tall bush. Then from the direction of the box, I heard a voice at the sound of which I stopped as if rooted to the spot.

'Did you get the surname of the pilot right? There's no mistake?'

I could not believe my ears. It was the voice of Volodya Markov, chief of our Novgorod flying club. The bush prevented me from seeing him. Then the guard spoke up.

'None at all, Comrade Major, there's no mistake.'

'And you say he's not tall?' continued the Major, trying to elicit the facts. 'Well then, show me this guardsman!'

But I was already running to meet him and in a few moments found myself in the strong embrace of a friend.

'Igoreshka, my friend! How on earth did you get here? What a meeting! Listen, I thought you would be somewhere on the Volkhov front.'

'And I thought you were in the north. Your letters took almost a month. I came here thinking to meet someone of the same name. . . .'

A big, broad-shouldered man in a long greatcoat like a cavalry officer, he was just as cheerful as he was before the war. We looked at one another and could not believe we had met.

'Yes,' Markov suddenly remembered, 'so was it you and the spotter plane above us?' he pointed at the sky.

'That's how it was, Volodya.'

He shook his head. 'I didn't know it was you but thought: "Suppose you are here somewhere, and this is you giving a display in the sky." And indeed, that's how it was!'

When he found that we were stuck in the mud, he came to the car with me. The driver had got a lever ready and thrust it under the wheel. But Markov took hold of the bumper and with one heave lifted the rear of the car and placed it on the log platform.

'There you are. Now you can drive,' he laughed.

When we were in battalion headquarters, the telephone rang. Volodya lifted the receiver, listened, gave brief instructions and wished the caller good luck.

'Scouts are going out to bring in prisoners for interrogation,' he explained to me. 'It's the usual practice for us, but you must wish them good luck.

Taking prisoners is not easy and very dangerous; but without it defence is impossible.'

He removed his greatcoat and straightened his tunic.

'Volodya, how did you come to be here? Surely, you're an air force reserve pilot.'

'Very simply. You went away to Eysk in the autumn of 1939 and I stayed at the flying club. Just before the war in May, they called me to Leningrad for military training. I changed and put on a sailor's uniform and joined a unit. There's a squadron of naval bombers there, the MBR 2s. You know, those enormous flying boats. I had only been flying in the U 2. During the training, they appointed me as commandant of the company of land forces defending the garrison. Soon the war started. When Hitler's armies approached our region, only a few aeroplanes were left in the squadron. From the crews without aircraft, they formed a company of marines. Then they appointed me as commander.'

A small barn near the command point, well concealed among the bushes and tall trees, served as a battalion mess. At the entrance, a slogan was written: 'A Fascist killed on the River Voronka will not storm Leningrad. Have you killed a Fascist?'

'This is our company cabin,' said Major Markov cheerfully as he entered the mess and introduced me to the staff officers, among them the Chief of Staff, Capt Chistyakov, and his political deputy, Capt G.N. Strelov.

'There's the galley,' he pointed at the door, 'and of course the cook. True, in breach of naval regulations, our cook is a woman, Vera Vasilyevna. But she makes excellent bortsch. The water's overboard,' laughed Volodya, looking through a small pothole at the swamp. 'Everything is as on a ship.'

After supper, our free and easy conversation continued. I told them how I shot down the spotter plane, then about my comrades in arms: about the feats of Hussein Aliyev, Volodya Tenyugin, our fighting commissar Matvey Yefimov – the first in the regiment to become a Hero of the Soviet Union.

It was already past midnight when Volodya brought my bayan and asked me to play, but quietly. It had happened that on one occasion, when the scouts, after a difficult but successful reconnaissance operation from which they returned not only with prisoners but with valuable trophies, rejoicing in the warm sunshine, decided to rest. They dried their equipment, cleaned their weapons and sang songs to the accompaniment of a captured accordion. With the help of a sound detector, Hitler's soldiers took bearings on the place where the music was being played and with five high explosive shells straddled the shelter. All fourteen men were killed.

Late at night, when everyone had left, Markov and I continued our chat in the command post. 'What did you receive the Order of the Red Star for?' I asked my friend.

Volodya looked at his medal and wiped it with his sleeve in order to make it shine brighter. 'It was in December 1941. I was still Company Commander then. Our brigade of marines were conducting reconnaissance operations in force. At the rocket signal, I sent the men on the attack and we literally dislodged the Fascists as we went from the front-line defences. We captured Krenovo, Sista-Palkino, Pernovo and Verkhnie Luzhki.'

'I can see that you've turned yourself into a good infantryman. Well done!' I was pleased for my friend and asked: 'But why are these inhabited posts on the map beyond the front line?'

'We carry out set exercises and return to our initial positions. This is reconnaissance in force.'

'Like fighters, they pounce, do their rustling and depart.'

'Ah, you're right,' Volodya again became lively. 'We really are destroyers. In the battalion, almost everyone is a sniper. Even the storekeepers, cooks, clerks in the companies have opened their personal score in revenge. Listen to what a sergeant, taken prisoner by us from the 207th Guards Division, which is now fighting against us, said: "The Russian fire power is terrible. You have driven us into our bunkers and compelled us to rot alive in the swamp water. The losses are enormous. We bury our dead almost every day. I'm glad to be a prisoner. I can stay alive."'

A light knock on the door stopped our conversation. The guard came in.

'Comrade Major, the scouts have returned.'

'How did they do?'

'Successfully. They've brought in a prisoner. Their leader was scratched. They're bandaging him.'

Markov turned to me. 'What lads we have!'

'Yes, you really do not allow the Fascists to rest,' I said. 'And it is certainly very difficult to take prisoners.'

'For the scouts, Igorek, the most difficult thing to do is to cross the front line,' replied Markov. 'In pitch darkness, you must pass quietly through barbed wire defences, mine fields and booby-traps. You mustn't cough nor rattle anything nor step on a twig. And there must be constant communication between the men in the group.'

'But if there's a mistake?'

'Mistake, you say. Well, there was a scout leader, Viktor Gomora, a cheerful and intelligent lad. Once, five of the scouts under his command set off for prisoners. They crawled noiselessly almost to the Fascist bunker itself. Suddenly there was an explosion. The leader had made a mistake by failing to notice a booby-trap mine placed by the enemy. The leader's face and chest were blood-stained, his left eye was damaged. What courage, what restraint he must have possessed in order not to shriek or moan, in no way to reveal his presence to the enemy. It would have destroyed them all. But Gomora endured his suffering.'

Furthermore, Markov said that Gomora had returned from the hospital to the unit and, despite the fact that he now had only one eye, had again led a platoon of scouts and continued to spread fear among the Fascists. He was killed by a sniper's bullet, which hit his Red Star medal, ricocheted from it and penetrated his heart. We sat long together, Volodya and I, remembering friends, acquaintances, talking about complex situations in which we had taken part.

I left after breakfast at ten o'clock. The driver had already started the car and we bade farewell to Volodya. But he suddenly begged me to wait and hurriedly went off somewhere. In twenty minutes, Markov returned accompanied by a large group of men serving with him. He stopped in front of me and unexpectedly said solemnly:

'Dear friend! As a mark of gratitude for shooting down the spotter plane, as a result of which the lives of many of our comrades were saved, for the interesting conversation and for your friendship in battle, on behalf of all the soldiers fighting here with the hated enemy, permit us to present to you our modest gift, a captured pistol taken last night from a captured sergeant-major. May you and all your comrades fly high!'

To the sound of approving exclamations, Markov handed me the gift.

The car moved away and was already gathering speed but Markov and his comrades in arms still stood and waved to us until we were hidden from sight at the turning.

'La Funf In Der Luft'

At last summer came. The evening before, I had prepared my fishing tackle and at first light ran to the river. The morning turned out warm; there was not a cloud in the sky. I walked along the river bank on a pathway winding through tall grass and bushes. We were once again at our base in the rear, more than 200 kilometres from Leningrad, on the shore of a picturesque river.

I went down to the river. Sedge swayed above the water; the submerged blackened branches of a tree were visible. I lifted one of the rods. The worm was there and the fish hadn't taken it. What was the matter? Very well, I'd try another. Lo and behold, the second float had gone. I took the fishing rod and there was a ruff on the hook! Never mind, that was better than nothing. But yet another float had gone to the bottom. I pulled on the line. There was something there, yes! I dragged it to the bank. What a fine perch it was! I took a new worm and my hands trembled with excitement. Again something took the float. Now, already dancing in the water, it thrashed, first towards the shore, then away. It mustn't get away, I thought. I struck and pulled. A chub! And what a big one! The fins red, the body silver. I threw it on the shore and cast again. I forgot about everything else in the world. My watch hands told me to hurry. What a pity there was so little time, otherwise I could have done some good fishing. Six chub and two perch. I'd left the basket at camp, so there was nowhere to put the catch. Never mind. I spread grass inside my service cap, placed my catch in it and walked back.

'Well then, welcome the fisherman then!' I roused Darmogray and Duk. 'What weather there is in the countryside here!'

'Look at the catch!' the adjutant enthused, wiping his eyes. 'Yevgeny, get up and clean the fish. We'll prepare fish soup.'

The CO was on leave, so we had much to worry about. The authorities wanted us to receive new aircraft, magnificent LaGG 5 fighters, which were undergoing military tests. We had to master the new technology and there wasn't much time for this. Moreover, as Lt Col Nikitin was away, I was ordered to stand in for him. The Regimental Chief of Staff, Dmitriyevsky, calmed me: 'Everything will be fine.' Of course everything would be fine, but it was necessary to work to achieve that.

The fighters, bought with the money raised by the Vologda district's workers, arrived at our aerodrome. Shining with new lacquer, two squadrons of LaGG 5s and a squadron of Yaks were lined up in a row at dispersal. Not aircraft but a dream! We could not wait and got on with the training flights. Soon the new machines had been mastered. Capt Viktor Terekhin's squadron in Yaks flew away to the front. A week later, on 18 July 1943, the remaining two squadrons, Capt Dmitry Tatarenko's and mine, left our base in the rear. Lt Col Nikitin returned from leave and also flew with us.

We flew without stops to Leningrad. We passed over the Finnish Gulf to the island of Lavansari, which translated from Finnish means 'island of happiness'. A week later, Viktor Terekhin's squadron landed there. I had to spend a couple of days at Lavansari. Then I was summoned by Lt Col Nikitin.

'Take strong lads with you,' he said. 'You're going to Seyskari Island. You'll be working with Stormoviks Il 2.'

Whom should I take? I took Sasha Shilkov, Nikolay Shestopalov, Pyotr Prasolov, Nikolay Mokshina and Aleksey Baranov. Soon our group were in their new place. Ivan Tsapov, my deputy, took command of those pilots who remained on Lavansari.

When we had landed on the airstrip at Seyskari, we paid a visit to the island's Commandant. Some time later, our technicians reported their arrival after making a sea trip in a naval cutter. We organized a meeting where we got to know the Stormovik crews. Capt Mikhail Romanov was their Commanding Officer. Of average height, far from athletic in build, but very decisive, strong willed and energetic, he told us about the situation around the island and showed us traces of enemy bombing raids.

The next morning, Vasiliy Chernyenko, commander of the reconn-aissance flight in Terekhin's squadron, climbed into his Yak, flew around the whole area of islands in the Finnish Gulf and landed on our aerodrome.

'Hallo, Igorek!' Chernyenko came up to me. 'It's me, Vasya. I've arrived from work,' he said, in keeping with his way of joking at every opportunity. Picking up a small stick from the ground, Vasya outlined at my feet the silhouette of the islands nearest to us. 'This is Gotland, and this is Great Tyuters. Here two enemy patrol ships are making for Finland. You'll catch them if you take off straight away.'

Vasya and I went to Capt Romanov. He sent eight Stormoviks accompanied by six of our Lavochkins. We had only just taken off when we identified our target. Two Fascist ships were making for Kotka. They sailed alone without aerial cover. Of course, the enemy's aviators knew that a dogfight with our fighters promised nothing good. They got to know what the La 5 fighters were like when the 4th Guards aviation regiment was flying there. It was as if the Fascist pilots now avoided meetings with Lavochkins. At dawn or towards evening, they would unexpectedly fly in to our aerodrome like a gang of robbers. But we only had to take off and the ether was filled with the cries of panic: '*Achtung, achtung, La funf in der Luft.*' ('Attention, attention, La 5s in the air.') However, this time there was no one to shout to. Our group were already approaching the target.

Anti-aircraft guns fired from the ships at the Stormoviks. But they dived, ignoring the flak. Enveloped in flames, the leading ship lifted its bow and sank into the water. It vanished in a moment. The deep waters literally swallowed it. Another patrol vessel poked half out of the water like a fishing float. Sloops scurried about it.

Observing this impressive picture, I thought of the bravery of our Stormovik aircrews, who had managed to deliver such a precise blow on manoeuvring ships, especially since they had no bomb sights in their aircraft. The second enemy ship disappeared beneath the waves.

The Stormoviks gathered together and in minutes we were back at our aerodrome. We warmly congratulated Capt Romanov and his subordinates on a successful attack.

'Friends! Today is 24 July – Navy Day, our holiday!' said squadron party organizer, Flight Technician A. Snigiryev. So we all joyfully shouted 'Hurrah' on the occasion of the holiday and the victory over the enemy, whom we had just overcome. And the nearby forest echoed that shout.

It was still only ten o'clock in the morning, but the sun had already managed to warm the earth and the air. I went to the Gulf to bathe. On the shore, Snigiryev, Sanoylov the armourer and one of the pilots caught up with me. They took hold of me and threw me in the air like a kitten.

'What's all this about?' I escaped but the lads threw me even higher.

'Devils, you'll drop me, injure me!' But they wouldn't leave off.

'Then tell me what all this is about.'

'It means that we are congratulating you on becoming a Hero of the Soviet Union.' Once more the whole island heard a deep throated 'Hurrah'.

'You're joking?'

'No, we're not.'

'Aren't you mistaken?'

'No, there's no mistake. It was broadcast over the radio. There are three new heroes: you, Semyon Lvov and Dmitry Tatarenko.'

'Then we need a "Hurrah" for them,' I suggested.

Having shouted till we were hoarse, we returned to the aerodrome. I walked as if in a dream. I could hardly believe it. But yet one more joyful piece of news had already been received at the aerodrome. A large group of our airfield workers had been awarded decorations and medals.

The next day was marked by an important event. It was announced that technicians Yevseyev and Baranov and our clerk Duk were to go to study at flying school. I tested the flying skills of Baranov and Yevseyev. They could pilot the U 2 aircraft excellently. At the same time, Zhenya Duk begged me to be tested:

'Comrade Commander, teach me to fly.'

'It's easy to say "teach me"!'

'But you've already promised. . . .'

I sat Zhenya in the cockpit. We made twelve circuits and two flights further afield in the area where we carried out flying manoeuvres. Then I told Zhenya that he should fly on his own, but I concealed myself, hidden in the forward cockpit. Duk rose confidently into the air, made a circuit and landed. His joy knew no bounds. Zhenya was accepted in the Eysk flying school with Yevseyev and Baranov.

On 25 July, a day memorable for all of us, we organized a warm sending-off for our three comrades. They went away and we stayed on the island and continued to fight.

I cannot resist telling the tale of one other curious incident which took place when we were on Seyskari Island. For some reason, I was called to regimental headquarters on Lavansari. A minute before take-off, an aviation engineer who had come to us from one of the aero-engine factories came up to me. He was carrying out so-called 'revision' work on an Ash 82 engine. Everything that had to be done on Seyskari was finished. Now he asked to be sent to Lavansari, but we didn't have a two-seater aircraft.

'Perhaps you had better go in a fighter,' I said. 'In six minutes, you'd be there.'

'You're joking, Comrade Captain – I'm serious.' The engineer was offended.

'No, why not? I'm also serious,' I said. 'Lay on the fuselage in here.' I opened the door used by technicians. 'The control cables are above you. Don't touch them.'

The engineer looked at me, thought for a moment and confidently stepped into the aircraft. He was a tall, lean man in a brown suit and plimsolls. He squeezed through the trapdoor with difficulty, turned over and lay down. I sat in the cockpit, started the engine, and looked through the armour-plated glass behind me. Only his legs, white socks and plimsolls were visible. In the air, once more I glanced at my passenger. He lay calmly without moving. The aircraft flew just above the water. Approaching the landing strip on Lavansari, I saw four Me 109s above us. They were already diving, trying to attack aircraft standing on the ground. I intercepted them and the Messerschmitts started to gain height. Then two of them came at me and the other two tried to strike our aircraft on duty. I had to pick a fight with all four. At a convenient moment, I opened fire on one of the enemy fighters. Starting to smoke, he flew off in the direction of Kurgalov Peninsula. Meanwhile, a flight of Yak 1s took off and the three remaining Messerschmitts hurried to their aerodrome. Disturbed by the fight, I landed, taxied, handed over the aircraft to the technician and went away to headquarters. As I remember, the Commanding Officer and I were talking when a sailor ran into the dug-out.

'Comrade Lieutenant Colonel – a stranger has been discovered.'

Nikitin looked at the sailor in astonishment. 'But where is he?'

'There. . . . We found him in the captain's aircraft.'

Only then did I understand what had happened, and with the permission of the CO, returned to dispersal. My passenger, whose existence I had unforgivably forgotten, had survived the fever of battle and was standing guarded by an armed sailor. The engineer's hair was dishevelled, his face was pallid.

At that moment, I probably appeared no less pitiable. I tried to explain things to the engineer, and begged his forgiveness. Coming to his senses, not without humour he spoke of what he had experienced and we laughed heartily. Then, I took him to headquarters, introduced him to the Regimental Commander and once more, this time together, we related this amusing story.

Nikitin said something reproachful to me. I felt I was at fault. But everything was settled. The engineer was advised to rest. But something quite unexpected awaited me. I had to leave the squadron and go to Moscow by order of the Commander in Chief of Naval Aviation, Col Gen S.F. Zhavoronkov.

Orders are orders, so on 18 August 1943, Aviation Day, I left the regiment. I handed over the squadron to Ivan Ivanovich Tsapov. He assembled the squadron on parade. In front of me stood men who, not long before, had been sergeant pilots, and were now already first lieutenants. Each one had a campaign medal on his chest. Orders and medals shone on the tunics of technicians and young specialists.

'Goodbye, comrades! Thank you for friendship, for fighting know-how and courage.' My voice broke (nerves, nerves – somehow, I had never noticed this before). 'Remember, always remember those who never returned from military operations. Patiently teach the novices. Do not forget the rule to which we have always been faithful: though you perish, rescue your comrades. I hope that you may all see the bright day of victory over Fascism.'

Sasha Shilkov (now he was Deputy Commander of the squadron) and my constant second-in-command, Kolya Shestopalov, accompanied me in flight. We made a circuit of the island, flew over dispersal at top speed and in a steep climb rose into the blue Baltic sky.

Before Kronstadt, Shilkov and Shestopalov turned back at my signal. 'Goodbye, friends!' I watched them go. 'Sometime, we'll meet again.'

At combined headquarters, the new divisional commander, Lt Colonel Koreshkov received me. I told him about the military situation on the islands. Then the telephone rang and the commander lifted the receiver. I looked round his modestly furnished study. On the wall to the left of me hung a portrait in a black frame. From the portrait the lively, thoughtful eyes of Pyotr Vasilyevich Kondratyev looked out. What a remarkable man Col

Kondratyev had been. Four rectangular tabs and the Gold Star of a Hero on his chest. In less than two years, he had made the journey from Squadron Commander to Brigade Commander. But on 2 July 1943, the day when the 61st Aviation Brigade was changed to the 1st Aerial Fighting Division, its commander was killed. Koreshkov finished his telephone conversation.

'So now I must say,' he came from behind the table, 'this is the time to congratulate you on your Gold Star.' The Divisional Commander shook my hand firmly. 'But I can inform you confidentially that your decoration has already come from Moscow. Presently, you will fly in a fighter for the medal. In the evening, a member of the military soviet will present you with the Order of Lenin and the Hero's Gold Star at a solemn parade on the occasion of the conferment of the status as guards to the 57th Regiment of assault aircraft. So don't delay. Tomorrow you will return here and we will send you in a U 2 to Vologda. A week at home and then to Moscow to Zhavaronkov.'

I shan't describe in detail the presentation of the award, except to say that I was agitated as I had never been in combat. At a modest dinner with comrades, Rear Adm N.K. Smirnov handed me the Order of Lenin and the Gold Medal of a Hero of the Soviet Union. It took place in an atmosphere of surprising cordiality and affection. Someone brought me a bayan. There were songs, dances, sincere speeches and pleasant parting words.

The next morning, Lt Col Koreshkov and I met again and once more he congratulated me and held my star in the palm of his hand as if he were testing its weight.

At that moment, an officer, short in stature, came up to us:

'Comrade Lieutenant Colonel, the machine is ready – may we start?'

'Do you know one another?' Koreshkov exchanged a glance with Tsaplin and me.

'We do.' I recalled how once, in wild stormy weather, 1/Lt Tsaplin had delivered the post to us on the island at night. We persuaded him to stay till morning but he flew off to neighbours. ('The lads are also waiting for letters,' he explained.)

Soon I was flying in the U 2 aircraft, piloted by Tsaplin, to my native Vologda.

As always, the days spent in my district passed quickly. In accordance with instructions, after a week I arrived in Moscow and attended a reception given by the Commander of the fleet's air force, Gen S.F. Zhavoronkov.

'So this is what you are like, Capt Kaberov!' said the General after I had introduced myself, measuring me with a glance and smiling. 'For some reason, I pictured you as a Hercules.'

'What can I do, Comrade General? I've failed to grow.'

'Never mind, in other things you have succeeded. Take a seat.' He pointed to an armchair.

The first thing that caught my eye in Zhavoronkov's study was a photo-portrait of Col Kondratyev – just the same as I had seen in the Divisional

Commander's study. We did not talk for long. Zhavoronkov informed me that from then on I was to be a flying instructor at the Eysk flying school. My plea to leave me at the front was politely heard and firmly refused.

'You have served in combat, Comrade Kaberov, and that's enough,' said the General. 'Youngsters have need of your battle experience.'

After a year of work in the Eysk flying school, I was sent on a course for senior officers. From there, I received an appointment in the Far East. I took part in the war with Japan. Then I wound up at the Moscow Air Force Academy which now carries the name of Y.A. Gagarin.

All this was extremely interesting, but I shall only tell of two peaceful days which have stirred in my memory all that I lived through in wartime.

CHAPTER THIRTEEN

The Stone Beside The Gate

By August 1961, exactly twenty years had passed since that memorable fight, memorable for me, after which my I 16 landed in a rye field beside the village of Bolshaya Vruda and struck a large stone boulder.

In 1960, I was demobilized and moved with my family to Novgorod. From there to Bolshaya Vruda is only a stone's throw. I wanted to take a look at those places, to visit Zinaida Mikhailovna Petrova, in whose house I found shelter after my unhappy landing. First I had to find out if she was still living in those parts. So I sent a letter to the Volosovo regional council. Soon, an answer came. 'Zinaida is expecting you to be her guest.' Zinaida Mikhailovna herself also sent me a letter, and it was so good and heartfelt, that not to go to Bolshaya Vruda would have been a sin.

The grey asphalt of the road moved beneath the wheels of my 'Volga'. I travelled by the route: Novgorod–Leningrad–Nizino–Gorelovo–Klopitsy–Volosovo–Bolshaya Vruda.

Nizino: how everything there had changed. The tall birch trees and poplars had not been there before. A shy little boy led me to places of burial for those who had died in the war. Along a pathway bordered by flowers, we approached the grave I was looking for, an obelisk towered above it. At the foot lay fresh flowers. In gold on the stone were clearly inscribed the words:

> Here are buried fighter pilots, who died heroically
> 16–21 August 1941 in aerial battles in defence of Leningrad.
> Hero of the Soviet Union, First Lieutenant Brinko, P.
> Major Novikov, I.
> First Lieutenant Sherstobitov, V.
> First Lieutenant Sobolyev, N.
> First Lieutenant Zhbanov, A.
> First Lieutenant Bagryantsev, M.
> Lieutenant Aliev, G.
> Second Lieutenant Sherchenko, N.

I stood benumbed. My friends, my dear brothers and comrades. I have come to you. I remember you. You are in my heart and mind forever, forever . . . .

In the inscription on the obelisk were many unfortunate inaccuracies. It would be necessary to correct them, but that was for later. At the time, I could not utter a word. Spasms squeezed my throat; my young guide stood beside me in silent understanding.

From my comrades' grave, I went towards the area where once our aerodrome had been. I walked slowly along the road, that very road along which I had accompanied my wife on the first day of the war. I stopped and listened. Behind the bushes, as then, a nameless rivulet was playing over pebbles, babbling and muttering something light-heartedly. Could twenty years have passed? Twenty years . . .?

The earth shelters had collapsed. There was a mound in place of our dug-out. It had also caved in – you couldn't get in. I returned to the river once again. Nearby I stumbled on something. I raked the grass aside and sticking up from the earth I discovered the metal ring of a stanchion to which we fastened the aircraft at dispersal. I ran to the car for a starting handle and used it to extract the trophy. Beside the river, where the armourers' tent was pitched, I found a cartridge case from a machine-gun. The corkscrew stanchion and the cartridge were dear to me for some reason. Memories . . . memories . . . .

From Nizino I arrived at Gorelivo. Zhenya, Zinaida Mikhailovna's son, lived there. The very same Zhenya who, in August 1941, had outstripped the other boys and run to my broken aircraft. A very tall, fair-haired man with broad shoulders met me on the threshold of his home. I told him my surname.

'Yevgeniy Georgevich,' he introduced himself to me, smiling with embarrassment. 'Please meet my wife, Katya.'

'I'm very pleased to meet you,' said Katya and, asking us to excuse her, hurried to the kitchen.

'But I think I know you,' boomed Yevgeniy Georgevich. 'You're the very same airman . . . .'

'Yes, yes, Zhenya, the same. Your mother asked me in her letter to call on you. So I have done so.'

Katya had already laid the table, placing glasses there.

'I'm driving – not for me,' I said.

'Yes, surely! Well, just a little. . . .'

'Thank you, no, no. . . .'

Zhenya and I had a bite and, taking leave of Katya, started on our way. On the road, he told me that he worked as a foreman in the water and sewerage service. The work wasn't bad; he liked it.

'Stop, Zhenya, we almost passed it.' I stopped the car. 'It's Klopitsy!'

'Yes, there ahead is the village.'

'But the aerodrome . . . it's not there now. . . .'

We drove up to the place where our canvas home had stood. I climbed out of the car, looked at the pine trees, listened to their noise and surrendered to the power of reminiscences. 'From this aerodrome, Zhenya, on 10 August 1941, I left on a flight, but landed beside your village in a field where you found me. . . .'

A short distance before arriving at Bolshaya Vruda, I drove into a thicket and changed my clothes. 'Zhenya, I must arrive in a proper fashion.'

'Well, quite right. . . .' He looked at my uniform, orders and medals with interest.

At last, we drove into the village and stopped by Zinaida Mikhailovna's house. I got out of the car and saw on the porch an elderly woman. She was dressed in her best holiday clothes. On her chest was an Order of the Red Banner for working people and an Economics Exhibition medal.

'Zinaida Mikhailovna?'

She embraced me like a mother. Tears, confused words. I noticed the boulder by the gate. 'As I remember, it wasn't here before.'

Zinaida Mikhailovna smiled and put her kerchief to her eyes. 'Do you recognize the stone?'

'Is it really the same?'

'Yes, after the war, the house was rebuilt and I asked the tractor driver to bring this boulder here from the field.'

We went to the club. The whole village was gathered there, from the smallest to the largest. In the hall you could not have dropped an apple. Guests arrived from the regional centre. The secretary of the collective farm party organization, A.Ya. Vlasova opened the evening. She made a short introductory speech and asked me to speak. I spoke of the far-off days of war, recalled with gratitude the brave and good people of the village of Bolshaya Vruda, who helped me in my hour of need, and read my poem 'Revenge'.

After me Zinaida Mikhailovna Petrova spoke. She was greeted with applause. It was immediately evident that the collective farm workers respected this simple, kind, hard-working woman. After the war, she had joined the party and laboured ceaselessly to improve and restore the ruined collective farm economy. For more than forty years, Zinaida Mikhailovna had organized the village amateur dramatic performances. Once she had described how we met in those grim times of war, she lapsed into silence and stood looking vacant, as if trying to overcome nervousness. Then she took from the pocket of her jacket the page of an exercise book folded into four and opened it.

'Permit me to read my poem.'

The hall became silent. As they told me later, no one had ever heard that Zinaida Mikhailovna wrote poetry. When she started to read, her voice shook, then became stronger, but in every word there was the sound of ineffable emotion.

> It was long ago, twenty years have already passed.
> In forty-one it was
> The enemy suddenly attacked our country
> And with flames everything was enveloped.
> To the defence of our country our army came.

In the sky aircraft clashed with the enemy.
Far to the rear of the country they sent the cattle
Much labour and trouble there was.
Our own aircraft flew over the village
And on the way met the enemy.
Fought long with the enemy and with a broken wing
Came down near our village.
Everyone ran to help, who saw that flight.
What could have happened to the airman!
Although the plane was shot down, the pilot lived.
The brave heart in him was preserved.
The enemy advanced strongly, everyone ran into the forest.
The airman could see only suffering.
And to take revenge for the spilt blood
He swore then when he bid farewell.
He kept that sworn oath.
In battles struck the enemy in deadly fights.
He took revenge for everything – even for my hut
And from the war returned a hero.

It is impossible to convey with what warmth everyone gathered in the club applauded Zinaida Mikhailovna. It was particularly touching to see how the little children, sitting on the floor in front of the stage, clapped their hands, how their eyes shone, how the expression on their faces changed to one of deep interest and sheer delight.

A little later, we were sitting at a hospitable table in Zinaida Mikhailovna's home. Conversations, recollections, tears of joy – I can't begin, I haven't the strength to write it all. I came to know much that interested me about Bolshaya Vruda, about its past and present life. The collective farm workers told me that the remains of the Junkers that I had shot down were still scattered behind the village in a swamp, beside a path leading to places where there were berries and mushrooms.

The next morning, at the invitation of the pioneers, I walked to the school. As I walked, I looked about me. 'Bolshaya Vruda, how unlike you are that front-line village, enveloped in flames, that I saw in 1941.' Now television aerials, family cars and motor cycles stood in the yards. The once dusty road, along which I had transported my aeroplane away from the village, was now dressed in asphalt. A five-storey block of flats was going up. The foundations of a new school had been laid. 'Nevertheless, Bolshaya Vruda, you are smaller. Half the inhabitants were killed on that tragic day, 10 August. And how many men did not return from the fields of war!'

But there was the school. It was the first day of a new school year. On this occasion there was a grand parade: children's faces shining with joy, snow-white shirts and blouses, red pioneer scarves.

I accepted a report from the chairman of the committee and wished the children well in the new school year. A boy came forward from the parade and announced the decision of the committee to confer on me the title of honorary pioneer. A little girl with blue eyes tied a pioneer's scarf around my neck, kissed me and ran into line. Suppressing emotion with difficulty, I told the children about the war, about the tragic days for Bolshaya Vruda, about my fighting comrades. As I talked, I looked at the children listening to me with concentration, and now and again my hidden thoughts returned: it was right, right for those who persistently advised me to write about everything I had been through. To write a book and give it to the children, our rising generation, our hope and joy.

So this book is written, written for you, my dear little boys and girls. Maybe not everything in it will seem to you equally interesting. But be lenient – I am not a literary man. I am simply one of those who, in his youth, helped our country to grow and strengthen. One of those who fought to the death with her enemies. I wrote this book in my spare time, between other work. My work, first and foremost, is in aviation. True, I no longer fly in fighter aircraft. Now I am the leader of a small flying club. The important thing to me is that I am in the sky, that I hold the control column of an aircraft. In the An 2 aircraft, I take up my pupils, fearless parachutists, to cloud level. At times, I forget my age and with them throw myself from on high to meet the ground. I leap and, embracing space with my arms, fly like a bird until, above my head, the canopy of my parachute opens. Then, once again at such moments, I'm as young as I was in those far-off years at the front.

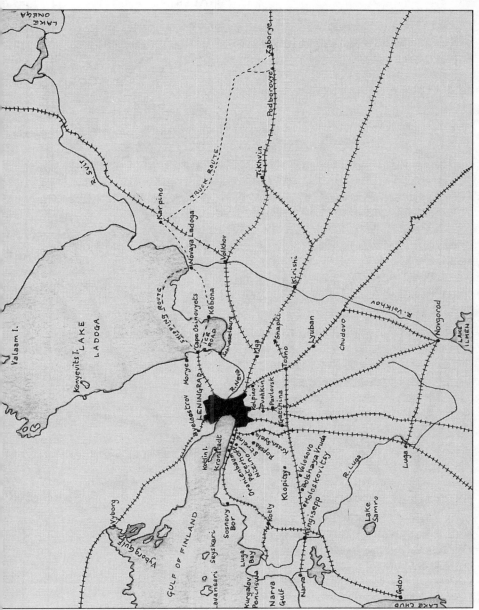

The area around Leningrad featuring most of the places mentioned in the text.

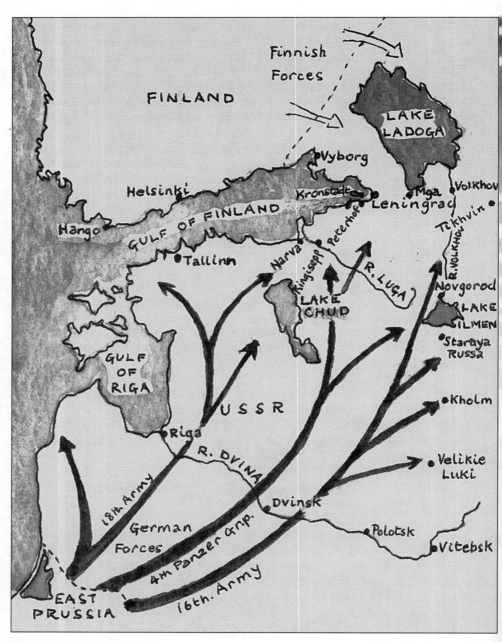

The German Advance, June–August 1941.

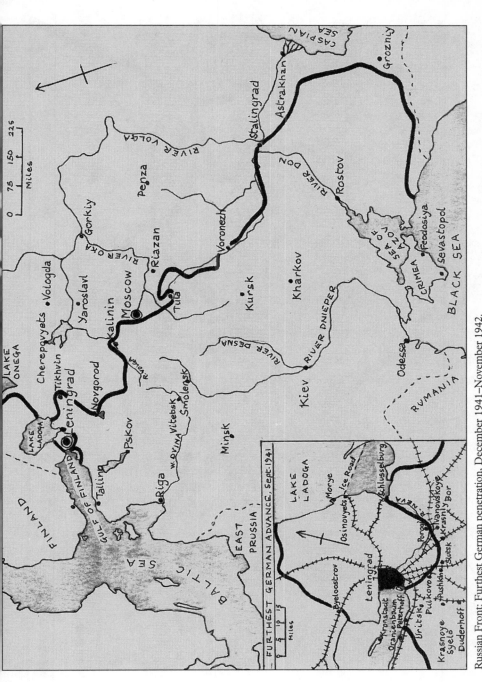

Russian Front: Furthest German penetration, December 1941–November 1942.

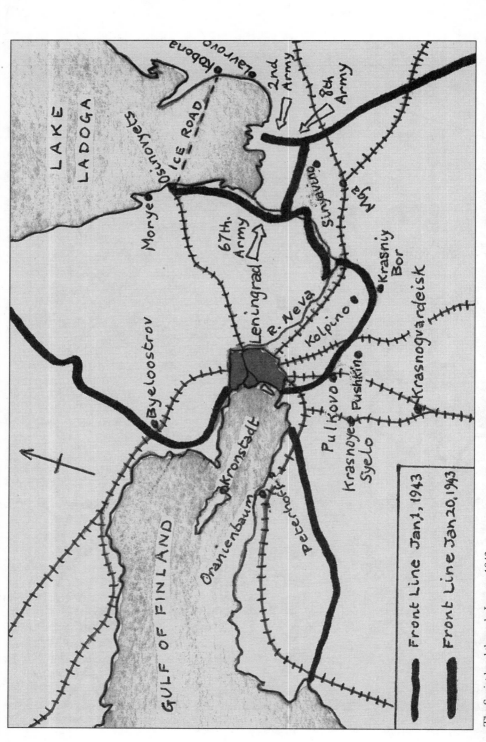

The Soviet breakthrough, January 1943.

Appendix 1

The Organization of the Soviet Air Force in the Second World War

During the Second World War, the Soviet Air Arm was divided into different units according to required duties and areas of operation.

On 22 June 1941 the division of the Soviet Air Force or the Air Force of the Red Army was as follows:

a. the air force of the Supreme Command (long-range bomber units), and
b. the air forces subordinate to the land forces, consisting of:
    1   the front air forces (formed from the air forces of the military districts),
    2   the army air forces (subordinate to the high command of the respective armies), and
    3   the liaison squadrons (subordinate to the commanders of different ground force units).

In addition to the above mentioned units, each fleet of the Soviet Navy had its own air force.

The naval air forces were designated an independent arm on 1 January 1938. Each of the Navy's Fleets had its individual air force:

1   the Red Banner Baltic Fleet Air Force,
2   the Northern Fleet Air Force,
3   the Black Sea Fleet Air Force,
4   the Pacific Fleet Air Force.

On 22 June 1941, 655 of the naval air forces' 1,445 aircraft were fighters. The naval air forces were commanded by Col Gen S.F. Zhavoronkov (25 September 1944 Air Marshal) from the beginning of June 1939 until the end of the war.

Guards Units

The first Guards Units of the Red Army were established on 18 September 1941. The epithet 'Guards' was an honorary title awarded to specially distinguished units. These were presented with a special Guards banner; the officers' ranks were prefixed 'Guards' (e.g. 'Guards Captain'), and the soldiers in service with the unit were awarded the Guards mark to bear on their uniforms. Also the number of the unit usually changed in connection with its nomination to Guards. The first Guards Aviation Regiments were nominated on 6 December 1941, and by the end of the war altogether 288 flying units had been awarded the honorary title of Guards.

Appendix 2

Fighter Equipment

During the latter half of the 1930s and still at the beginning of the Great Patriotic War, the most common Soviet fighter types were the I 16, I 15bis (I 152), and I 153 designed by Polikarpov. Production of the new fighter generation (LaGG 3, MiG 3, and Yak 1 fighters) began in 1940.

On June 22 1941, the air forces of the Baltic, Byelo-Russian, Kiev and Odessa Military Districts included about 5,540 aircraft of which about 3,270 were fighters, and of these, only 980 belonged to the new fighter generation.

During the Blitzkrieg attacks of the first days of the Great Patriotic War, the Germans destroyed as many as 1,136 Soviet aircraft (800 of them on the ground). From 1942 the war industry, which had been evacuated to Siberia, was, however, capable of replacing the serious losses of the first year of the war with new high-performance Yak 7, Yak 9, La 5, La 7, and Yak 3 fighters.

From autumn 1941, the United States and Britain provided the Soviet Union with additional aircraft under the 'lend-lease' agreement, including Airacobra, Kingcobra, Kittyhawk, Tomahawk, Thunderbolt, Hurricane and Spitfire fighters. The number of these aircraft represented, however, only a small part of the total number of fighters in the Soviet Air Force. During the war, the Soviet aircraft industry produced a total of 136,800 aircraft of which 108,028 were actual warplanes, while the lend-lease deliveries totalled 17,834 aircraft. In the table below are given the total number of Soviet wartime fighters produced in the Soviet Union or imported under the lend-lease agreement.

Fighter type	Number	Fighter type	Number
I 16	6,555	La 7	5,753
I 15bis	2,408	Yak 3	4,848
I 153	3,437	P 39 Airacobra	5,707
LaGG 3	6,528	P 63 Kingcobra	2,400
MiG 3	3,322	P 40 Tomahawk,	
Yak 1	8,721	Warhawk	2,397
Yak 7	6,399	P 47 Thunderbolt	195
La 5	c. 10,000	Hurricane	2,952
Yak 9	16,769	Spitfire	1,331

The information, given here under the titles The Organization of the Soviet Air Force in the Second World War, Guards Units and Fighter Equipment, is taken from the 1979 Finnish publication *Red Stars in the Sky*, Book 1 (ISBN 951 9035 50 8).

Appendix 3

Aircraft Included in the Text of Igor Kaberov's Memoirs

Soviet and Allied Aircraft

(Data taken from official history of the Soviet Air Force in the Second World War)

	Engine	Horse power	Wing-span	Length	Fuel gals	Speed mph	Range miles
Fighters							
MiG 3	AM 35A	1,350	33 ft 9 in	26 ft 9 in	171	398	776
I 16	M 62	1,000	26 ft 6 in	20 ft 1 in	67	304	460
Yak 1	VK 105PF	1,100	32 ft 10 in	27 ft 9 in	108	360	528
I 15 (Kings)	M 25	715	32 ft	20 ft	69	225	450
LaGG 3	VK 105PF	1,100	32 ft 1 in	29 ft	127	354	400
I 153	M 62	1,000	32 ft 10 in	20 ft 3 in		275	432
Hurricane (Mk 2B)	Merlin XX	1,185	40 ft	31 ft 5 in		340	
La 5	M 82FN	1,850	32 ft 1 in	28 ft 5 in	140	404	475
Bombers and Ground Attack Aircraft							
SB 2 (high-speed bomber)	2 × M 103	960	66 ft 8 in	40 ft 3 in		279	745
Pe 2 (ground attack)	2 × M 105R	1,100	56 ft 3 in	41 ft 6 in		335	745
Il 2 (ground attack)	AM 38	1,600	47 ft 11 in	38 ft		292	465
Il 4 (bomber)	2 × M 88B	1,100	70 ft 4 in	48 ft 6 in		276	2,360
Li 2 (transport)	2 × M 62	900	94 ft 6 in	64 ft 6 in		174	1,552
MBR 2 (flying boat)	M 17	680	44 ft			136	745

Enemy Aircraft

(Data taken from *Jane's Fighting Aircraft of World War 2*)

	Engine	Horse power	Wing-span	Length	Fuel gals	Speed mph	Range miles
Fighters							
Messerschmitt 109	DB 601a	1,150	32 ft 6 in	29 ft 6 in	99	354	621
Focke-Wulf 190	BMW 801C		34 ft	29 ft	272	402	950
Bombers and Ground Attack Aircraft							
Messerschmitt 110	2 × DB 601 Aa	1,150	53 ft 4 in	40 ft 6 in		365	1,750
Junkers 87	Jumo 211	1,050	45 ft 4 in	35 ft 6 in		242	498

	Engine	Horse power	Wing-span	Length	Fuel gals	Speed mph	Range miles
Junkers 88	2 x Jumo211a	1,200	59 ft	46 ft 6 in		317	1,310
Heinkel 111	2 x DB 601 A	1,150	74 ft 3 in	54 ft 6 in	880	274	2,140
Dornier 217	2 x BMW 801 A		62 ft 5 in	56 ft 6 in		330	2,400
Caproni	2 x Piaggio V11C16	460	53 ft 2 in	44 ft		218	620
Junkers 86	2 x Jumo	207	74 ft		462	260	980
Henschel 126 (reconnaissance aircraft)	BMW 132 DC	870	47 ft 7 in	35 ft 7 in	120	221	620

Notes to Text of Translation

1 Volodya – The diminutive form of Vladislav is usually Vladik or Slava. For some reason Dikov preferred Volodya.
2 Kotovsky – A hero of the Civil War who always cut off all his hair.
3 Anikanich – The patronymic suffix -ich is often used as a familiar alternative to the usual -ov as here with Anikanov.
4 Marzikovaya Luzha – Part of a bay on the Finnish Gulf between Leningrad and Kronstadt.
5 'Shurochka, direct your eyes at us, the peasants have come from work.' – Here Kaberov uses a phrase used by Godunov and pronounces it in Boris's Finnish accent.
6 bayan – A kind of accordion. The word also means an Old Russian bard or minstrel.

7 lapotnik – Slang expression used to describe the Junkers 87, probably because the aircraft's undercarriage reminded the Soviet pilots of peasants in 'lapti' – bast sandals.
8 DOSAAF – A society of volunteers who give support and training to the Army, Air Force and Navy.
9 GTO – Award recognizing service to the nation for labour and defence.
10 Kokkinaki – Vladimir Kokkinaki, like Chkalov and other Soviet aviators, was famous for his long-range flights in the 1930s. In April 1939 he flew from Moscow to Canada in the DB 3 prototype.
11 Sukho – In Russian the word means 'It is dry'.
12 Furmanov – Dmitry Andreyevich Furmanov (1891–1926) – during the Civil War he was Commissar of the 25th (Chapaev) Division. Later he became secretary of the Moscow Writers' Association.

Index